Clive Phillipps-Wolley

Gold, gold, in Cariboo

a Story of Adventure in British Columbia

Clive Phillipps-Wolley

Gold, gold, in Cariboo
a Story of Adventure in British Columbia

ISBN/EAN: 9783743320680

Manufactured in Europe, USA, Canada, Australia, Japa

Cover: Foto ©ninafisch / pixelio.de

Manufactured and distributed by brebook publishing software (www.brebook.com)

Clive Phillipps-Wolley

Gold, gold, in Cariboo

CONTENTS.

CHAP.		Page
I.	THE GOLD FEVER,	9
II.	A "GILT-EDGED" SPECULATION,	23
III.	A LITTLE GAME OF POKER,	33
IV.	THE MOTHER OF GOLD,	41
V.	"IS THE COLONEL 'STRAIGHT?'"	52
VI.	THE WET CAMP,	64
VII.	FACING DEATH ON THE STONE-SLIDE,	73
VIII.	THEIR FIRST "COLOURS,"	82
IX.	UNDER THE BALM-OF-GILEAD TREE,	89
X.	THE SHADOWS BEGIN TO FALL,	97
XI.	"JUMP OR I'LL SHOOT,"	107
XII.	A SHEER SWINDLE,	117
XIII.	THE BULLET'S MESSAGE,	125
XIV.	WHAT THE WOLF FOUND,	132
XV.	IN THE DANCE-HOUSE,	144
XVI.	THE PRICE OF BLOOD,	153
XVII.	CHANCE'S GOLD-FEVER RETURNS,	162
XVIII.	ON THE COLONEL'S TRAIL AGAIN,	170
XIX.	"GOOD-BYE, LILLA,"	177
XX.	THE ACCURSED RIVER,	184

CONTENTS.

CHAP.		Page
XXI.	Pete's Creek,	192
XXII.	Gold by the Gallon!	203
XXIII.	The Hornet's Nest,	211
XXIV.	Drowning in the Forest,	222
XXV.	In the Camp of the Chilcotins,	234
XXVI.	Rampike's Winter Quarters,	243
XXVII.	The Search for Phon,	250
XXVIII.	The King of the Big-horns,	258
XXIX.	Phon's Return,	266
XXX.	Cruickshank at Last!	276

ILLUSTRATIONS.

	Page
Steve Chance exhibits his Map to the Colonel, *Front.*	14
Corbett seizes his one chance for Life,	80
"With a scream of fear the Chinaman sprang out,"	116
Lilla accosts the Colonel in the Dance-house,	146
"Gold—Gold in Flakes, and Lumps, and Nuggets,"	210
Corbett and Chance are found by a Friendly Indian,	234

"GOLD, GOLD IN CARIBOO!"

A TALE OF ADVENTURE IN BRITISH COLUMBIA.

CHAPTER I.

THE GOLD FEVER.

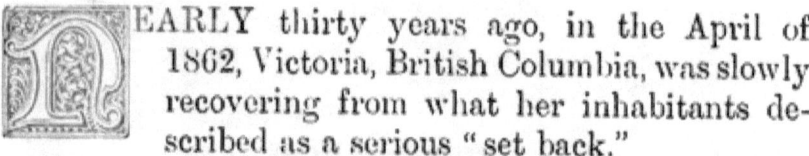EARLY thirty years ago, in the April of 1862, Victoria, British Columbia, was slowly recovering from what her inhabitants described as a serious "set back."
From the position of a small Hudson Bay station she had suddenly risen in '58 to the importance of a city of 17,000 inhabitants, from which high estate she had fallen again with such rapidity, that in 1861 there were only 5000 left in her to mourn the golden days of the "Frazer river humbug."

In '48 the gold fever broke out in California, and for ten years, in the words of an eye-witness, 50,000 adventurers of every hue, language, and clime were drifting up and down the slopes of the Great Sierra, in search of gold, ready to rush this way or that at the first rumour of a fresh find.

In '58 California's neighbour, British Columbia, took the fever. The cry of "Gold, gold!" was raised upon the Frazer, and the wharves of San Francisco groaned beneath the burden of those who sought to take ship for this fresh Eldorado.

In a year most of these pilgrims had returned from the new shrine, poorer by one year of their short lives, beaten back by the grim canyons of the Frazer river, or cheated of their reward by those late floods, which kept the golden sands hidden from their view. In '58 and '59 the miner cursed Victoria as a city of hopes unfulfilled, and left her to dream on undisturbed of the greater days to come.

She looked as if, on this April day of '62, her dreams were of the fairest. The air, saturated with spring sunshine, was almost too soft and sweet to be wholesome for man. There was a languor in it which dulled the appetite for work; merely to live was happiness enough; effort seemed folly, and if a man could have been found with energy enough to pray, he would have prayed only that no change might come to him, that the gleam of the blue waters of the straits and the diamond brightness of the distant snow-peaks might remain his for ever, balanced by the soft green of the island pine-woods: that the hollow drumming of the mating grouse and the song of the meadow lark, and the hum of waking nature might continue to caress his ear, while only the scent of the fresh-sawn lumber suggested to him that labour was the lot of man.

And yet, in spite of this seeming dreaminess in nature, the old earth was busy fashioning new things out of the old, and the hearts of men all along the Pacific slope were waking and thrilling in answer to the new message of Mammon—"Gold! gold by the ton, to be had for the gathering in Cariboo!" The reports which had come down from Quesnel, of the fortunes made in '61 upon such creeks as Antler and Williams, had restored heart to the Victorians, and even to those Californian miners who still sojourned in their midst, so that quite half the people in the town, old residents as well as new-comers, were only waiting for the snows to melt, ere they rushed away to the mining district beyond the Bald Mountains.

But the snows tarry long in the high places of British Columbia, and the days went on in spite of the men and their desire, and bread had to be earned even in such an Elysium as Vancouver Island, with all the gold which a man could want, as folks said, within a few weeks' march of them; so that hands and brains were busy, in spite of the temptations of Hope and the spring sunshine. Moreover, there were dull dogs even then in Victoria, who believed more in the virtue of steady toil than in gold-mining up at Cariboo.

Thus it happened, then, that a big, yellow-headed axeman, and a ray of evening sunlight, looking in together through an open doorway upon Wharf Street, found a man within in his shirt sleeves, still busily engaged upon his daily task.

"Hullo, Corbett, how goes it? Come right in and take a smoke."

The voice, a cheery one with a genuine welcome in it, came from the inside of the house, and in answer the axeman heaved his great shoulder up from the door-post and loafed in.

In every movement of this man there was a suggestion of healthy weariness, that most luxurious and delightful sensation which comes over him who has used his muscles throughout the day in some one of those outdoor forms of labour which earn an appetite, even if they do not gain a fortune.

As he stood in the little room looking quizzically at his friend's work, Ned Corbett, in his old blue shirt and overalls, with the axe lying across one bare brown forearm, might have served an artist as a model for Labour; but the artist into whose studio he had come had no need for such models. There was no money in painting such subjects, and Steve Chance painted for dollars, and for dollars only. Round the room at the height of a man's shoulder was stretched a long, long strip of muslin (not canvas, canvas would cost six bits a picture), and this strip had been sized and washed over with colour. When Corbett entered, Chance had just slapped on the last patch of this preliminary coat of paint, so that now there was nothing more to be done until the morrow.

"Well, Steve, how many works of art have you knocked off to-day?" asked Corbett.

"Works of art be hanged!" replied his friend. "I've covered about twenty feet of muslin, and that at five dollars a picture isn't a bad day's work. What have you done?"

"Let me see, I've cut down a tree or two and earned an appetite, and—oh, yes, a couple of dollars to satisfy the same. Isn't that enough?"

"All depends upon the way you look at things. I call it fooling your time away."

"And I call this work of yours a waste of talent worse, fifty times worse, than my waste of time. Look at that thing, for instance;" and Ned pointed to a large canvas, bright with all the colours of the rainbow.

"That! Well, you needn't look as if the thing might bite, Ned. That is the new map of Ophir, a land brimming 'ophir'—forgive the joke—with coarse gold, and, what is more important, bonded by those immaculate knights of the curbstone, Messrs. Dewd and Cruickshank."

"An advertisement, is it? Well, it is ugly enough even for that. How much lower do you mean to drag your hapless art, you vandal? 'Auctioning pictures,' as you call it, is bad enough, but this is simple sign-painting!"

"Well, and why not, if sign-painting pays? You take my advice, Ned; get the 'sugar' first, the fame will come at its leisure. Sign-painting is honest anyway, and more remunerative than felling trees, you bet."

"That may be," replied the younger man, balancing his axe in his strong hands, "and more intellectual, I suppose; but, by George, there's a pleasure in every ringing blow with the axe, and the scent of the fresh pine-wood is sweeter than the smell of your oil-paints."

"Pot-paints, Ned, two bits a pot. We don't run to tube-paints in this outfit."

"Well, pot-paints if you like; but even so you are not making a fortune. We can't always sell those panoramas of yours, you know, even at a dollar a foot."

"That's *your* fault, Ned; you've no eye for the latent merits of my pictures, and therefore make a shocking mess of the auctioneer's department. However, I am not wedded to my art. If lumbering and painting don't pay, what do you say to real estate?" and as he spoke, Chance put his "fixins" together and proceeded to lock up the studio for the night.

"Real estate! Why, fifty per cent of the inhabitants of the Queen City are real estate agents professionally, and most of the others are amateurs. Be a little original, outside your art anyway, old fellow. I don't want anything to do with real estate, except in acre blocks beyond the city limits, and a jolly long way beyond at that!"

"Is that so?" asked a mellow voice from behind the last speaker. "Then, my dear sir, Messrs. Dewd and Cruickshank can fix you right away. What do you say to a little farm on the gorge, fairly swarming with game, and admirably suited for either stock raising or grain growing?"

"Viticulture, market-gardening, or a gentleman's park! Better go the whole hog at once, Cruickshank," laughed Chance, turning round to greet the new-comer, a dark, stout man with an unlit cigar stuck in the corner of his mouth.

"You must have your joke, Mr. Chance; but the farm is really a gem for all that, and with the certainty of a large advance in price this summer, a man could not do better than buy."

"What, is the farm better than a claim in Ophir?" laughed Chance.

"Ah, well, that is another matter!" said Cruickshank. "The farm is a gilt-edged investment. There is, of course, just a suspicion of speculation in all gold-mining operations, though I can't see where the risk is in such claims as those you mention. By the way, have you finished the map?"

"Yes, here it is," replied the artist, producing a roll from under his arm, and partly opening it to show it to his questioner. "I call it rather a neat thing in sign-boards, don't you? I know I've used up all my brightest colours upon it."

"Yes, it will do; and though I don't suppose Williams Creek is quite that colour," laughed Cruickshank, "I am happy to say that our reports are not over-coloured, even if our map is. Do you know the Duke of Kent, Mr. Corbett?"

"No. Who is the Duke of Kent? I'd no idea that we had any aristocrats out here."

"Oh, the duke's is only a fancy title; most titles are that way in the far west."

"My sentiments exactly, Colonel Cruickshank," replied Corbett; and anyone inclined to quarrel with him might have thought that Corbett dwelt just a thought too long upon the "colonel."

But Cruickshank was not inclined to quarrel with a man who stood six feet two, and girthed probably forty inches round the chest, and who was reported, moreover, to be master of quite a snug little sum in good English gold.

"The Duke of Kent has a claim alongside those which we bonded last fall, and he tells me that he has already refused a hundred thousand dollars for a half share in it."

"A hundred thousand dollars for a half share! Great Cæsar's ghost, why, you could buy half Victoria for the money!" cried Chance.

"Well, not quite, but a good deal of it, and yet I've no doubt but that we have quite as rich claims amongst those we offer for sale. How can it be otherwise? They lie side by side on the same stream."

"Have you seen any of these claims yourself, colonel?" asked Corbett.

"Every one of them, my good sir. My clients are for the most part my own countrymen, and you may bet that I won't let them be done by any beastly Yank."

"Civil to you, Steve," laughed Corbett.

"I beg your pardon, Mr. Chance, but there are Americans *and* Americans; and you can understand that a man who has spent the best years of his life wearing the Queen's uniform feels hotly about some of the frauds practised upon tender-feet by Californian bilks."

"Why, certainly; don't apologize. I suppose there are a few honest men and a good many rogues in every nation. Did you say you had seen the claims yourself? I thought you were in Victoria in the fall."

"No; Dewd and I were up together. I came down and he stayed there. There is big money in them. Change your minds, gentlemen, and give up art for gold-mining."

"No, thanks; I think not," replied Corbett.

"No! Well, you know best. Good-day to you. You won't take a drink, will you?"

"No, I won't spoil my appetite even for a cock-tail."

"So long, then!" and with a flourish of his gold-headed cane, which was meant to represent a military salute, the somewhat florid warrior dived through a swing-door, over which was written in letters of gold, "The Fashion Bar."

"Say, Corbett," remarked Chance as Cruickshank disappeared, "don't you make yourself so deuced disagreeable to my best customers. Cruickshank's orders keep our firm in bread and cheese, and I can see you want to kick the fellow all the time he is in your company."

"All right, old chap; but I didn't say anything rude, did I? If he would only drop the 'British army' and 'we English' I wouldn't even want to be rude. What the deuce does he care whether he gets his dollars from a Britisher or a Yank?"

"Not much, you bet! But here we are. Hullo, Phon, have you got the muck-a-muck ready?"

"You bet you! Soup all ready. Muck-a-muck heap

good to-day you see;" and laughing and chattering Phon dived into the tent, and rattled about the tin plates and clucked as if he were calling chickens to be fed.

Phon was a character in his way, and a good one at that; a little wizen, yellow body, with an especially long pig-tail coiled up on his head like a turban; eyes and tongue which were in perpetual motion, and a great affection for the two white men, who treated him with the familiarity of old friendship.

"What are you in such a deuce of a hurry for to-night, Phon?" asked Corbett a little later, when the Chinaman rushed in to take away the remains of dinner.

"S'pose I tell you, you no let me go?" replied the fellow, half interrogatively.

"Go! of course I'll let you go. I couldn't help myself, I suppose. Where are you going to—the hee-hee house?"

"No, no. Hee-hee house no good. No makee money there. Pay all the time. Me go gamble."

"Gamble, you idiot! What, and lose all your pay for a month?"

"'Halo' (*anglice* not) lose. Debbil come to me last night; debbil say, 'Phon, you go gamble, you win one hundred dollars.' I go win, you see."

"Please yourself. You'll see as much of that hundred dollars as you did of the devil. Who's that calling?"

Phon went out of the tent for a moment and then returned, and holding up the tent flap for someone to enter, said:

"Colonel Cruickshank want to see you. Me go now?"

"All right! go to blazes, only don't expect us to pay you any more wages if you lose. Come in, colonel."

"Won't you come out instead, Mr. Corbett? It's better lying on the grass outside than in to-night."

"Guess he is right, Ned. Come along, you lazy old beggar!" cried Chance. And the three men in another minute were all lying prone on a blanket by the embers of a camp-fire, smoking their pipes and chatting lazily.

Corbett's tent—a marvel of London make, convertible into anything from a Turkish bath to a suit of clothes, and having every merit except the essential one of portability—stood upon the very edge of the encampment, commanding a view of the sea and the Olympic Range on the farther shore.

The encampment itself was a kind of annexe of the town of Victoria, standing where James Bay suburb now stands, although what is to-day covered with villas and threatened by an extension of the electric tramway was in '62 a place of willows and wild rose-bushes.

Here lived part of the floating population of Victoria, miners *en route* to Cariboo, remittance-men sent away from home to go to the dogs out of sight of their affectionate relatives, and a good many other noisy good-fellows who liked to live in their shirt sleeves in the open air.

Corbett and Chance were the aristocrats of this quarter, thanks to the magnificence of their abode and the general "tonyness" of their outfit. In their own hearts they knew that they were victims to their outfitter—that they were living where they were instead of in a house merely out of regard for their tent, and for those mysterious camp appliances which all fitted into one another like Chinese puzzles.

That was where the shoe pinched. In a moment of

pride they had pitched their tent (according to written instructions) and unpacked their "kitchen outfits," and *they had never been able to repack them.*

It was all very well to advertise the things as packing compactly into a case two feet by one foot six inches, but it required an expert to pack them; and so, unless they were minded to abandon their "fixings," they had to stay by them. Therefore they stayed, and said they preferred the open air, even when it rained, as it sometimes does even on Vancouver Island.

Later on they learnt better, and were consoled for their losses by the sight of the hundred and one "indispensable requisites of a camp life" cast away by weary pilgrims all along the Frazer river road. It is a pity that the gentlemen who sell camp outfits cannot be compelled to pass one year in prospecting before they enter upon their trade.

But an April evening by the Straits of Fuca, with a freshly-lit pipe between your teeth, will put you in charity even with a London outfitter. The warm air was full of the scent of the sea and the sweet smoke of the camp-fires, while the chorus of the bull-frogs sounded like nature's protest against the advent of man.

As the darkness grew the forest seemed to close in round the intruding houses, and for a while even the estate agent was silent, oppressed by the majesty of night and nature.

It was Corbett who broke the silence at last.

"Do you know that long, blue valley, Steve—you can hardly see it now,—the one that goes winding away back into the mountains from the gate of the Angels?"

Steve nodded. He was too lazy to answer.

"That valley is my worst tempter. I know I ought

to settle here and work: keep a store and grow up with the country; but I can't do it. That valley haunts me with longings to follow it through the blue mists to—"

"To the place where the gold comes from—eh, Ned? To the place where it lies in lumps still, not worn into dust by its long journey down stream from the heart of its parent mountain. Old Sobersides, you have been reading your *Colonist* too much lately."

Ned smiled, and knocking the ashes out of his pipe, began to refill it.

"How much of all these yarns about gold up at Antler and Williams Creek do you believe, colonel?" he asked, turning to Cruickshank. "Do you really think anyone ever took out fifty ounces in a day with a rocker?"

"I know it, my good sir. I have seen it. When Antler was found in 1860 the bed-rock was paved with gold, and you could not wash a shovelful of dirt that had not from five to fifty dollars' worth of dust in it."

"Oh, there's gold up in Cariboo, Ned, but it wants finding. You've only got to go into the saloons to know that there is plenty of dust for the lucky ones. Fellows pay with pinches of dust for liquors whose names they did not know a year ago."

"*Paid*, you mean, Chance," corrected Cruickshank. "They are all pretty near stone-broke by now. But are you longing to go and bail up gold in your silk hat, Mr. Corbett?"

"I am longing to be doing something new, colonel. I've taken the prevalent fever, I think, and want to make one in this scrimmage. I can't sit still and see band after band of hard-fists going north any longer.

Town life may be more profitable, perhaps, but I want to be with the men."

"Bully for you, Ned! English solidity of intellect for ever! Why, you villain, you're as bad a gambler as Yankee Chance."

"Worse, I expect, Mr. Chance," remarked Cruickshank, eyeing the two young men critically. "You would play to win, he would play for the mere fun of playing."

"Which would give me the advantage," retorted Corbett; "because in that case I should stop when I was tired of the game."

"Never mind the argument," broke in Chance; "gambler or no gambler, if you go I go. I'm sick of that picture of the pines and the waterfall, anyway."

"So is Victoria. 'Bloomin' red clothes'-props and a mill-race,' one chap called the last copy I tried to sell," muttered Corbett.

"Well, why not buy a couple of those claims of mine?" suggested Cruickshank. "I always like to do a fellow-countryman a good turn, and it would really be a genuine pleasure to me to put you two into a good thing."

"How many have you left, Colonel Cruickshank?" He could not help it for the life of him, but the moment Cruickshank became more than ordinarily affectionate and open-hearted Corbett put on the colonel, and, as it were, came on guard. He was angry with himself directly afterwards for doing so, but he could no more help it than a man can help pulling himself together when he hears the warning of the rattlesnake.

"Only three, Mr. Corbett; and I doubt whether I can hold those till to-morrow morning. I am to meet a man in town at nine about them."

"What do you want for the three?"

"As a mere matter of curiosity?" put in Chance.

"Well, let me see. They are '100-foot' claims, right alongside the places where the big hauls were made last year; but they are the last, and as you are an Englishman and a friend—"

"Oh, please be good enough to treat this as a purely business matter," ejaculated Corbett, blushing up to the temples, whilst anyone looking at Cruickshank might for the moment have thought that his speech had had exactly the effect he intended it to have.

"Well, say two thousand dollars apiece; that is cheap and fair."

"Two thousand dollars apiece! What a chap you are to chaff, Cruickshank!" cried Chance, breaking in. "Do you take us for millionaires?"

"In embryo if you buy my shares, certainly, my dear sir."

"Perhaps. But look here, say a thousand dollars apiece, half cash, and half when we make our pile."

"Can't do it; but I'll knock off a hundred dollars from each claim, as we are friends."

"The market value is two thousand dollars, you say, Colonel Cruickshank (my dear Chance, do leave this to me), and you have yourself inspected these claims?"

"Certainly."

"And they are good workable claims, adjoining those you spoke of?"

"Undoubtedly, that gives them their principal value."

"Very well then, I'll buy the three. Here is a hundred dollars to bind our bargain. We'll settle the rest tomorrow. Now, let me give you a drink."

"Thank you. Are the claims to stand in your name?"

"In Chance's, Phon's, and mine. How will that do, Steve?"

"Settle it your own way; if you have gone crazy I suppose I must humour you. But there is a good deal owing to our firm from yours, colonel, isn't there?"

"Of course. That can be set off against a part of the sum due as payment for the claims. Good-night, Mr. Corbett. Thank you for the confidence you show in me. Treat a gentleman like a gentleman, and an honest man like an honest man, say I."

"And a thief or a business man like a thief or a business man," muttered Chance, as Cruickshank walked away. "Oh, Ned, Ned! What a lot nature wasted on your muscles which she had much better have put into your head!"

CHAPTER II.

A "GILT-EDGED" SPECULATION.

"NED, were you drunk last night, or am I dreaming?" asked Chance next morning, as the two sat over their breakfast, while the canoes of the early Indian fishers stole out along the edges of the great kelp beds.

It was a lovely scene upon which Corbett's tent looked out, but Chance at the moment had no eyes for the blue water, or the glories of the snow range beyond, all he could think of was "three claims at two thousand dollars apiece."

"Neither, that I am aware of, Steve. You eat as if you had all your faculties about you, and I've no headache."

"Then you did not buy three claims from Cruickshank at two thousand dollars apiece?"

"Yes, I did; and why not?"

'Where is the money to come from?'

"I'll see to that," replied Corbett. "I am quite aware that six thousand dollars is twelve hundred pounds; but if you don't want to take a share in my speculation, I propose to invest that much of my capital in the venture, and even if I lose it all I shall still have something left, besides my muscles, thank God. You two, Phon and yourself, can work for me on wages if you like, or we'll make some other arrangement to keep the party together."

For a minute or two Chance said nothing, and then he began laughing quietly to himself.

"Say, Ned, you took scarlatina pretty bad when you were a kiddy, didn't you?"

"I don't remember, old chap. Why do you ask?"

"And whooping-cough, and measles, and chicken-pox, and now its gold fever, and my stars isn't it a virulent attack?" and Chance broke out laughing afresh.

"I don't see," began Corbett, growing rather red in the face.

"Oh, no: you don't see what all this has to do with me," interrupted Chance, "and it's infernal impertinence on my part to criticise your actions, and if I wasn't so small you would very likely punch my head. I know all that. But, you see, we two are partners, and I am not going to dissolve partnership because I think you are taking bigger risks than you ought to. If you put up three thousand dollars I will put up as much, and part of it can come out of the money owing to the firm."

"But why do this if you think the risk too big?" asked Corbett.

"Why ask questions, Ned? I feel like taking the risk; I am a Yankee, and therefore a natural gambler. You of course are not, are you? And then it's spring-time, and from twenty-three to the other end of threescore years and ten is a long, long time; and even if we 'bust,' there'll be lots of time to build again. So we will go halves, the third claim to be held in Phon's name, and Phon to work on wages."

"Let us have old Phon in. Phon! Phon!" shouted Corbett.

The Chinaman, who was cleaning the tin plates by a creek hard by, came slowly towards them.

"Well, Phon, did you lose all your dollars last night?" asked his master.

"Me tell you debbil say me win—debbil know, you bet," replied Phon coolly.

"And did you win?"

"Me win a hundred dollars—look!" and the little man held out a roll of dirty notes, amounting to something more than the sum named.

"You were in luck, Phon. 'Spose I were you, I no go gamble any more," remarked Corbett, dropping into that pigeon English, which people seem to think best adapted to the comprehension of the Chinaman.

"Oh yes, you go gamble too. Debbils bodder me very bad last night. They say you go gamble, Chance he go gamble, Phon he go gamble too. All go gamble to-gedder. And then debbil he show me gold, gold,—so much gold me no able to carry it. Where you goin' now?"

"I guess your friends, the devils, might have told you that too," remarked Chance. "Don't you know?"

"No, me no savey. You tell me."

'Corbett and myself are going up to Cariboo mining, and if you like you can come as cook, or you can come and work on wages in our claims. How would you like that?"

"Me come, all-lite me come; only you give me one little share in the claims—you let me put in one hundred dollars I win last night."

"Better keep what you've got and not gamble any more," replied Corbett kindly.

"Halo! Halo keep him. 'Spose you not sell me share I go gamble again to-night."

"Better let him have his way, Ned. Let the whole crowd go in together, 'sink or swim.'"

"Very well, Phon, then you will come."

"You bet you, Misser Corbett. Who you 'spose cook for you 'spose I no come?" And having proposed this final conundrum, Phon retired again to his kitchen.

"Rum, the way in which he seemed to know all about our movements, Ned," remarked Chance, when the Chinaman had done.

"Oh, he overheard what we said last night, or at breakfast this morning," replied Corbett.

"He wasn't here last night, and he was down by the stream whilst we were at breakfast."

"All right, old man, perhaps his 'debbil' told him. It doesn't much matter anyway. Did you see this piece in the *Colonist?*"

"About us? No. Read it out."

"'We understand that Colonel Cruickshank, the Napoleon of Victorian finance, the mammoth hustler of the Pacific coast, has determined to conduct those gentlemen who have bought his bonded claims to the fortunes which await them. This additional proof of the colonel's belief in the property which he offers for sale should ensure a keen competition for the one claim still left upon his hands, which we understand will be raffled for this afternoon at 4 p.m. at Smith's saloon. Tickets, ten dollars each. We are informed that amongst the purchasers of claims in the Cruickshank reserve are an English gentleman largely interested in the lumber business, and an American artist rapidly rising into public notice.'"

"What cheer, my lumber king!" laughed Chance as Corbett laid down the paper. "These journalists are wonderful fellows, but I suspect most of that paragraph was inspired and paid for by the 'mammoth hustler.' By the way, if it is true that he means to personally conduct a party to Williams Creek, it does really look as if he had some belief in the claims."

"Yes, IF he means to; but I expect that is simply to draw people to his raffle this afternoon."

"Probably; but if he were to go up to Williams Creek we might as well go up with him. You see, he has travelled along the trail before."

"Well, I'll see about that, and make any arrangements I can for getting up to Cariboo, if you will try to get our accounts settled up, Steve. I'm no good at figures, as you know."

"That's what!" replied Chance laconically; and the two young men got upon their legs and prepared to start on their day's business.

It will be as well here to enter upon a short explanation of the law as it then stood in British Columbia with regard to the bonding of claims. Experience had shown that in the upper country, early winters and late springs, with their natural accompaniment of deep snows, made mining impossible for about half the year. In consequence of this a law had been passed enabling miners to "bond" claims taken up late in the fall until the next spring. Upon claims so bonded it was not necessary to do any work until the 1st of June of the ensuing year, so that from November to June the claims lay safe under the wing of the law; but should their owners neglect to put in an appearance or fail to commence work upon the 1st of June, they forfeited all right to the claims, which could then be "jumped" or seized upon by the first comer.

It was under this law that Corbett and Chance had bought, so that it was imperatively necessary that they should reach their claims by the 1st of June; and although there was still ample time in which to make the journey, there was no time to waste. The Cariboo migration had already begun, and every day saw fresh bands of hard-fists leave Victoria for the mines. Already the gamblers had gone, the whisky trains and other pack trains had started, and the drain upon the stock of full-grown manhood in Victoria was easily noticeable. It was no vain boast which the miners made that the men of Cariboo were the pick of the men of their day. Physically, at any rate, it would have been hard indeed to find a body of men tougher in fibre and more recklessly indifferent to hardships than the pioneers who pushed their way through the Frazer valley to the gold-fields beyond. In that crowd there was no room for the stripling or the old man. The race for gold upon the Frazer was one in which only strong men of full age could live even for the first lap.

And this was the crowd which Corbett and Chance sought to join. To some men the mere idea of a railway journey, entered upon without due consideration and ample forethought, is fraught with terrors. Luckily neither Corbett nor Chance were men of this sort. Chance was a Yankee to the tips of his fingers, and had therefore no idea of distance or fear of travel. The world was *nearly* big enough for him, and he cared just as little about "crossing the herring-pond" as he did about embarking on a ride in a 'bus. As for Corbett, nature had made him a nomad—one of those strangely restless beings, who, having a lovely home, and knowing it to be lovely, still long for constant change, and circle the world with tireless feet, only to bring home the report that "after all England is the only place fit for a fellow to live in." The odd part of it all is, that that being their conviction, most of these wanderers contrive to live out of England for three parts of their lives.

It was no wonder, then, that when Corbett and Chance met again at dusk everything had been, as Chance said, "fixed right away."

"It's a true bill about Cruickshank, old man," Corbett said. "And if you can get the bills paid and our kit packed he wants us to start with him on the *Umatilla* for Westminster the day after to-morrow."

"I don't know about getting the bills paid," replied Chance. "A good many fellows who owe us money appear to have gone before to Cariboo, but I reckon we must look upon that as the opening of an account to our credit in the new country."

"Not much of an account to draw upon; but I suppose it can't be helped. I believe, though, that to do the thing properly we ought both to get stone-broke before starting," remarked Corbett.

"That will come later. Hullo, Cruickshank! what is in the wind now?" cried Steve, turning to the newcomer.

"Gold, gold, nothing but gold, Chance. But I say, gentlemen, are those your packs?" asked the colonel, pointing to two small mountains of luggage which nearly filled the interior of the tent.

"Yes. That is Chance's pack, and this is mine. There will be a sort of joint-stock pack made up to-morrow of the kitchen stuff and the tent. And I think that will be all."

"And you think that will be all, Mr. Corbett?" repeated Cruickshank. "You are a strong man; can you lift that pack?" and he pointed to the biggest of the two.

"Oh yes, easily; carry it a mile if necessary," replied Corbett, swinging the great bundle up on to his shoulders.

"You *are* a stout fellow," admitted Cruickshank admiringly; "but hasn't it occurred to you that you may have to carry all you want for a good many miles? And even if you can do that, who is to carry the joint-stock pack? Not Phon, surely?"

"Well, but won't there be any pack ponies?" asked Corbett.

"For hire on the road, do you mean? Certainly not."

"All right, then," replied Corbett, after a minute or two spent in solemnly and somewhat sadly contemplating all the neatly-packed camp equipage. "I can do with two blankets and a tin pannikin if it comes to that. Can't you, Steve?"

"A tin pannikin and blanket goes," answered Chance. "To blazes with all English outfits anyway!"

"Well, I don't know about that," put in Cruickshank, who seemed hardly as well pleased at his comrade's readiness to forswear comfort as might have been expected. "I thought that you fellows might like to take a few comforts along with you, so I had mentally arranged a way in which we might combine pleasure with profit."

"Pleasure with profit by all means, my boy. Unfold your scheme, colonel; we are with you," cried Chance.

"Well, stores are terribly high up in Cariboo. Whisky is about the only thing these packers think of packing up to the mines, and if you fellows had the coin I could easily buy a little train of cayuses down at Westminster pretty cheap, and load them up with stuff which would pay you cent per cent, and between us the management of a little train like that would be a mere nothing."

"How about packing? You cain't throw a diamond hitch by instinct," remarked Chance, who knew a little from hearsay of the life of the road.

"Oh, I can throw the hitch, and so I guess can your heathen, and we'll deuced soon teach both of you to take the on-side if you are wanted to."

"How much would such a train cost?"

"The ponies ought not to cost more than fifty dollars apiece; as to the stores, of course it depends upon what you choose to take. The ponies will carry about two hundred pounds apiece, if they are good ones."

"What do you say to it, Steve?" asked Ned.

"Seems a good business," replied Chance, "and we may as well put our last dollars into a pack-train as leave them in the bank or chuck them into the Frazer. A pack-train goes."

And so it was settled that the two friends should invest the balance of their funds in a pack-train and stores for Cariboo. The venture looked a promising one, with no possibility of failure or loss, and even if things went wrong the boys would only be stone-broke; and who cares whether he is stone-broke or not at twenty-three, in a new country with no one dependent upon him?

It was only eighteen months before that Edward Corbett had left home, a home in which it was part of the duty of about five different human beings to see that Master Edward wanted for nothing. At about the same time one of the finest houses in New York would have been disturbed to its very foundations if it were suspected that Mr. Steve Chance wanted for any of the luxuries of the nineteenth century, and yet here were Steve Chance and Ned Corbett, their last dollar invested in a doubtful venture, their razors abandoned, their toilet necessaries reduced to one cake of soap and a towel between two (Cruickshank condemned the habit of washing altogether upon the road), and their whole stock of household goods reduced to two light packs, to be carried mile after mile upon their own strong shoulders. There was daily labour ahead of them such as a criminal would hardly have earned for punishment at home, there was a certainty before them of bad food, restless nights, thirst, hunger, and utter discomfort, and yet this life was of their own choosing, and a smile hovered round the lips of each of them as the pipes dropped out of their mouths and they turned over to sleep.

As for "gold," the prize which both of them appeared to be making all these sacrifices for, neither of the boys, oddly enough, had thought of it that night. With Phon it was different, but then he was a celestial. He played for the stakes. Both the whites played, though in different ways, for the fun of the game.

CHAPTER III.

A LITTLE GAME OF POKER.

"WELL, Ned, how do our fellow-passengers strike you? This is a pretty hard crowd, isn't it?" asked Chance, as his eyes wandered over the mob of men of every nationality, who were jostling one another on board the steamer *Umatilla*, ten minutes after she had left Victoria for New Westminster.

"Yes, they look pretty tough, most of them," assented Corbett; "but a three-weeks' beard, a patch in the seat of your pants, and a coat of sun-tan, will bring you down to the same level, Steve. Civilized man reverts naturally to barbarism as soon as he escapes from the tailor and the hair-dresser."

"That's what, sonny! And I believe the only difference between a white man and a siwash, is that one has had more sun and less soap than the other."

"Oh, hang it, no! I draw the line there," cried Corbett. "But look, there go the gamblers already;" and Ned pointed to a little group which had gathered together aft, the leading spirit amongst them appearing to be a dark, overdressed person, who was inviting everybody at the top of his voice to "Chip in and take a drink."

"They don't mean to lose much time, do they?" remarked Chance. "And, by the way, do you see that the 'mammoth hustler,' our own colonel, is among them?"

"And seems to know every rascal in the gang," muttered Corbett.

"Come and look on, Ned, and don't growl. You

don't expect a real-estate agent to be a saint, do you?" remonstrated Chance.

"Not I. I don't care a cent for cards. You go if you like. I'll just loaf and look at the scenery."

"As you please. I don't take much stock in scenery unless I have painted it myself, and even that sours on me sometimes;" and with this frank and quaintly expressed confession, Steve Chance turned and pushed his way through the crowd to a place behind Cruickshank, who welcomed him effusively, and introduced him to his friends.

Ned saw the artist gulp down what looked like a doctor's prescription, and light up a huge black cigar, and then turning his back upon the noisy expectorating crowd, he leant upon the bulwarks and forgot all about it.

Before his eyes stretched a vast field of blue water; blue water without a ripple upon it, save such as the steamer made, or the diving "cultus" duck, which the boat almost ran down, before the bird woke and saw its danger. Here and there on this blue field were groups of islands, wooded to the water's edge, and inhabited only by the breeding ducks and a few deer. As yet no one owned these islands, and, except for an occasional fishing Indian, no one had ever set foot on most of them. Everything spoke of rest and dreamful ease. What birds there were, were silent and asleep, rocked only in their slumbers by the swell from the passing boat, or else following in her wake on gliding wings which scarcely seemed to stir. There was no wind to fret the sea, or stir an idle sail. Nature was asleep in the spring sunlight, her calm contrasting strangely with the noise, and passion, and unrest on board the tiny boat which was puffing and churning its way through the still waters of the straits.

As for Ned, his ears were as deaf to the oaths and noise behind him as his eyes were blind to the calm beauty beneath them. His eyes were wide open, but his mind was not looking through them. As a matter of fact Ned Corbett, the real Ned Corbett, was just then day-dreaming somewhere on the banks of the Severn.

"Can you spare me a light, sir?"

This was the first sound that broke in upon his dreams, and Ned felt instinctively in his waistcoat pocket, and handed the intruder the matches which he found there.

"Thank you. I was fairly clemmed for a smoke."

"*Clemmed*" for a smoke! It was odd, but the dialect was the dialect of Ned's dream still, and as he looked at the speaker, a broad burly fellow, who evidently had made up his mind to have a chat, a pouch of tobacco was thrust out to him with the words: "Won't you take a fill yourself. It's pretty good baccy, and it ought to be. I had it sent to me all the way from the Wyle Cop."

"The Wyle Cop!" ejaculated Ned. "I thought there was only one Wyle Cop. Where do you come from, then?"

The stranger's face broadened into an honest grin.

"What part do I come from? Surely you ought to guess. Dunno yo' know a Shropshire mon, when yo' sees un?" he added, dropping into his native dialect, and holding out to Corbett a hand too broad to get a good grip of, and as hard as gun-metal.

Ned took the proffered hand eagerly. The sound of the home dialect stirred every chord in his heart.

"How did you know I was Shropshire?" he asked, laughing.

"How did I know? Well, I heard your friend call you Corbett, and that and your yellow head and blue eyes were enough for me. But say," he continued, resuming the Yankee twang which he had acquired in many a western mining camp, "if that young man over there is any account to you, you'd better go and see after him. They'll skin him clean in another half hour unless he owns the Bank of England."

Corbett's eyes involuntarily followed those of his newly-found friend, and he started as they rested upon Steve Chance, who now sat nervously chewing at the end of an unlit cigar in the middle of the poker players.

"Your friend ain't a bad player, but he ain't old enough for that crowd," remarked Roberts; and so saying he pushed a way for himself and his brother Salopian through the crowd to the back of Chance's chair.

Except for the addition of Chance, and another youngish man who appeared to be at least half-drunk, the party of poker players was the same which sat down to play when the *Umatilla* left the Victoria wharf.

Cruickshank faced Chance, and the same noisy dark fellow, who had been anxious to assuage everyone's thirst in the morning, appeared to be still ready to stand drinks and cigars. But the little crowd was quieter than it had been in the morning. The players had settled down to business.

"How deuced like Cruickshank that fellow is!" whispered Corbett to Roberts.

"Which?" answered his friend. "There are two Cruickshanks playing—Dan and Bub."

"But is the colonel any relation to the other?"

"I do not know which you call the colonel: never heard him called by that name before; but that's Bub" (pointing to the ringleader of the party), "and that's Dan" (pointing to the colonel). "Some say they are brothers, some say they are cousins. Anyway, I know *one* is a scoundrel."

"The deuce you do. Which of them?" But his inquiries were cut short and his attention diverted by the action of a new-comer, who just then pushed past him with a curt, "'Scuse me, sir."

"Let him through," whispered Roberts. "I tipped him the wink, and if you let him alone he'll fix them."

Ned was mystified, but did as he was bid. Indeed it was too late to attempt to do otherwise, for the last-joined in that little crowd, a withered gray man, whose features looked as if they had been hardened by a hundred years of rough usage, had quietly forced his way to the front until he had reached a seat at Steve Chance's elbow. It was noticeable that though the crowd was by no means tolerant of others who tried to usurp a front place amongst them, it gave way by common consent to the new-comer, who was moreover specially honoured with a nod and a smile from each of the Cruickshanks.

Steve only seemed inclined to resent the old man's familiarity, and for any effect it had he might as well have hidden his resentment.

"Pretty new to this coast, ain't you, sir?" remarked Mr. Rampike, after he had watched the game in silence for some minutes.

"Yes, I've only been out from the East a year," replied Steve shortly, as he examined his hand.

"Bin losing quite a bit, haven't you?" persisted his

tormentor. Steve growled out that he *had* lost "some," and turned his back on old Rampike with an emphatic rudeness which would have silenced most men.

"'Scuse me, sir, one moment," remarked Rampike utterly unabashed, and half rising to inspect Steve's hand over his shoulder.

A glance seemed to satisfy him.

"Who cut those cards?" he sung out.

"Dan Cruickshank," answered a voice from the crowd.

"Who dole those cards?" he persisted.

"Bub Cruickshank," replied the voice.

"Then, young man, you pass;" and without stirring a muscle of his face he coolly took from the astounded Steve four queens, and threw them upon the table.

For a moment Steve sat open-mouthed, utterly astounded by his adviser's impudence, and when he tried to rise and give vent to his feelings, Corbett's heavy hand was on his shoulder and kept him down.

Meanwhile an angry growl rose from the gamblers, but it was drowned at once in the laugh of the crowd, as without a sign of feeling of any kind, or a single comment, old Rampike slowly pulled from a pocket under his coat-tails an old, strangely-fashioned six-shooter, which he began to overhaul in the casual distrait manner of one who takes a mild interest in some weapon of a remote antiquity.

One by one, as the old hard-fist played with his ugly toy, those who objected to his intervention found that they had business elsewhere, so that when at last he let down the hammer, and replaced his "gun" under his coat-tails, Steve and the two Shropshiremen alone remained near him. Glancing round for a moment, the old man came as near smiling as a man could with features such as his, and then recovering himself he turned to Steve and remarked:

"This ain't no concern of mine, mister, but my pardner there, Roberts, I guess he takes some stock in you and he called me, so you'll 'scuse my interfering, but ef you should happen to play agen with California bilks, you mout sometimes go your pile on a poor hand, but pass four aces, quicker nor lightning, if Bub Cruickshank deals 'em," with which piece of advice the old man retired again into his shell, becoming, as far as one could judge, an absolutely silent machine for the chewing of tobacco.

Chance, now that he had had time to pull himself together, would gladly have had a talk with his ally; but old Rampike would have none of him, and Corbett, in obedience to a sign from Roberts, put his arm through his friend's and carried him off to another part of the ship.

"Let the old man alone," remarked Roberts, "talking isn't in his line. That is my share of the business. I sing and he fiddles."

"All right, as you please; but I say, Mr. Roberts," said Chance, "what in thunder did your partner mean by making me throw down four queens?"

"Mean! why, that Bub Cruickshank had four kings or better. You don't suppose that those chaps are here for their health, do you?"

"Here for their health?"

"Well, you don't suppose that they have come all the way to British Columbia to play poker on the square?"

"Then who are the Cruickshanks?" demanded Chance.

"That is more than I know. Bub Cruickshank is just about as low-down a gambler as there is on the coast; not a chap who pays up and stands drinks when he is bust, like the count and that lot."

"And is the colonel his brother?"

"Some say he is, some say he isn't. But I never knew him regularly on the gambling racket before, though he won a pile of money up at Williams Creek last fall."

"Then you have been in Cariboo," Corbett remarked.

"In Cariboo? Rather! I was there when Williams Creek was found, and for all that had to sing my way out with a splinter in my hand, and not a nickel in my pocket."

"How do you mean 'sing your way out?'"

"I mean just what I say. My hand went back on me and swelled, so that I couldn't work, and I just had to sing for my grub as I went along. Old Rampike had a fiddle and used to play, and I used to make up the songs and sing 'em. Perhaps you've heard the 'Old pack mule.' It's a great favourite at the mines:

"Ted staked and lost the usual way,
    But his loss he took quite cōōl;
  He was near the mines, and he'd start next day
    Riding on his old pack mūle."

"Riding, riding, riding on his old pack mule," sang Chance.

"Oh, you know it, do you? Seems to me it suits your case pretty well. Well, *I* made that;" and so saying the poet protruded his portly bosom three inches further into space, with the air of one who had done well by his fellow-men and knew it.

"Are you coming up to Cariboo this spring?" asked Corbett.

"No, we haven't dust enough to pay our way so far, more's the pity."

"Why not come with us? I'll find the dollars if you'll lend a hand with our pack-train," suggested Corbett.

"Well, I don't know, perhaps I might do worse; and as to that, if you are taking a pack-train along I daresay I could pretty nearly earn my grub packing. But I must talk it over with Rampike."

"All right, do you fix it your own way," put in Chance; "but mind, if you feel at all like coming, there need be no difficulty about the dollars either for you or your partner. I am pretty heavily in your debt anyway."

"Not a bit of it. Those bilks owe us something perhaps, and if they get a chance they won't forget to pay their score. But I guess they'll hardly care to tackle Rampike, or me either for the matter of that;" and whistling merrily his favourite tune, "Riding, riding, riding on the old pack mule," the Cariboo poet went below for refreshment.

CHAPTER IV.

"THE MOTHER OF GOLD."

FROM Victoria to the mouth of the Frazer river is about seventy miles, and thence to New Westminster is at least another sixteen. As the steamers which used to ply between the two young cities in '62 were by no means ocean racers, none of the passengers on board the s.s. *Umatilla* were in the least degree disappointed, although the shadows of evening were beginning to fall before they passed the Sandheads, and ran into the yellow waters of the Frazer.

Very few of those on board had eyes for scenery.

A rich-looking bar or a wavy riband of quartz high up on a mountain-side would have attracted more attention from that crowd than all the beauties of the Yosemite, and even had they been as keen about scenery as Cook's tourists, there was but little food for their raptures in the delta they were entering. The end of a river, like the end of a life, is apt to be ugly and dull, and the Frazer exhibits no exception to this rule. Child as she is of the winter's snows and the summer's sun, she loses all the purity of the one and the gleam of the other long before she attains her middle course, and at her mouth this "mother of gold" is but a tired, dull, old river, sordid and rich with golden sands, glad, so it seems, to slip by her monotonous mud-banks and lose herself and her yellow dross in the purifying waters of the salt sea.

As Corbett gazed upon the wide expanse of dun-coloured flood, he saw no sign even of that savage strength of which he had heard so much, except one. Far out, and looking small in the great waste of waters, was a stranded tree—a great pine, uprooted and now stranded on a sunken bank, its roots upturned, its boughs twisted off, and its very bark torn from its side by the fury of the riffles and whirlpools of the upper canyons. To Corbett there was something infinitely sad in this lonely wreck, though it was but the wreck of a forest tree. Had he known the great sullen river better he would have known that she brought down many sadder wrecks in those early days—human wrecks, whose wounds were not all of her making, though the river got the evil credit of them.

As it was, the first sight of the Frazer depressed him, and his depression was not dispelled by the sight of New Westminster. The idea of a new city hewed by man out of the virgin forest is noble enough, and whilst the sun is shining and the axes are ringing, the life and energy of the workers makes some compensation for the ugliness of their work. But it is otherwise when the sun is low and labour has ceased. Then "Stump-town" seems a more appropriate title than New Westminster, and a new-comer may be forgiven for shuddering at the ugliness of the new frame-houses, at the charred stumps still left standing in the main streets, at the little desolate forest swamps still left undrained within a stone's-throw of the Grand Hotel, and at all the baldness and beggarliness of the new town's surroundings. To Ned Corbett it looked as if Nature had been murdered, and civilization had not had time to throw a decent pall over her victim's body. Certainly in 1862 New Westminster might be, as its citizens alleged, an infant prodigy, but it was not a picturesque city.

However, as the s.s. *Umatilla* ran alongside her wharf, a voice roused Corbett from his musings, and turning he found Cruickshank beside him.

"What do you think about camping to-night, Corbett?" asked the colonel. "It will be rather dark for pitching our tent, won't it?"

Now, since the poker-playing incident Corbett had not spoken to Cruickshank. Indeed he had not seen him, and he had hardly made up his mind how to treat him when they met. That Cruickshank had a good many objectionable acquaintances was clear, but on the other hand there was nothing definite which could be alleged against him. Moreover, for the next month Ned and the estate-agent were bound to be a good deal together, and taking this into consideration,

Ned decided on the spur of the moment to let all that had gone before pass without comment. Cruickshank had evidently calculated upon Corbett taking this course, for though there had been a shade of indecision in his manner when he came up, he spoke quietly, and as one who had no explanations to make or apologies to offer.

"Yes, it is too dark to make a comfortable camp to-night," assented Corbett. "What does Chance want to do?"

"Oh, I vote for an hotel," cried Steve, coming up at the moment. "Let us be happy whilst we may, we'll be down to bed-rock soon enough."

"All right, 'the hotel goes,' as you would say, Steve;" and together the young men followed the crowd which streamed across the gangway to the wharf.

There the arrival of the s.s. *Umatilla* was evidently looked upon as the event of the day, and a great crowd of idlers stood waiting for the disembarkation of her passengers; and yet one man only seemed to be there on business, the rest were merely loafing, and would as soon have thought of lending a hand to carry a big portmanteau to the hotel as they would have thought of touching their hats.

This one worker in the crowd was an old man in his shirt sleeves, who caught Ned by the arm, as he had caught each of his predecessors, as soon as his foot touched the wharf, and in a tone of fatherly command bade him "Go up to the Mansion House. Best hotel in the city. It's the miners' house," he added. "Three square meals a day every time, and don't you forget it."

Ned laughed. The last recommendation was certainly worthy of consideration, and as no one else seemed anxious for his patronage he turned to Cruickshank with, "Is it to be the Mansion House?"

"Oh yes," replied the latter, "all the hard-fists stay with Mike."

"How long do you mean to stay here anyway?" asked Chance.

"Four or five days,—perhaps a week," replied Cruickshank. "There is a boat for Douglas to-night, but we could not buy the horses and the stores so as to be ready in less than a couple of days."

"That is so. We shall have to stay a week then?" asked Steve.

"Unless you like to intrust me with the purchase of your train. I could hire a man to help me and come on by the next boat if you want particularly to catch this one—"

The eyes of Corbett and Chance met, and unluckily Cruickshank saw the glance, and interpreted it as correctly as if the words had been spoken.

Corbett noticed the flush on the man's face and the ugly glitter in his eye, and hastened to soothe him.

"Oh no, colonel, it is deuced good of you," he said; "but we would rather wait and all go together. We are looking to you to show us a good deal besides the mere road in the next six weeks. But what are we to do with our packs now?"

"We can't leave them here, can we?" asked Chance, pointing to where their goods lay in a heap on the wharf.

"I don't see why not," growled Cruickshank; and then added significantly, "Murder or manslaughter are no great crimes in the eyes of some folk around here, but miners are a bit above petty larceny;" and so saying he turned on his heel and left Chance and Corbett to shift for themselves.

"Better take care what you say to that fellow," remarked Corbett, looking after the retreating figure; "although I like him better in that mood than in his oily one."

"Oh, I think he is all right; at any rate you won't want my help to crush him, Ned, if he means to cut up rough."

"Not if he fights fair, Steve; but I don't trust the brute—I never did."

"Just because he plays cards and calls himself a colonel? Why, everyone is a colonel out here. But to blazes with Cruickshank anyway. Come and get some grub."

And so saying Steve Chance entered the principal hotel of New Westminster, down the plank walls of which the tears of oozing resin still ran, while the smell of the pine-forest pervaded the whole house.

The "newness" of these young cities of the West is perhaps beyond the imagination of dwellers in the old settled countries of Europe. It is hard for men from the East to realize that the hotel, which welcomes them to all the comforts and luxuries of the nineteenth century, was standing timber a month before, that the walls covered with paper in some pretty French design, and hung with mirrors and gilt-framed engravings, were the homes of the jay and the squirrel, and that the former tenants have hardly had time yet to settle in a new abode.

And yet so it is: we do our scene-shifting pretty rapidly out West, and though there may not be time to perfect anything, the general effect is wonderful in the extreme.

The Westminster hotel was a gem of its class, and even Ned and Steve, who had become fairly used to Western ways, were a little aghast at the contrast between the magnificence of some of the new furniture and the simplicity of the sleeping accommodation, as illustrated by the rows of miners' blankets neatly laid out along the floor. Luckily Cruickshank had cautioned them to take their bedding with them, or they might have been obliged to pass a cheerless night in one of the highly-gilded arm-chairs, which looked as comfortless as they were gaudy.

The old tout upon the wharf, who owned what he advertised, had not misrepresented his house. As he had said, the meals were square enough even for the hungry miners who swarmed around his board, and though it was dull to lie upon their oars and wait, Steve and Ned might have found worse places to wait in than the Mansion House. For at Westminster a delay arose, as delays will the moment a man begins packing or touches cayuses out West. Of course there were a few horses to be bought, but equally, of course, everyone in the city and its suburbs seemed to know by instinct that Corbett & Co. were cornered, and must buy, however bad the beasts and however high the prices.

An old Indian, one Captain Jim, who with the assistance of all his female relatives used to pack liquor and other necessaries to the mines, had part of an old train to sell, horses, saddles, and all complete, and for the first three days of their stay at Westminster Corbett & Co. expected every minute to become owners of this outfit. But the business dragged on, until the noble savage upon whom they had looked as the type of genial simplicity had become an abomination in their eyes, and they had decided to leave the management of him to Cruickshank, resolving that if the train was not bought and ready to be shipped on the next boat to Douglas that they would go without a pack-train altogether. In the meanwhile they had to get through the time as best they could, assisted by the Cariboo poet, who had stayed on like themselves at Westminster.

To Chance this was no hardship; what with a little sketching, a little poker, and a great deal of smoking, he managed to get through the days with a good deal of satisfaction to himself. As to Ned, the delay and inaction disgusted him and spoilt his temper, which may account in some measure for an unfortunate incident which occurred on the second day of his stay at the Mansion House.

As the day was hot and he had nothing to do, the big fellow had laid out his blankets in a shady corner and prepared to lie down and sleep the weary hours away. Before doing so he turned for a minute or two to watch a game of piquet, in which Roberts appeared to be invariably "piqued, repiqued, pooped, and capoted," as his adversary, a red-headed Irishman, announced at the top of his voice.

Tired of the game, Ned turned and sought his couch, upon which two strangers had taken a seat. Going up to them, Ned asked them to move, and as they did not appear to hear him he repeated his request in a louder tone. Perhaps the heat and the flies had made him irritable, and a tone of angry impatience had got into his voice which nettled the men, one of whom, turning towards him, but not attempting to make room, coolly told him "to go to blazes."

As the man turned, Ned recognized him as Bub Cruickshank, the brother or cousin of the Colonel; but it needed neither the recognition nor the laugh that ran round the room to put Ned's hackles up.

Without stopping to think, he picked up the fellow by the scruff of his neck and the slack of his breeches and deposited him with the least possible tenderness upon an untenanted piece of the floor.

Before he had time to straighten himself, the dislodged Bub aimed a furious kick at Ned, and in another minute our hero was in the thick of as merry a mill as any honest young Englishman could desire. Time after time Ned floored his man, for though Bub knew very little of the use of his hands he was a determined brute, and kept rushing in and trying to get a grip of his man at close quarters, and, moreover, it was a case of one down the other come on, for as soon as Ned had floored one fellow and put him *hors de combat* for a short time, his companion took up the battle.

"Take care, Corbett,—take care of his teeth!" shouted Roberts all at once; and Ned felt a horrible faint feeling come over him, robbing him for the moment of all his strength, as Bub fastened on his thumb.

For a moment the Shropshireman almost gave up the battle. Those only who have suffered from this dastardly trick of the lowest of Yankee roughs, can have any idea of the effect it has upon a man's strength. But Corbett was almost as mad with rage at what he considered unsportsman-like treatment as he was with pain, so that he managed to wrench himself free and send his man to earth again with another straight left-hander.

Meanwhile the red-haired Irishman, who had been playing piquet with Roberts, had lost all interest in his game since the fight began, and was fairly writhing in his seat with suppressed emotion.

At last flesh and blood (or at least *Irish* flesh and blood) could endure it no longer, so that, jumping up from his seat, he took Ned just by the shoulders and lifted him clean out of the way as if he had been a baby, remarking as he did so—

"You stay there, sonny, and let me knock 'em down awhile."

But the poor simple Celt was doomed to disappointment. The truth was that Ned had been greedy, and taken more than his share of this innocent game of skittles, so that, as Mr. O'Halloran remarked sorrowfully at supper, he did but get in "one from the shoulther, and thin them two murtherin' haythens lit right out."

When the scrimmage was over Roberts took Ned on one side, and after looking at the bitten thumb and bandaging it up for his friend, he gave Ned a little advice.

"Fighting is all very well, Mr. Corbett, where people fight according to rules, but you had better drop it here. If you don't, some fellow will get level on you with the leg of a table or a little cold lead. If you must fight, you had better learn to shoot like old Rampike."

"Where is old Rampike now?" asked Ned, anxious to turn the conversation, and feeling a little ashamed of his escapade.

"Rampike went right on by the boat that met the *Umatilla*. He got a job up at Williams Creek, and will be there ahead of us."

"Then you mean to come up too, Roberts, that's right," said Corbett genially.

"Yes, I am coming up with your crowd. I met the count in town last night and borrowed the chips from him. I am thinking that if you make a practice of quarrelling with Cruickshank and all his friends you will need someone along to look after you"

"But who is the count, and why could you not have borrowed the money from us?" asked Corbett in a tone of considerable pique.

"The count! Oh, the count is an old friend, and lends to most anyone who is broke. It's his business in a way. You see, he is the biggest gambler in the upper country. Skins a chap one day and lends him a handful of gold pieces the next. He'll get it back with interest from one of us even if I don't pay him, so that's all right;" and honest Roberts dismissed all thought of the loan from his mind, as if it was the most natural thing in the world for a professional gambler to lend an impecunious victim a hundred dollars on no security whatever.

Luckily for Ned his fellow countryman took him in hand after this, and what with singing and working managed to keep him out of mischief. For Roberts found Corbett work in Westminster which just suited his young muscles, though it was as quaint in its way as Roberts' own financial arrangements in their way.

It seemed that in the young city there was no church and no funds to build one, but there was a sturdy, energetic parson, and a mob of noisy, careless miners, who rather liked the parson; not, perhaps, *because* he was a parson, but because he had in some way or other proved to them that he was a "man."

Had they been on the way down with their pockets full of "dust" the boys would soon have built him anything he wanted, whether it had been a church or a gin-shop. I am afraid it would have mattered little. As it was they were unluckily on their way up, and their pockets were empty.

But as the will was there the parson found the way, and all through that week of waiting Ned and a gang of other strong hardy fellows like himself made their axes glitter and ring on the great pines, clearing a site, and preparing the lumber for the first house of God erected in New Westminster.

Who shall say that their contribution had not as much intrinsic value as the thousand-dollar cheque which Crœsus sends for a similar object. A good deal more labour goes to the felling of a pine ten feet through than to the signing of a cheque, anyway.

CHAPTER V.

"IS THE COLONEL 'STRAIGHT?'"

AT the very last moment, when all Corbett's party, except Cruickshank, had yielded to despair, the Indian Jim gave in, and sold his animals as they stood for sixty dollars a head. This included the purchase of pack-saddles, cinches, and other items essential to a packer's outfit.

The steamer for Douglas started at 8 p.m., and it was long after breakfast on the same day that the eyes of Corbett and Chance, who were smoking out-

side their inn, were gladdened by the sight of Phon
and Cruickshank driving ten meek-looking brutes up
to the front of the Mansion House.

Having tied each pony short by the head to the
garden rail, Cruickshank began to organize his forces.
There were the ponies, it was true, but their packs and
many other things had still to be bought. There was
much to be done and very little time to do it in. Then
it was that Cruickshank showed himself to the greatest
advantage. For days he had appeared to dawdle over
his bargaining with Jim, until Ned almost thought that
Indian and white together were in league against him;
now he felt miserable at the mere memory of his former
suspicions. Cruickshank knew that no man can hurry
an Indian, and therefore abstained from irritating Jim
by attempting the impossible. The result of this was
that at the end of the time at his disposal Cruickshank
had by his indifference convinced Jim that he cared
very little whether he got the horses or not, so that
now the Indian was in a hurry to sell before the
steamer should carry Cruickshank and his dollars away
to Douglas. So Cruickshank bought the ponies, bought
them cheap, and, moreover, just in time to catch the
boat. This was all he had struggled for.

But now that he had white men to deal with his
tactics changed. These men knew the value of time
and could hurry, therefore Cruickshank hurried them.
To every man he gave some independent work to do.
No one was left to watch another working. Whilst
one dashed off to buy stores another took the horses
to the forge to be shod, and old Phon was left to repair
the horse furniture and overhaul the outfit generally.
Cruickshank himself went off to buy gunny sacks,
boxes, ropes, and such-like, rendered necessary by the

absence of *aparejos*, needing the knowledge of an expert in their selection.

It was already late in the afternoon, and Ned, hot and dusty, and as happy as a schoolboy, was helping the smith to shoe the last of the ponies, when Roberts, who had done his own work, walked into the forge.

For a minute or two Roberts stood unnoticed, observing his fellow-countryman with eyes full of a sort of hero-worship, commoner at a public school than in the world.

But Ned was one of those fellows who win men's hearts without trying to do so; a young fellow who said what he thought without waiting to pick his words, who did what he liked, and luckily liked what was good, and honest, and manly, and who withal looked the man he was, upstanding, frank, and absolutely fearless. Ned had been in the forge for perhaps half a day or more, and had already so won the heart of the smith that that good man with his eyes on the boy's great forearm had been hinting that there was "just as much money in a good smithy as there was in most of them up-country claims."

But Ned was bent on gold-mining and seeing life with the hard-fists, so though he loved to swing the great smith's hammer he was not to be tempted from his purpose, though he was quite ready to believe that a smith in New Westminster could earn more by his hands than many a professional man by his brains in Westminster on the Thames.

"Hullo, Rob! have you got through with your work?" cried Ned, catching sight of his friend at last.

"Yes. I've done all I've got to do; can I lend you a hand?"

"Why, no, thanks; my friend here is putting on the

last shoe. But what is the matter? you look as if you had got 'turned round' in the bush, and were trying to think your way out;" and Ned laid his hand laughingly on his friend's shoulder.

Roberts laughed too, but led the younger man outside, and once there blurted out his trouble.

"Look here, Corbett, ever since that gambling row I've had my eye on Cruickshank, and I thought that I knew him for a rascal, but blow me if he hasn't got beyond me this time."

"How so, Rob?"

"Well, I'm half-inclined to think he's honest after all. He is a real rustler when he chooses anyway," added the poet admiringly.

"Oh, I expect he is as honest as most of his kind. Why shouldn't he be? All men haven't the same ideas of honesty out here; and if he isn't honest it doesn't matter much to us, does it?" asked Ned carelessly.

"Doesn't it? Ain't you trusting him with a good many thousand dollars?" asked Roberts with some asperity.

"No, I don't think so. You see, Rob, if he is, as you thought, a card-sharper and a bogus estate-agent, my money is lost already; he can't clear out with the claims or the packs even if he wants to. But why do you think he is a rogue?"

"I tell you I'm beginning to think that he isn't."

"Bully for you, that's better!" cried Ned approvingly; "but what has worked this change in your opinions, Rob?"

"Well, last night that scoundrelly siwash, Captain Jim, tried to work a swindle with those pack-ponies, and Cruickshank wouldn't have it. Jim was to sell you a lot of unsound beasts at eighty dollars a head.

You would never have noticed that they had healed sores on their backs, and if Cruickshank had held his tongue he was to have had twenty dollars a pony, and the way he 'talked honest' to that Indian was astonishing, you bet."

"How did you find all this out?" asked Ned.

Roberts looked a little uncomfortable and flushed to the roots of his hair, but at length made the best of it, and admitted that he had followed the two men and overheard their conversation.

"You see, Ned," he added, "it's not very English, I know, but you must fight these fellows with their own weapons."

For a while Ned said nothing, though he frowned more than Roberts had ever seen him frown before, and his fingers tugged angrily at his slight moustache.

"Roberts," he said at last, "I agree with you, this sort of thing isn't very English, I'm hanged if it is; but I've been pretty nearly as suspicious as you have, so I can't afford to talk. Once for all, do you know anything against the colonel?"

"No," hesitated Roberts, "I don't know anything against Dan, but Bub—."

"Oh, to blazes with Bub!" broke in Corbett angrily. "A man cannot be responsible for every one of his cousins and kinsmen. From to-day I mean to believe in Cruickshank as an honest man, until I prove him to be a knave. You had better do the same, Rob; spying after a fellow as we have been doing is enough to make an honest man sick;" and Ned Corbett made a wry face as if the mere thought of it left a bad taste in his mouth.

"All right, that's a-go then. He was honest about these cayuses anyway, and if he does go back on us we'll fire him higher than a sky-rocket;" and so saying Roberts lent Ned a hand to collect the said cayuses. These at the first glance would have struck an English judge of horseflesh as being ten of the very sorriest screws that ever stood upon four legs; but at least they showed to Roberts' practised eye no signs of old sore backs, none of those half-obliterated scars which warn the *cognoscenti* of evils which have been and are likely to recur.

Taken in a body, they were a little too big for polo ponies, and a little too ragged, starved, and ill-shaped for a respectable costermonger's cart. There was one amongst them, a big buckskin standing nearly 14·2 hands, which looked fairly plump and able-bodied, but atoned for these merits by an ugly trick of laying back her ears and showing the whites of her eyes whenever she got a chance.

The most typical beast of his class was one Job, a parti-coloured brute (or pinto as they call them in British Columbia), with one eye brown and the other blue, and a nose of the brightest pink, as if he suffered from a chronic cold and a rough pocket-handkerchief. Job's bones stared at you through his skin, his underlip protruded and hung down, giving him an air of the most abject misery, and even a Yorkshire horsedealer could not have found a good point to descant upon from his small weak quarters to his ill-shaped shoulder.

But though Job's head was fiddle-shaped there was a good deal in it, as those were likely to discover who had given sixty dollars for him, and expected to get sixty dollars' worth of work out of him. He had not been packing since the days when he trotted as a foal beside a "greasers'" train for nothing. At present he was the meekest, most ill-used-looking brute on the Pacific coast, and Corbett was just remarking to Roberts "that that poor devil of a pony would never be able to carry a hundred and fifty pounds let alone two hundred over a bad road," when the buckskin let out, and caught the bay alongside of him such a kick on the stifle as made that poor beast go a little lame for days. No one noticed that the bite which set the buckskin kicking was given by old Job, who moved his weary old head sadly, just in time, however, to let the kick go by and land on the unoffending body of his neighbour.

An hour later all the horses were up again at the hotel, and the bill having been settled Phon and Roberts drove the train down to the wharf, where the steamer for Douglas, a small stern-wheeler, was waiting for her passengers and her cargo. With the exception of Job, all the cayuses were put on board at once and secured, but seeing that there was still a good deal of luggage in small parcels up at the hotel, Chance kept "that quiet old beast Job, just to carry down the odds and ends;" and Job, with a sigh which spoke volumes to those who could understand, plodded away to do the extra work set aside as of right for the meek and long-suffering.

It is an aggravating employment under any circumstances, the employment of packing. Many men, otherwise good men, swear naturally (and freely) as soon as they engage in it; but then, why I know not, the very presence of a horse makes some men swear. Steve knew very little about packing anyway, and had he known more he would not have found it easy to fasten his bundles on to the back of a beast which shifted constantly from one leg to another, and always seemed to be standing uphill or downhill, with one leg at least a foot shorter than the other three.

When Steve spoke to him (with an angry kick in the stomach), Job would lift his long-suffering head with an air of meek dejection, and shifting his leg as required plant a huge hoof solidly upon Steve's moccasined foot. If I could paint the look on that great ugly equine head as it turned with leering eye and projecting nether lip, and looked into the anguished face of Steve Chance, I should be able to teach my reader more of cayuses (the meanest creatures on God's earth) than I can ever hope to do. But even with Job to *help* him, Steve got his load down to the boat at last, and put all aboard except a new pack-saddle, which he had taken off the pack-horse and laid down on the ground beside him.

With lowered head and half-shut eyes Job stood for some minutes patiently waiting, and then, as Steve came over the side to drive him on board with his fellows, the old horse heaved a long, long sigh, and before Steve could reach him lay down slowly and gently upon that pack-saddle. Of course when he got up, the pack-saddle was demolished, and as the last whistle had sounded, there was no time to get another before leaving Westminster.

A new saddle would have to be bought at Douglas, and that would cost money, or made upon the road, and that would mean delay, so Job, with a cynical gleam in his wall-eye, trotted meekly and contentedly on board. He had entered his first protest against extra work.

Five minutes later the steamer *Lillooet* cast loose from her moorings, the gangway was taken in, and the gallant little stern-wheeler went cleaving her way up through the yellow Frazer, on her forty-mile run to the mouth of Harrison river, steaming past long mud-flats and many a mile of heavy timber.

A day and a half was the time allowed for the journey from New Westminster to Douglas, but Corbett and Chance could hardly believe that they had taken so long when they came to their moorings again at the head of the Harrison Lake.

To them the hours had seemed to fly by, for their eyes and thoughts were busy, intent at one moment upon the bare mud-banks, watching for game or the tracks of the game, the next straining to catch a glimpse of deer feeding at dawn upon the long gray hills—hills which were a pale dun in the light of early morning, but which became full of rich velvety shadows as the day wore on.

Overhead floated the fleecy blue and white sky of spring-time; on the hills patches of wild sunflower mingled with the greenish gray of the sage brush, and here and there, even on the arid barren banks of the Frazer itself, occurred little "pockets" of verdure—hollows with fresh-water springs in them, where the tender green of the young willows, and the abundant white bloom of the choke cherries and olali bushes, made Edens amongst the waste of alkaline mud-banks, Edens tenanted and made musical by all the collected bird-life of that barren land.

The only difficult bit of water for the little steamer was the seven miles of the Harrison river, a rapid, turbulent stream, up which the s.s. *Lillooet* had to fight every inch of the way; but beyond that lay the lake, a broad blue lake, penned in by steep and heavily-timbered mountains, and beyond the one-house town of Douglas, at which Ned and his fellow-passengers disembarked about noon of the second day out from Westminster.

From Douglas the ordinary route was by river and lake, with a few short portages to *Lillooet* on the Frazer; and in 1862 there were steamers upon all the lakes (Lillooet, Anderson, and Seton), and canoes (with a certainty of a fair breeze in summer) for such as preferred them.

But Ned and his friends had decided that as they had a pack-train, and would be compelled to pack part of the way in any case, they might just as well harden their hearts and pack the whole distance, more especially since they had ample time to make their journey in, and not too much money to waste upon steamboat fares. So at Douglas Cruickshank bought another pack-saddle for about twice what it would have cost at Westminster (freight was high in the early days), and suggested that as the one house (half store, half hotel) was full to overflowing, they might as well strike out for themselves, and as it was only mid-day make a few miles upon their road before camping for the night.

"You see," argued Cruickshank, "it's no violet's camping where so many men have camped before, and a good many of them greasers and Indians."

Corbett and Chance were new to the discomforts of the road, and had still to learn the penalty for camping where Indians have camped; but for all that they took the colonel's advice and assented to his proposal, though it meant bidding good-bye to their fellow-men a day or two sooner than they need have done.

Once the start had been decided upon Cruickshank lost no time in getting under weigh. The diamond hitch had no mysteries for him, the loops flew out and settled to an inch where he wanted them to, every strand in his ropes did its share of binding and holding fast; his very curses seemed to cow the most stubborn cayuse better than another man's, and when he cinched the unfortunate beasts up you could almost hear their ribs crack.

Job alone nearly got the better of the colonel, but even he just missed it. Cruickshank cinched this wretched scarecrow a little less severely than the rest, but when later on he saw old Job with his cinch all slack, a malevolent grin came over his face, and he muttered, "Oh, that's your sort, is it, an old-timer? So am I!" And after giving Job a kick which would have knocked the wind out of anything, he cinched him up again before he could recover himself, and then led him to drink. As the horse sucked down the water greedily Cruickshank muttered to himself, "*Bueno*, I guess your load will stick now until you are thirsty again." After this Job and the colonel seemed to have a mutual understanding, and as long as he was within hearing of Cruickshank's curses there was no better pack-pony on the road than old Job.

It seems as if men who have been used to packing, and have had a spell of rest from their ordinary occupation, itch to handle the ropes again; at least, it is only in this way that I can explain the readiness displayed by so many of Ned's fellow-passengers to lend a hand in fixing his packs for him.

In an hour from the time of disembarkation the train was ready to start, and the welcome cry of "All set!" rang out, after which there was a little hand-shaking, a lighting of pipes, and the procession filed away up the river, Cruickshank leading the first five ponies, then Roberts plodding patiently along on foot, then another five ponies, and then, as long as the narrow train would permit of it, Ned and Steve trudging along, chatting and keeping the ponies on the move.

Cruickshank was already some distance ahead, and even Steve and Ned were almost outside the little settlement, when a big red-headed Irishman, whom Corbett remembered as his fighting friend at Westminster, came running after him.

"Say," asked Mr. O'Halloran, rather out of breath from his run. "Say, are you and that blagyard partners?"

"Which?" asked Ned in amaze. "My friend Chance?"

"No, no, not this boy here—that fellow riding ahead of the train."

"Cruickshank? Yes, we are partners in a way," replied Ned.

"And you know it was his brother you laid out? Faith, you laid him out as nate as if it was for a berryin'," he added with a grin.

"I've heard men say that the colonel is Bub Cruickshank's brother," admitted Ned; "but the colonel is all right, whatever Bub is."

"And you and he ain't had no turn-up along of that scrimmage down at Westminster?" persisted O'Halloran.

"Not a word. I don't think he knew about it."

"Oh yes, he did. I saw Bub and him talking it over, and you may bet your boots the only reason he didn't bark is that he means to bite—yes, and bite hard too. It's the way with them dark, down-looking blagyards," added the honest Irishman, in a tone of the deepest scorn.

"Ah, well, I don't think Cruickshank is likely to try his teeth on me," laughed Ned. "If he does I must try that favourite rib-bender of yours upon him," and Ned gripped O'Halloran's hand and strode gaily after his train.

For a moment the red-headed one stood looking after his friend, and then heaving a great sigh remarked:

"Indade and I'd like a turn wid you mesilf, but if that black-looking blagyard does a happorth of harm to you, it's Kornaylius O'Halloran as 'll put a head on him."

CHAPTER VI

THE WET CAMP.

AS his pack-train wound away along the trail from Douglas, Ned Corbett gave a great deep sigh as if there was something which he fain would blow away from him. And so there was.

As he left the last white man's house between Douglas and Lillooet, he hoped and believed that he left behind him towns and townsmen, petty delays, swindlings, and suspicions of swindlings.

He was going to look for gold, and give a year at least of his young life to be spent in digging for it, and yet this absurd young Englishman was actually thanking his stars that now, at last, he was rid of dollars and dollar hunters, business and business men, for at least a month.

There was food enough on the beasts in front of him to last his party for a year. He was sound in wind and limb, his rifle was not a bad one, and he had seen lots of game tracks already, and that being so he really cared very little whether he reached his claims in time or not. But of course, as Cruickshank said, there was ample time to make the journey in, time indeed and to spare, as every one he had met admitted, so that no doubt Steve and he would reach Williams Creek in time, find the claims as Cruickshank had represented them, and make no end of money.

That would just suit Steve; and after all a lot of money would be a good thing in its way. It would make a certain old uncle at home take back a good many things he had once said about his nephew's "great useless body and ramshackle brains," and besides, he would like a few hundred pounds himself to send home, and a bit in hand to hire a boat to go to Alaska in. That had been Ned's day-dream ever since he had seen a certain cargo of bear-skins which had come down from that ice-bound *terra incognita* to Victoria.

So Ned sighed a great sigh of relief and contentment, took off his coat and slung it on his back, opened the collar of his flannel shirt and let the soft air play about his ribs, turned his sleeves up over his elbows, tied a silk handkerchief turban-wise on his yellow head, and having cut himself a good stout stick trudged merrily along, sucking in the glorious mountain air as greedily as if he had spent the last six months of his life waiting for briefs in some grimy fog-haunted chamber of the Temple.

He would have liked the ponies to have moved along a little faster, because as it was he found it difficult to keep behind them, five miles an hour suiting his legs better than two. But this was his only trouble, and as every now and then he got a breather, racing up some steep incline to head back a straggler to the path of duty, Ned managed to be perfectly happy in spite of this little drawback.

As for the others, Cruickshank, who had seemed restless and nervous as long as he had been with the crowd of miners on the boat and at Douglas, had now relapsed into a mere automaton, which strode on silently ahead of the pack-train, emitting from time to time little blue jets of tobacco smoke. Steve seemed buried in calculations, based on a miner's report that the dirt at Williams Creek had paid as much as fifty cents to the shovelful, an historical fact which Phon and the young Yankee discussed occasionally at some length: and old Roberts, having agreed to leave his suspicions behind him, shared his tobacco cheerily with Cruickshank, and from time to time startled the listening deer with scraps of his favourite ditties.

It was the refrain of the old pack mule, "Riding, riding, riding on my old pack mule," which at last roused Steve Chance's indignation against the songster.

"Confound the old idiot!" growled the Yankee; "I wish he wouldn't remind me of the unattainable. I shouldn't mind riding, but I am getting pretty sick of tramping. Isn't it nearly time to camp, Ned?"

"Nearly time to camp? Why, we haven't made eight miles yet," replied Corbett.

"Oh, that be hanged for a yarn! We have been going five solid hours by my watch, and five fours are twenty."

"That may be, but five twos are ten, and what with stoppages to fix packs, admire the scenery, and give you time to munch a sandwich and tie up your moccasins, I don't believe we have been going two miles an hour. But are you tired, Steve?"

"You bet I am, Ned. If there really is no particular hurry let us camp soon."

"All right, we will if you like. Hullo, Cruickshank!" Cruickshank turned.

"Steve is tired and wants to camp—what do you say?"

Cruickshank hesitated a moment and then agreed to the proposition, beginning at once to loosen the packs upon the beasts nearest to him.

'Here, I say, steady there!" cried Corbett; "you take me too literally. Steve can go another mile if necessary. We'll stop at the next good camping-ground."

"I'm afraid you won't get anything better than this," replied the colonel. "Why, what is the matter with this? You didn't expect side-walks and hotels on the trail, did you, Corbett?"

Even in his best moods there was a nasty sneering way about Cruickshank, which put his companions' backs up.

"No, but I did think we might find a flat spot to camp on."

"Did you? Then I'm sorry to disappoint you. You won't find anything except a swamp meadow flatter than this for the next ten miles or so, and the swamps are a little too wet for comfort at this time of year."

"Do you mean to say, Cruickshank, that we can't find a flatter spot than this? Why, hang it, man, you couldn't put a tea-cup down here without spilling the contents," remonstrated Corbett.

"Well, if you think you can better this, let us go on; perhaps you know best. What is it to be, camp or 'get?'"

"Oh, if you are certain about it I suppose we may as well stay here; but, by Jove, we shall have to tie ourselves up to trees when we go to sleep to prevent our straying downhill." And Ned laughed at the vision he had conjured up.

A minute later a bale,—bigger, heavier, and more round of belly than its fellows,—escaped from Steve Chance's grip and fell heavily to the earth. Steve was not a strong man, certainly not a man useful for lifting weights, besides he was a careless fellow, and tired. For a moment Steve stood looking at the bale as it turned slowly over and over. Twice it turned round and Steve still looked at it. The next moment it gathered way, and before Steve could catch it was hopping merrily downhill, in bounds which grew in length every time it touched the hillside. Steve, assisted by Phon, had the pleasure of recovering that bale from the group of young pines amongst which it eventually stuck, and brought it with many sobs and much perspiration to the point from which it originally started. It took Steve and Phon longer to get over that two hundred feet of hillside than it had taken the bale.

That first camp of theirs has left an impression upon Ned's mind and Steve's which years will not efface. Ned was too tough to look upon it as more than a somewhat rough practical joke, likely to pall upon a man if repeated too often, but to Chance that camp was a camp of misery and a place of tears. There was water, but it was a long way downhill; there was, as Cruickshank said, timber enough to keep a mill going for a twelvemonth, but whatever was worth having for firewood was either uphill or downhill—you had to climb for everything you happened to want; and to wind up with, you absolutely had to dig a sort of shelf out of the hillside upon which to pitch your tent.

It was here, too, that Steve had his first real experience of camping out. He helped to unpack the horses, but he took so long to retrieve the bale which had gone downhill that some one had to lend him a hand even with the one beast which he unpacked. He volunteered to cook, but when on investigation it was discovered that he would have fried beans without boiling them, a community unduly careful of its digestion scornfully refused his assistance. In despair he seized an axe, and went away as "a hewer of wood and a drawer of water." By and by the voice of his own familiar friend came to him again and again in tones of cruel derision:

"Where is that tree coming down, Steve?"

"I don't know and don't care, but it's got to come somewhere," replied the operator angrily, as he hewed blindly at the tough green pine.

"But it won't do for firewood anyway, Steve, this year, and if you don't take care you will never need firewood again. Don't you know how to make a tree fall where you want it to?" and Ned took the tool from his hand, and completing what his companion had so badly begun, laid the tree out of harm's way.

"Well, it seems that I can't do anything to please you," grumbled Steve, now thoroughly angry. "When there is anything that you and Cruickshank reckon you want my help in you can call me, Corbett. I'll go and smoke whilst you run this show to your own satisfaction."

"No you won't, old man, and you won't get riled either. Just be a good chap and go and cut us some brush for bedding. See, this is the best kind," and Ned held out to his friend a branch of hemlock. Although an hour later Ned noticed that there was every kind of brush *except* hemlock in the pile which Steve had collected, he wisely complimented him on his work, and said nothing about his mistake. A man does not become a woodsman in a week.

Meanwhile the tent had been pitched; Cruickshank was just climbing up the hill again after driving the ponies to a swamp down below, and old Phon was handling a frying-pan full of the largest and thickest rashers of bacon on record. Little crisp ringlets of fried bacon may serve very well for the breakfast of pampered civilization, but if you did not cut your rashers thick out in the woods you would never stop cutting.

Lucky would it have been for Steve and Ned if rough fare and a rocky camp had been the worst troubles in store for them, but unluckily, even as they lit their post-prandial pipes, the storm-clouds began to blow up the valley, ragged and brown, and whilst poor Steve was still tossing on a sleepless pillow, vexed by the effects of black tea on his nerves, and crawling beasts upon his sensitive skin, the first great drops of the coming storm splashed heavily on the sides of the tent.

Of course the tent was new. Everything the two young miners had was new, brand-new, and made upon the most recent and improved lines. None of the old, time-tried contrivances of practical men are ever good enough for beginners. So the fourth or fifth drop of rain which hit that tent came through as if it had been a sieve, and when well-meaning Steve rubbed his hand over the place "feeling for the leak," the water came in in a stream.

When the next morning broke, the wanderers looked out upon that most miserable of all things, a wet camp in the woods. The misery of a wet camp is the one convincing argument in favour of civilization.

It was still early in the year, and the season was a late one even for British Columbia, amongst whose mountains winter never yields without a struggle. On the dead embers of last night's camp-fire were slowly melting snowflakes, and a chill wet wind crept into Ned's bosom, as he looked out upon the morning, and made him shudder.

But Ned was hard, so that careless of rain and puddles he splashed out past the camp-fire, and after a good many failures kindled a little comparatively dry wood, over which to make the morning tea, and then drew upon himself the scorn of that old campaigner Cruickshank by washing.

What work they could find to do the men did, but even so the hours went wearily by. Cruickshank was opposed to making a start, for fear lest the rain should damage the packs, which now lay all snug beneath their *manteaux*. So they waited until Cruickshank was tired of smoking, and Roberts of hearing himself sing; until Corbett could sleep no more, and Steve was hoarse with grumbling. Only Phon, lost in thought which white men cannot fathom, and the pack animals full of sweet young grass, seemed content.

For three whole days the party stopped in the same camp, gazing hour after hour upon a limited view of stiff burnt pines, with the melting snow drifting down through them, and the fog wrapping them and hiding away all the distance. Even the fire of piled logs shone, *not* with heat but with damp, and the monotonous splash of the drops as they fell from a leak in the tent into the frying-pan set to catch them, combined with Phon's harsh cough, to break the silence.

At last, when even Ned was beginning to think of rheumatism, and to long for a glass of hot toddy and a Turkish bath, the sun came back again, and cast long rich shadows from the red stems of the bull-pines across the trail, over which Steve nearly ran, in his anxiety to leave the wet camp as far behind him as possible.

But even the wet camp was only the beginning of troubles. Three days they lost waiting for the sun, and in the next camp they waited three more days for their horses.

At the first camp Cruickshank had been careful to hobble the horses, which would not have strayed had he left them free in a small naturally inclosed pasture, like that swamp at the foot of the side hills. But at the second camp, where the feed was bad and the ways open, he neglected to hobble any of them, and, oddly enough, old packer though he was, he overlooked the whole band in his first day's search, so that no one went that way to look for them again, until it occurred to Corbett to try to puzzle out their tracks in that direction for himself. There he found them, in the very meadow in which they had pastured the first night, all standing in a row behind a bush no bigger than a cabbage, old Job at their head, every nose down, every ear still, even Job's blue eye fixed in a kind of glassy stare, and the bell round Job's neck dumb, for it was full of mud and leaves. It was deuced odd, Ned thought, as he drove the beasts home. Cruickshank didn't seem to know as much of packing and the care of horses as he appeared to know at first; but if he knew too little, that wall-eyed fiend, Job, knew too much.

Anyway, they had taken eight days to do two days'

travel, up to that time. It was well that they had ample time in which to make their journey to Cariboo.

CHAPTER VII.

FACING DEATH ON THE STONE-SLIDE.

IT was the last day of Corbett's journey between the Harrison and the Frazer, and a boiling hot day at that. With the exception of Corbett himself, and perhaps Cruickshank, whose back alone was visible as he led the train, the whole outfit had relapsed into that dull mechanical gait peculiar to packers and pack animals. To Chance it seemed that he was in a dream— a dream in which he went incessantly up and up or down, down day after day without pause or change. To him it seemed that there was always the same gray stone-slide under foot, the same hot sun overhead, and the same gleaming blue lake far below; like the pack animals, he was content to plod along hour after hour, seeing nothing, thinking of nothing, unless it was of that blessed hour when the camp would be pitched and the tea made, and the soothing pipe be lighted.

But though Chance had no eyes for it, the end of this first part of his journey was near at hand. Fourteen miles away the great grisly mountains came together and threw a shadow upon Seton Lake, building a wall and setting a barrier over or through which there seemed no possible way of escape. As Corbett looked at it, he could see the trees quite plainly on the narrow rim of grass between that mountain wall and the lake, and though he could not see that too, he knew that through them ran a trail which led to Lillooet on the Frazer. Even Ned longed to reach that trail and catch a glimpse of the little town, in which he and his weary beasts might take at least one day's rest and refreshment.

Since leaving Douglas, Cruickshank and Corbett had been upon the best of terms. Cruickshank knew how everything ought to be done, and Corbett was quick and tireless to do it, so that between them these two did most of the work of the camp; and though Ned noticed that his guide was not as anxious to get to Lillooet as he had been to get away from Douglas, he made allowances for him. Cruickshank was hardly a young man, and no doubt his strength was not equal to his will.

As to the straying of the horses at the second camp, there could be but one opinion. It was a bad mistake to leave them unhobbled; but after all everyone made mistakes sometimes, and though that mistake had involved the loss of a great deal of time, it was the only one which could be laid to Cruickshank's account. So far not one single thing, however unimportant, had been left behind in camp or lost upon the trail; there had been no accidents, no lost packs, nor any sign of sore backs. Day after day Cruickshank himself had led the train, choosing the best going for his ponies, and seeing them safely past every projecting rock and over every *mauvais pas*.

On this day for the first time Cruickshank proposed to give up his position in front of the train to Ned. Stopping at a place where there was room to shunt the rear of his column to the front, the colonel hailed Ned, and suggested that they should change places.

"Come on and set us a quick step, Corbett. Even

if you do overtire the ponies a bit, it doesn't matter now that we are so near Lillooet. They can rest there as much as they like."

"Very well. I expect *you* must want a change, and I'll bet old Steve does. Why, you have hardly had anyone to speak to for a week," replied Corbett good-naturedly.

"That's so, but I must save my breath a little longer still. If Roberts will go behind with Phon and Chance, I'll keep the first detachment as close to your heels as I can; and, by the way, we had better make a change with the horses whilst we are about it."

"Why?" asked Ned. "What is the matter with them?"

"Not much, but if we are to have any more swimming across places where the bridging is broken down, we may as well have the horses that take kindly to water in front, and send that mean old beast to the rear;" and the colonel pointed to Job, which with its head on one side and an unearthly glare in its blue eye, appeared to be listening to what was being said.

"All right, we can do that here if you will lend a hand. Which shall we put the bell on?" and Ned took the bell off Job, and turned that veteran over to the second half of the train.

"Put it on this fellow; he takes to the water like an otter, and he will make a good leader. Wherever his packs can go, any of the others can follow;" and Cruickshank pointed to the great bulging bales upon the back of the buckskin.

"I expect Steve and Roberts packed him, didn't they?" Cruickshank added. "Well, they aren't pretty to look at, but I guess they'll stick;" and so saying, he gave the buckskin a smack on his quarters which sent that big star-gazing brute trotting to the front, where Ned invested him with the order of the bell.

"Is it all right now, Cruickshank?" asked Corbett.

"All right."

"Forrard away then!" cried Ned, and turning he strode merrily along a narrow trail, which wound up and up across such sheer precipitous side hills as would make some men dizzy to look at. A slip in some places would have meant death to those who slipped, long before their bruised bodies could reach the edge of the lake glittering far below; but neither men in moccasins nor mountain ponies are given to slipping.

After the rain had come the sunshine and the genial warmth of spring, under the influence of which every hill was musical with new-born rivulets, and every level place brilliant with young grass. The very stone-slides blossomed in great clumps of purple gentian, and over even the stoniest places crept the tendrils of the Oregon vine, with its thorny shining leaves and flower-clusters of pale gold.

Now and again the trail rose or fell so much that it seemed to Ned as if he had passed from one season of flowers to another. Down by the lake, where the pack animals splashed along the bed of a little mountain stream, the first wild rose was opening, a mere speck of pink in the cool darkness made by the overhanging bushes. Here by the lake side, too, were numerous butterflies—great yellow and black "swallow tails," hovering in small clouds over the damp stones, or Camberwell beauties in royal purple, floating through sun and shadow on wings as graceful in flight as they were rich in colour. Higher up, where the sun had heated the stone-slides to a white heat, were more butterflies (fritillaries and commas and tortoise-shells), while now and again a flash of orange and a shrill little screech told Ned that a humming-bird went by.

In the highest places of all, where the snow still lingered in tiny patches, the red-eyed spruce-cocks hooted from the pines, the ruffed grouse strutted and boomed in the thickets, and the yellow flowers of lilies gave promise of many a meal for old Ephraim, when their sweet bulbs should be a few weeks older.

To Ned, merely to swing along day after day in the sunshine and note these things, was gladness enough, and it was little notice he took of heat, or thirst, or weariness. Unfortunately he became too absorbed, and as often happens with men unused to leading out, forgot his train and walked right away from his ponies.

When this fact dawned upon him it was nearly mid-day, and he found himself at the highest point which the path had yet reached, from which, looking back, he could see the train crawling wearily after him. He could see, too, that Cruickshank was signalling him to stop, so nothing loth Ned sat down and waited. The path where he sat came out to a sharp promontory, and turning round this it began to pass over the worst stone-slide Ned had yet seen. Most of those he had hitherto encountered had been mere narrow strips of bad going from fifty to a hundred yards across, but this was nearly five hundred yards from side to side, and except where the trail ran, there was not foothold upon it for a fly. Properly speaking it was not, as the natives called it, a stone-slide at all, but rather the bed or shoot, by which, century after century, some hundreds of stone-slides had gone crashing down into the lake below.

As soon as Ned had assured himself that the train was

once more as near to him as it ought to be, he knocked off as much of the projecting corner as he could, and passed round it on to the slide.

Looking up from the narrow trail, the young Englishman could see the great rocks which hung out from the cliffs above: rocks whose fellows had been the makers of this slide, letting go their hold up above as the snows melted and the rains sapped their foundations, and then thundering down to the lake with such an army of small stones and debris that it seemed as if the whole mountain-side was moving. When this stone-avalanche crashed into the water a wave rolled out upon the lake big as an ocean swell from shore to shore.

Looking down, a smooth shoot sloped at an angle from him to the blue water.

"Well, that is pretty sheer," muttered Ned, craning his neck to look down to where the lake glistened a thousand feet below, "and if one of our ponies gets his feet off this trail, there won't be anything of him left unbroken except his shoes;" and so saying, he turned to see how the leader would turn the awkward corner which led on to this *via diabolica*.

As he did so the report of a pistol rang out sharp and clear, followed by a rush and the clatter of falling stones, and the next moment Ned saw the leading pony dash round the overhanging rocks, its ropes all loose, its packs swinging almost under its belly, its bell ringing as if it were possessed, and its eyes starting from its head in the insanity of terror.

At every stride it was touch-and-go whether the brute would keep its legs or not. Each slip and each recovery at that flying pace was in itself a miracle, and Ned hardly hoped that he could stop the maddened beast before it and the packs went crashing down to the lake.

Stop the pony! He might as well have tried to stop a stone-slide. And as he realized this, the danger of his own position flashed across him for the first time.

Coming towards him, now not fifty yards away, was the maddened horse, which probably could not have stopped if it wanted to in that distance, and on such a course. Behind Ned was four hundred yards of such a trail as he hardly dared to run over to escape death, and even if he had dared, what chance in the race would he have had against the horse? Above him there was nothing to which even his strong fingers could cling, and below the trail—well, he had already calculated on the chances of any living thing finding foothold below the trail. Instinctively Ned shouted and threw up his hands. He might as well have tried to blow the horse back with his breath. In another ten seconds the brute would be upon him; in other words, in another ten seconds horse and packs and Ned Corbett would be the centre of a little dust-storm bounding frantically down that steep path to death!

In such a crisis as this men think fast, or lose their wits altogether. Some, perhaps, rather than face the horror of their position shut their eyes, mental and physical, and are glad to die and get it over. Ned was of the other kind: the kind that will face anything with their eyes open, and fight their last round with death with eyes that will only close when the life is out of them.

There was just one chance for life, and having his eyes open, Ned saw it and took it.

Twenty yards from him now was that hideous maddened brute, with its ears laid back, its teeth showing, the foam flying from its jaws, and its great blood-shot eyes almost starting from their sockets. Twenty yards, and the pace the brute was coming at was the pace of a locomotive!

And yet, though Corbett's face was gray as a March morning, and his square jaws set like a steel trap, there was no blinking in his eyes. He saw the blow coming, and quick as light he countered. Never on parade in the old school corps did his rifle come to his shoulder more steadily than it came now; not a nerve throbbed as he pressed (not pulled) the trigger, nor was it until he stood *alone* upon that narrow path that his knees began to rock beneath him, while the cold perspiration poured down his drawn white face in streams.

One man only besides Corbett saw that drama; one man, whose features wore a look of which hell might have been proud, so fiendish was it in its disappointed malice, when through the dust he saw the red flame flash, and then, almost before the report reached him, saw the body of the big buckskin, a limp bagful of broken bones, splash heavily into the Seton Lake.

But the look passed as a cloud passes on a windy morning, and the next moment Cruickshank was at Corbett's side, a flood of congratulations and inquiries pouring from his ready lips. As for Ned, now that the danger was over, he was utterly unstrung, and a bold enemy might have easily done for him that which the runaway horse had failed to do. Perhaps that thought never occurred to any enemy of Ned's; perhaps the quick, backward glance, in which Cruickshank recognized old Roberts' purple features, was as effectual a safeguard to the young man's life as even his own good rifle had been; be that as it may, a few moments

CORBETT SEIZES HIS ONE CHANCE FOR LIFE.

later Ned stumbled along after his friend to a place of safety, and there sat down again to collect himself.

Meanwhile, Roberts and Cruickshank stood looking at one another, an expression in the old poet's face, which neither Corbett nor Cruickshank had ever seen there before, the hand in his coat pocket grasping a revolver, whose ugly muzzle was ready to belch out death from that pocket's corner at a moment's notice. At last Cruickshank spoke in a voice so full of genuine sorrow, that even Roberts slackened his hold upon the weapon concealed in his coat pocket.

"You've had a near shave to-day, Corbett, and it was my fault. I am almost ashamed to ask you to forgive me."

"How—what do you mean? Did you fire that shot?"

"I did, like a cursed idiot," replied Cruickshank.

Roberts' face was a study for an artist. Speechless surprise reigned upon it supreme.

"I did," Cruickshank repeated. "I fired at a grouse that was hooting in a bull-pine by the track, and I suppose that that scared the cayuse—though I've never known a pack-horse mind a man shooting before."

"Nor I," muttered Roberts. "I suppose you didn't notice if you hit that fool-hen, Colonel Cruickshank?"

"No; I don't suppose I did. I'd enough to think of when I saw what I had done."

"Well, it didn't fly away, and it ain't there now," persisted Roberts. "Perhaps you'd like to go and look for it."

However, Cruickshank took no notice of Roberts' speech, but held out his hand to Corbett with such an honest expression of sorrow, that if it was not sincere, it was superb as a piece of acting.

Without a word Corbett took the proffered hand. There are some natures which find it hard to suspect evil in others, and Ned Corbett's was one of these. Only he made a mental note, that though Cruickshank had only made two mistakes since starting from Douglas, they had both been of rather a serious nature.

Only one man climbed down to look at the dead cayuse as it lay half hidden in the shallow water at the edge of the lake, and that was only a Chinaman. Of course he went to see what he could save from the wreck; equally, of course, he found nothing worth bringing away; found nothing and noticed nothing, or if he did, only told what he had seen to old Roberts. There seemed to be an understanding between these two, for Phon trusted the hearty old Shropshireman as much as he seemed to dread and avoid the colonel.

CHAPTER VIII

THEIR FIRST "COLOURS."

"LILLOOET at last!"

Steve Chance was the speaker, and as his eyes rested upon the Frazer, just visible from the first bluff which overlooks the Lillooet, his spirits rose so that he almost shouted aloud for joy. There beneath him, only a short mile away, lay most of the things which he longed for: rest after labour, good food, and pleasant drinks. Steve's cravings may not have been the cravings of an ideal artist's nature, but let those who would cavil at them tramp for a week over stone-slides and through alkaline dust, and then decide if these are not the natural longings of an ordinary man.

To tell the whole truth, Steve had amused himself and his comrade Roberts for more than a mile by discussing what they would order to eat and drink when once they reached comparative civilization again. Even the hardest of men tire in time of bacon and beans and tea.

A "John Collins," a seductive fluid, taken in a long glass and sipped through a straw, was perhaps what Steve hankered after most; but there were many other things which he longed for besides that most delectable of drinks, such for instance as a "full bath," a beefsteak, and clean sheets to follow.

Alas, poor Steve! There was the Frazer to wash in if he liked, and no doubt he could have obtained something which called itself a steak at the saloon, but a "John Collins" and clean sheets he was not likely to obtain west of Chicago.

Indeed, to this day long glasses and "drinketty drinks" are rare in the wild west; "drunketty drinks" out of short thick vulgar little tumblers being the order of the day. And apart from all this, Lillooet, though larger in 1862 than it is to-day, was even then but a poor little town, a town consisting only of one long straggling street, which looked as if it had lost its way on a great mud-bluff by the river. Benches of yellow mud and gray-green sage-brush rose above and around the "city," tier above tier, until they lost themselves in the mountains which gathered round, and deep down at the foot of the bluffs the Frazer roared along.

Since Chance had last seen the Frazer at Westminster its character had considerably changed. There it was a dull heavy flood, at least half a mile in breadth from bank to bank; here it was an angry torrent, roaring between steep overhanging banks, nowhere two hundred yards apart. There the river ran by flat lands, and fields which men might farm; here the impending mountains hung threateningly above it. The most daring steamboat which had ever plied upon the Frazer had not come nearer to Lillooet than Lytton, and that was full forty miles down stream.

In one thing only the Frazer was unchanged. At Lillooet, as at Westminster, it was a sordid yellow river, with no sparkle in it, no blue backwaters, no shallows through which the pebbles shone like jewels through liquid sunshine. And yet, artist though he was in a poor tradesman-like fashion, Steve gazed on the Frazer with a rapture which no other stream had ever awakened in him. At the portage between Seton and Anderson lakes he had passed a stream such as an angler dreams of in his dusty chambers on a summer afternoon, but he had hardly wasted a second glance upon it. Only trout lay there, great purple-spotted fellows, who would make the line vibrate like a harp string, and thrash the water into foam, ere they allowed themselves to be basketed; but in the Frazer, though the fish were only torpid, half-putrid salmon, that would not even take a fly, there was gold, and gold filled Steve's brain and eyes and heart just then to the exclusion of every other created thing. All he wanted was gold, gold; and his spirits rose higher and higher as he noted the flumes which ran along the river banks, and saw the little groups of blue-shirted Chinamen who squatted by their rockers, or shovelled the gravel into their ditches.

So keen, indeed, was Steve to be at work amongst

his beloved "dirt," that tired though he was, he persuaded Ned to come with him and wash a shovelful of it, whilst dinner was being prepared.

Right at the back of the town a little company of white men had dug deep into the gravel of the beach, set their flumes, and turned on a somewhat scanty supply of water, and here Steve obtained his first "colours."

A tall old man who ran the mine lent him a shovel, and showed him where to fill it with likely-looking dirt: taught him how to dip the edge of his shovel in the bucket, and slowly swill the water thus obtained round and round, so as to wash away the big stones and the gravel which he did not want.

The operation looks easier than it is, and at first Steve washed his shovel cleaner than he meant to, in a very short time. By and by, however, he learnt the trick, and was rewarded by seeing a patch of fine gravel left in the hollow of the shovel, with here and there a tiny ruby amongst it, and here and there an agate. The next washing took away everything except a sediment of fine black sand,—sand which will fly to a magnet, and is the constant associate and sure indication of gold.

Steve was going to give this another wash when old Pete stopped him. "Steady, my lad, don't wash it all away; there it is, don't you see it!" and sure enough there it was, up by the point of the shovel, seven, eight—a dozen small red specks, things that you almost needed a microscope to see, not half as beautiful as the little rubies or the pure white agates; but this was gold, and when the old miner, taking back his shovel, dipped it carelessly into the water of his flume, Chance felt for a moment a pang of indignation at seeing his first "colours" treated with such scant ceremony, although the twelve specks together were not, in all probability, worth a cent.

But the sight of the gold put new life into Chance and filled Phon's veins with fever. One night at Lillooet, Steve said, was rest enough for him; and most of that night he and Phon spent either down by the river or in the saloon, watching the Chinese over their rockers, or listening to the latest accounts from Cariboo. Men could earn good wages placer mining at Lillooet in '62, even as they can now, but all who could afford it were pushing on up stream to golden Cariboo. What was five dollars a day, or ten, or even twenty for the matter of that, when other men were digging out fortunes daily on Williams Creek and Antler Cunningham's, and the Cottonwood?

And in this matter Cruickshank humoured Steve's feverish impatience to get on. Here, as at Douglas, the gallant colonel showed a strange reluctance to mingle with his fellows, or at least with such of them as had passed a season in the upper country, and even went so far as to camp out a mile away from the town, to give the pack animals a better chance of getting good feed, and to secure them, so he said, against all temptations to stray up stream with somebody else. Horseflesh was dear at Lillooet in '62; and the colonel said that morals were lax, though why they should have been worse than at Westminster, Ned could not understand.

However, it suited him to go on, so he raised no objection to Cruickshank's plans, more especially as the rest did not seem beneficial to his honest old chum, Roberts, who had been the centre of a hard-drinking, hard-swearing lot of mining men, ever since

he arrived at Lillooet. Whenever Ned came near, these
men sunk their voices to a whisper, and once when
Cruickshank came in sight, the scowl upon their brows
grew so dark, and their mutterings so ominous, that
the colonel took the hint and vanished immediately.
When Ned saw him next he was at their trysting-
place, a mile and a half from the saloon, and very
impatient to be off,—so impatient, indeed, that he absolutely refused to wait for Roberts, who, he "guessed,"
was drunk.

"Those old-timers are all the same when they get
amongst pals, and as for Roberts, we are deuced well
rid of him, he is no use anyway," said the colonel.

This might very well be Cruickshank's opinion.
It was not Ned's, and Ned had a way of thinking and
acting for himself, so without any waste of words he
bade his comrades "drive ahead," whilst he turned
back in search of Roberts.

By some accident this worthy had not heard of the
intended start, and was, as Ned expected, as innocent
of any intention to desert as he was of drunkenness.

When Ned found him he was sitting in the bar-
room with a lot of his pals, and the conversation
round him had grown loud and angry; indeed, as Ned
entered, a rough, weather-beaten fellow in his shirt
sleeves was shouting at the top of his voice, "What
the deuce is the good of all this jaw? Lynch the bilk,
that's what I say, and save trouble."

But Ned's appearance put a stop to the proceedings,
though an angry growl broke out when he was overheard to say that Cruickshank and Steve had started
half an hour ago, and that he himself had come back
to look for old Roberts.

"Don't you go, Bob," urged one of his comrades;

"them young Britishers are bound to stay by their packs, but you've no call to."

"Not you. You'll stay right here, if you ain't a born fool," urged another.

But Bob was not to be coaxed or bantered out of his determination to stay by his brother Salopian.

"No, lads," he retorted, "I ain't a born fool, and I ain't the sort to go back on a pal. If Corbett goes I'm going, though I don't pretend to be over-keen on the job."

"Wal, if you will go, go and be hanged to you; only, Bob, keep your eye skinned, and, I say, *shoot fust* next time, *shoot fust;* now don't you forget it!" with which mysterious injunction Bob's big friend reeled up from the table (he was half-drunk already), shook hands, "liquored" once more, and left. He said he had some business to attend to down town; and as it was nearly noon, and he had done nothing but smoke and drink short drinks since breakfast-time, he was probably right in thinking that it was time to attend to it.

Whilst this gentleman rolled away down the street with a fine free stride, requiring a good deal of sea-room, Ned and his friend had to put their best feet foremost (as the saying is) to make up for lost time. When you are walking fast over rough ground you have not much breath left for conversation, and this, perhaps, and the roar of the sullen river, accounts for the fact that the two men strode along in silence, neither of them alluding to the conversation just overheard in the saloon, although the minds of both were running upon that subject, and Ned noticed that the pistol which Roberts pulled out and examined as they went along was a recent purchase.

"Hullo, you've got a new gun, Rob," he remarked. Everything with which men shoot is called a gun in British Columbia.

"Yes, it's one I bought at Lillooet. I hadn't got a good one with me."

"Well, I don't suppose you'll want it, now you have got it," replied Corbett.

"Well, I don't know. I *might* want it to shoot grouse with by the side of the trail."

And the old fellow laid such an emphasis upon his last words and chuckled so grimly, that Ned half suspected that he had wetted his whistle once too often after all.

CHAPTER IX.

UNDER THE BALM-OF-GILEAD TREE

FROM noon of the day upon which Ned Corbett and old Roberts strode out of Lillooet until the night upon which we meet them again was a fortnight and more, a fortnight of which I might, if I chose, write a history, but it would only be the history of almost every mining party and pack-train that ever went up the Frazer. The incidents of those days are indelibly engraved upon the memories of Steve and of Corbett, but to Roberts they passed without remark and left no impression behind. The life was only the ordinary miner's life; and there was nothing new to the old-timer in buoyant hopes wearing away day by day; nothing new in the daily routine of camps broken by starlight and pitched again at dusk; in trails blocked by windfalls or destroyed by landslips; in packs which would shift, tie them ever so tightly; in stones which cut the moccasins, and prickly pears which filled the sole with anguish; or in cruel fire-hardened rampikes, which tore the skin to rags and the clothes to ribands. Three weeks upon the road had done its work upon the party, had added much to their knowledge, and taken much away that was useless from their equipment.

When they left Westminster they were five smart, well-fed, civilized human beings; when they struggled up out of the valley of the Frazer towards Cariboo, at Soda Creek, they were five lean, weather-hardened men, their clothes all rags and patches, their skin all wounded and blistered, every "indispensable adjunct of a camp," as made by Mr. Silver, discarded long ago; but every article of camp furniture which was left, carried where it could be got at, ready when it was wanted, and thoroughly adapted to the rough and ready uses of those who took the trouble to "pack it along."

Even to Steve it seemed ages now since his nostrils were used to any other odour than the pungent scent of the pines; ages since his ears listened to any other sound than the roar of the yellow river and the monotonous tinkle of the leader's bell; ages even since washing had been to him as a sacred rite, and a clean shirt as desirable as a clean conscience.

And yet Corbett and Chance had seen, on their way up, men who led harder lives than theirs; blue-shirted, bearded fellows, who carried their all upon their own shoulders; and others who had put their tools and their grub in the craziest of crafts, and, climbing one moment and wading the next, strove to drag it up stream in the teeth of the Frazer.

As Ned saw the frail canoes rear up on end against

the angry waters, he understood why the old river carried so many down stream whose dead hands grasped no dollars, whose dead lips told no tales. But the river trail had come to an end at last, and the five were now steering north-east for the bold mountains and their gold-bearing rivers and creeks. They had now put many a mile between themselves and Soda Creek, and were lying smoking round their camp-fire, built under a huge balm-of-gilead tree, which stood in the driest part of what we call a swamp, and Canadians a meadow. The pack-saddles were set in orderly line, with their ropes and cinches neatly coiled alongside them; the packs were snug under their *manteaux*, and the tent was pitched as men pitch a tent who are used to their work, not with its sides all bellying in, strained in one place slack in another, but just loose enough to allow for a wetting if it should happen to rain in the night. Now and again the bell of one of the pack animals sounded not unmusically from some dark corner of the swamp, or the long "ho-ho" of kalula, the night-owl, broke the silence, which but for these sounds would have been complete.

Suddenly a voice said:

"Great Scott! do you know what the date is?"

Since the pipes had been lighted no one had spoken, and as Cruickshank broke the silence, it was almost under protest that Ned rolled round on his blanket to face the speaker, and dropped a monosyllabic "Well?" The men were too tired to talk, and night, which in these northern forests is very still, had thrown its spell upon them. Steve and Phon merely turned their heads inquiringly to the speaker, who sat upon a log turning over the leaves of a little diary, and waited.

"To-morrow will be the 27th of May."

"The 27th of May—what then?" asked Ned dreamily. He was hardly awake to everyday thoughts yet.

"What then! What then! Why, if you are not at Williams Creek by the 1st of June your claims can be jumped by anyone who comes along."

"But can't we get there by the 1st of June?" asked Ned, sitting up and taking his pipe out of his mouth.

"Impossible. If you could drive the ponies at a trot you could only just do it. It is five good days' journey with fresh animals, and we have only four to do it in, and grizzlies wouldn't make our ponies trot now."

"Well, what are we to do?" broke in Chance. "You calculated the time, and said that we had enough and to spare."

"I know I did, but I made a mistake."

"Oh to blazes with your *mistakes*, Colonel Cruickshank," cried Chance angrily; "they seem to me a bit too expensive to occur quite so often."

"Don't lose your temper, my good sir. I couldn't help it, but I am willing to atone for it. I calculated as if April had thirty-one days in it, and it hasn't; and, besides, I've dropped a day on the road somehow."

"Looking for horses," growled Roberts, "or shooting grouse, maybe."

"What do you propose to do, Colonel Cruickshank?" asked Corbett, whose face alone seemed still perfectly under his own control.

"Well, Mr. Corbett, I've led you into the scrape, so I must get you out of it. If either you or Roberts will stay with me I'll bring the horses on for you to Williams Creek, whilst the rest can start away right now and make the best of their time to the claims.

You could do the distance all right if it wasn't for the pack-ponies."

"But how could *I* stay?" asked Corbett.

"Well, you needn't, of course, if Roberts doesn't mind staying; otherwise you could assign your interest in your claim to him, and he could go on and hold it for you."

"But it will be deuced hard work for two men to manage nine pack-ponies over such a trail as this."

"It won't be any violets," replied Cruickshank, "you may bet on that; but it's my fault, so I'll 'foot the bill.'"

"I don't know about its being your fault either," broke in Corbett, "I was just as big an ass as a man could be. I ought to have calculated the time for myself. Can't we all stop and chance it?"

"What, and lose a good many thousand dollars paid, and every chance of making a good many thousand more, for which we have been tramping over a month—that would be lunacy!" broke in Chance.

"Well, if you don't mean to lose the claims, I know no other way of getting to Williams Creek in time," said Cruickshank; and, looking up at the sky, he added, "you might have two or three hours' sleep, and then be off bright and early by moonlight. The moon rises late to-night."

It was a weird scene there by that camp-fire; and there were things written on the faces of those sitting round it, which a mere outsider could have read at a glance.

The moon might be coming up later on, but just at that moment there was neither moon nor star, only a black darkness, broken by the occasional sputtering flames of the wood fire. Out of the darkness the men's faces showed from time to time as the red gleams flickered over them; the faces of Corbett, Steve, and Roberts full of perplexity and doubt; the eyes of Phon fixed in a frightened fascinated stare upon the colonel; and Cruickshank's face white with suppressed excitement, the coarse, cruel mouth drawn and twitching, and the eyes glaring like the eyes of a tiger crouching for its prey.

"Well, what had we better do?" asked Corbett at last from somewhere amongst the shadows, and Cruickshank's eyes shifted swiftly to where Steve and Roberts lay, as if anxious to forestall their answer.

"I'll stay, Ned Corbett. It's safer for me than it would be for you," said Roberts. "I can only lose a little time, not much worth to anyone, and you have a good deal to lose."

After all it was only a small question. They had driven the pack animals now for a month, and, whoever stayed, would only at the worst have to drive them for another week. The work, of course, would be rather heavy with only two to divide it among; but on the other hand those who went ahead would have to make forced marches and live upon very short rations.

Ned was rather surprised then that Roberts answered as if it was a matter of grave import, and that his voice seemed to have lost the jolly ring which was natural to it.

"Don't stop if you don't like to, old chap. Phon can assign his interests to you and stay behind instead."

"No, no, me hālō stay. Hālō! hālō!" and the little Chinaman almost shrieked the last word, so emphatic was his refusal.

"It's no good leaving Phon," replied Roberts, casting

a pitying look towards that frightened heathen; "he would see devils all the time, and be of no use after it got dark. I tell you, I'll stay and take care of the ponies; and now you had better all turn in and get some sleep. You will have to travel pretty lively when you once start. I'll see to your packs."

Probably Ned had been mistaken from the first, but if any feeling had shaken his friend's voice for a moment, it had quite passed away now, and Roberts was again his own genial, helpful self.

After all, he was the very best person to leave behind. Except Cruickshank, he was the only really good packer amongst them. He was as strong as a horse, and besides, he had no particular reason for wanting to be at Williams Creek by the 1st of June.

"You really don't mind stopping, Rob?" asked Corbett.

"Not a bit. Why should I? I'd do a good deal more than that for you, if it was only for the sake of the dear old country, my lad."

Again, just for a moment, there seemed to be a sad ring in his voice, and he stretched out his hand and gripped Ned's in the darkness.

Ned was surprised.

"The old man is a bit sentimental to-night," he thought. "It's not like him, but, I suppose, these dismal woods have put him a little off his balance. They *are* lonesome."

With which sage reflection Ned turned his eyes away from the dark vista down which he had been gazing, and rolling round in his blankets forgot both the gloom and the gold.

For two or three hours the sleepers lay there undisturbed by the calls of the owls, or the stealthy tread of a passing bear, which chose the trail as affording the best road from point to point. At night, when there is no chance of running up against a man, no one appreciates a well-made road better than a bear. He will crash through the thickest brush if necessary, but if you leave him to choose, he will avoid rough and stony places as carefully as a Christian.

Towards midnight Cruickshank, who had been tossing restlessly in his blankets, sat up and crouched broodingly over the dying embers, unconscious that a pair of bright, beady eyes were watching him suspiciously all the time.

But Phon made no sign. He was only a bundle of blankets upon the ground, a thing of no account.

By and by, when Cruickshank had settled himself again to sleep, this bundle of blankets sat up and put fresh logs on the camp-fire. The warmth from them soothed the slumberers, and after a while even Cruickshank lay still. Phon watched him for some time, until convinced that his regular breathing was not feigned, but real slumber, and then he too crept away from the fire-side, not to his own place, but into the shadow where Roberts lay.

After a while an owl, which had been murdering squirrels in their sleep, came gliding on still wings, and lit without a sound on the limb of a tall pine near the camp. The light from the camp-fire dazzled its big red-brown eyes, but after a little time it could see that two of the strange bundles, which lay like mummies round the smouldering logs, were sitting up and talking together. But the owl could not catch what they said, except once, when it saw a bright, white gleam flash from the little bundle like moonlight showing through a storm-cloud, and then as the bigger bundle snatched the white thing away, the listening owl heard a voice say:

"No, my God, no! That may do very well for a Chinee; it won't do for a Britisher, Phon!"

And another voice answered angrily:

"Why not? You white men all fool. You savey what *he* did. S'pose you no kill him, by 'm bye he—"

But the rest was lost to the owl, and a few minutes later, just as it raised its wings to go, it saw the smaller bundle wriggle across the ground again to its old place by the embers.

CHAPTER X

THE SHADOWS BEGIN TO FALL.

WHEN Corbett woke, the first beams of the rising moon were throwing an uncertain light over the forest paths, and the children of night were still abroad, the quiet-footed deer taking advantage of the moonlight to make an early breakfast before the sun and man rose together to annoy them.

The camp-fire had just been made up afresh, and a frying-pan, full of great rashers, was hissing merrily upon it, while a kettle full of strong hot coffee stood beside it, ready to wash the rashers down.

Men want warming when they rise at midnight from these forest slumbers, and Roberts, knowing that it would be long ere his friends broke their fast again, had been up and busy for the last half-hour, building a real nor'-west fire, and preparing a generous breakfast.

Cruickshank too was up, if not to speed the parting,

at any rate to see them safely off the premises, a smile of unusual benevolence on his dark face.

Between them, he and Roberts put up the travellers' packs, taking each man's blankets as he got out of them, and rolling in them such light rations as would just last for a four days' trip. In twenty minutes from the time when they crawled out of their blankets, the three stood ready to start.

"Are you all set?" asked Cruickshank.

"All set," replied Chance.

"Then the sooner you 'get' the better. It will be as much as your heathen can do to make the journey in time, I'll bet."

"Why, is the trail a very bad one?"

"Oh, it's all much like this, but it's most of it uphill, and there may be some snow on the top. But you can't miss your way with all these tracks in front."

"You will be in yourself a day or two after us, won't you?" asked Corbett.

"Yes. If you don't make very good time I daresay I shall, although the snow may delay the ponies some. But don't you worry about them. I'll take care of the ponies, you can trust me for that."

"Then, if you will be in so soon, I won't trouble to take anything except one blanket and my rifle," remarked Ned.

"Oh, take your rocker. It looks more business-like; and, besides, all the millionaires go in with 'nothing but a rocker-iron for their whole kit, and come out worth their weight in gold.'"

There was a mocking ring in Cruickshank's voice as he said this, at variance with his oily smile, but Steve Chance took his words in good faith. Steve still believed in the likelihood of his becoming a millionaire at one stroke of the miner's pick.

"I guess you're right, colonel. I'll take my rocker-iron, whatever else I leave behind. Lend a hand to fix it on to my pack, will you?" and then, when Cruickshank had done this, Steve added with a laugh: "I shall consider you entitled to (what shall we say?) one per cent on the profits of the mine when in full swing, for your services, colonel."

"Don't promise too much, Chance. You don't know what sort of a gold-mine you are giving away yet;" and the speaker bent over a refractory strap in Steve's pack to hide an ugly gleam of white teeth, which might have had a meaning even for such an unsuspicious fool as Ned Corbett, who at this moment picked up his Winchester and held out his hand to Cruickshank.

"Good-bye, colonel," he said. "What with the claims and the packs, we have trusted you now with every dollar we have in the world. Lucky for us that we are trusting to the honour of a soldier and a gentleman, isn't it? Good-bye to you."

It was the kindliest speech Ned had ever made to Cruickshank. Weeks of companionship, and the man's readiness to atone for his mistake, had had their effect upon Corbett's generous nature; but its warmth was lost upon the colonel.

Either he really did not see, or else he affected not to see the outstretched hand; in any case he did not take it, and Ned went away without exchanging that silent grip (which a writer of to-day has aptly called "an Englishman's oath") with the man to whom he had intrusted his last dollar.

As for old Roberts, he followed his friends for a

couple of hundred yards upon their way, and then wrung their hands until the bones cracked.

"Give this to Rampike when you see him, Ned. I guess he'll be at Williams Creek, or Antler; Williams Creek most likely," said the old poet in parting, and handed a note with some little inclosure in it to Ned.

"All right, I won't forget. Till we meet again, Rob;" and Corbett waved his cap to him.

"Till we meet again!" Roberts repeated after him, and stood looking vacantly along the trail until Steve and Corbett passed out of sight. Then he, too, turned and tramped back to camp, cheering himself as he went with a stave of his favourite ditty.

The last the lads heard of their comrade on that morning was the crashing of a dry twig or two beneath old Roberts' feet, and the refrain of his song as it died away in the distance—

"Riding, riding, riding on my old pack-mule."

Ned Corbett could not imagine how he had ever thought that air a lively one. It was stupidly mournful this morning, or else the woods and the distance played strange tricks with the singer's voice. But if Ned was affected by an imaginary minor key in his old friend's singing, a glimpse at the camp he had left would not have done much to restore his cheerfulness.

The embers had died down, and looked almost as gray and sullen as the face of the man who sat and scowled at them from a log alongside. The only living thing in camp besides the colonel was one of those impudent gray birds, which the up-country folk call "whisky-jacks." Of course he had come to see what he could steal. That is the nature of jays, and the whisky-jack is the Canadian jay. At first the bird stood with his head on one side eyeing the colonel, uncertain whether it would be safe to come any closer or not. But there was a fine piece of bacon-rind at the colonel's feet, so the bird plucked up his courage and hopped a few paces nearer. He had measured his distance to an inch, and with one eye on the colonel and one on the bacon, was just straining his neck to the utmost to drive his beak into the succulent morsel, when the man whom he thought was asleep discharged a furious kick at an unoffending log, and clenching his fist ground out between his teeth muttered:

"A soldier and a gentleman! a soldier and a gentleman! Yes, but it came a bit too late, Mr. Edward Corbett. Hang it, I wish you had stayed behind instead of that fool, Roberts."

Of course the "whisky-jack" did not understand the other biped's language, but he was a bird of the world, and instinct told him that his companion in camp was dangerous; so, though the bacon-rind still lay there, he flitted off to a tree hard by, and spent the next half-hour in heaping abuse upon the colonel from a safe distance.

That "whisky-jack" grew to be a very wise bird, and in his old days used to tell many strange stories about human bipeds and the Balm-of-Gilead camp.

But there was half a mile of brush between Ned and their old camp, so he saw nothing of all this; and after the fresh morning air had roused him, and the exercise had set his blood going through his veins at its normal pace, he went unconcernedly on his way, talking to Steve as long as there was room enough for the two to walk side by side, and then gradually forging ahead, and setting that young Yankee a step which kept him extended, and made poor little Phon follow at a trot.

Though Ned and Steve had grown used to isolation

upon the trail with ten laden beasts between the two, they made several attempts upon this particular morning to carry on a broken conversation, or lighten the road with snatches of song.

Perhaps it was that they were making unconscious efforts to drive away a feeling of depression, which sometimes comes over men's natures with as little warning as a storm over an April sky.

But their efforts were in vain; nature was too strong for them. In the great silence amid these funereal pines their voices seemed to fall at their own feet, and ere long the forest had mastered them, as it masters the Indians, and the birds, and the wild dumb beasts which wander about in its fastnesses. The only creature which retains its loquacity in a pine-forest is the squirrel, and he is always too busy to cultivate sentiment of any kind.

Cruickshank had warned them that the trail led uphill, and it undoubtedly did so. At first the three swung along over trails brown with the fallen pine needles of last year, soft to the foot and level to the tread, with great expanses of fruit bushes upon either side,—bushes that in another month or two would be laden with a repast spread only for the bear and the birds. Salmon-berry and rasp-berry, soap-berry and service-berry, and two or three different kinds of bilberry were there, as well as half a dozen others which neither Ned nor Steve knew by sight. But the season of berries was not yet, so they wetted their parched lips with their tongues and passed on with a sigh.

Then the road began to go uphill. They knew that by the way they kept tripping over the sticks and by the increased weight of their packs. By and by Steve thought they would come to a level place at the top,

and there they would lie down for a while and rest.
But that top never came, or at least the sun was going
round to the south, and it had not come yet. And then
the air began to grow more chill, and the trees to change.
There were no more bushes, or but very few of them;
and the trees, which were black dismal-looking balsams,
were draped with beard-moss, the winter food of the
cariboo, and there was snow in little patches at their
feet. When the sun had gone round to the west the
snow had grown more plentiful, and there were glades
amongst the balsams, and at last Steve was glad, for
they had got up to the top of the divide.

But he was wrong again, for again the trail rose,
and this time through a belt of timber which the wind
had laid upturned across their path. Heavens! how
heavy the packs grew then, and how their limbs
ached with stepping over log after log, bruising their
shins against one and stumbling head-first over another.
At first Steve growled at every spiked-bough which
caught and held him, and groaned at every sharp stake
which cut into the hollow of his foot. But anger in
the woods soon gives place to a sullen stoicism. It is
useless to quarrel with the unresponsive pines. The
mountains and the great trees look down upon man's
insignificance, and his feeble curse dies upon his lips,
frozen by the terrible sphinx-like silence of a cold
passionless nature.

As long as the sunlight lasted the three kept up
their spirits fairly well. The glades in their winter
dress, with the sunlight gleaming upon the dazzling
snow and flashing from the white plumes of the pines,
were cheery enough, and took Corbett's thoughts back
to Christmas in the old country; besides, there were
great tracks across one glade—tracks like the tracks

of a cow, and Ned was interested in recognizing the footprints of the beast which has given its name to Cariboo.

But when the sun went, everything changed. A great gloom fell like a pall upon man and nature: the glitter which made a gem of every lakelet was gone, and the swamps, which had looked like the homes of an ideal Father Christmas, relapsed into dim shadowy places over whose soft floors murder might creep unheard, whilst the balsam pines stood rigid and black, like hearse plumes against the evening sky.

"Ned, we can't get out of this confounded mountain to-night, can we?" asked Chance.

"No, old man, I don't think we can," replied Ned, straining his eyes along the trail, which still led upwards.

"Then I propose that we camp;" and Chance suited the action to the word, by heaving his pack off his shoulders and dropping on to it with a sigh of relief.

Perhaps the three sat in silence for five minutes (it certainly was not more), asking only for leave to let the aching muscles rest awhile; though even this seemed too much to ask, for long before their muscles had ceased to throb, before Steve's panting breath had begun to come again in regular cadence, the chill of a winter night took hold upon them, stiffened their clothes, and would shortly have frozen them to their seats.

"This is deuced nice for May, isn't it, Steve?" remarked Ned with a shiver. "Lend me the axe, Phon; it is in your pack. If we don't make a fire we shall freeze before morning. Steve, you might cut some brush, old chap, and you and Phon might beat down some of the snow into a floor to camp on. I'll go and get wood enough to last all night;" and Corbett walked off to commence operations upon a burnt "pine stick," still standing full of pitch and hard as a nail. But Ned was used to his axe, and the cold acted on him as a spur to a willing horse, so that he hewed away, making the chips fly and the axe ring until he had quite a stack of logs alongside the shelter which Steve had built up.

Then the sticks began to crackle and snap like Chinese fireworks, and the makers of the huge fire were glad enough to stand at a respectful distance lest their clothes should be scorched upon their backs. That is the worst of a pine fire. It never gives out a comfortable glow, but either leaves you shivering or scorches you.

Having toasted themselves on both sides, the three travellers found a place where they would be safe from the wood smoke, and still standing pulled out the rations set apart for the first day's supper, and ate the cold bacon and heavy damper slowly, knowing that there was no second course coming.

When you are reduced to two slices of bread and one of bacon for a full meal, with only two such meals in the day, and twelve hours of abstinence and hard labour between them, it is wonderful how even coarse store bacon improves in flavour. I have even known men who would criticise the cooking at a London club, to collect the stale crumbs from their pockets and eat them with apparent relish in the woods, though the crumbs were thick with fluff and tobacco dust! As they stood there munching, Ned said:

"I suppose, Steve, we did wisely in coming on?"

"What else could we have done, Ned?"

"Yes, that's it. What else could we have done? And yet—"

"And yet?" repeated Steve questioningly. "What is your trouble, Ned?"

"Do you remember my saying, when I bought the claims, that with Cruickshank under our eyes all the time we should have a good security for our money?"

"Yes, and now you have let him go. I see what you mean: but you can rely upon Roberts, can't you?"

"As I would upon myself," replied Corbett shortly. "But still I have broken my resolution."

"Oh, well, that is no great matter; and besides, I don't believe that the colonel would do a crooked thing any more than we would."

"He-he! He-he-he!"

It was a strangely-harsh cackle was Phon's apology for a laugh, and coming so rarely and so unexpectedly, it made the two speakers start.

But they could get nothing out of the man when they talked to him. He was utterly tired out, and in another few minutes lay fast asleep by the fire.

"I am afraid that quaint little friend of ours doesn't care much for the colonel," remarked Ned.

"Oh, Phon! Phon thinks he is the devil. He told me so;" and Steve laughed carelessly.

What did it matter what a Chinaman thought! A little yellow-skinned, pig-tailed fellow like Phon was not likely to have found out anything which had escaped Steve's Yankee smartness.

CHAPTER XI.

"JUMP OR I'LL SHOOT."

THREE days after they left the Balm-of-Gilead camp, Ned Corbett and his two friends stood upon a ridge of the bald mountains looking down upon the promised land.

"So this is Eldorado, is it?"

Ned Corbett himself was the speaker, though probably those who had known him at home or in Victoria would have hardly recognized him. All the three gold-seekers had altered much in the last month, and standing in the bright sunlight of early morning the changes wrought by hard work and scanty food were very apparent.

Bronzed, and tired, and ragged, with a stubble of half-grown beards upon their chins, with patches of sacking or deer-skin upon their trousers, and worn-out moccasins on their feet, none of the three showed signs of that golden future which was to come. Beggars they might be, but surely Crœsus never looked like this!

"We shall make it to-day, Ned," remarked Chance, taking off his cap to let the cool mountain breeze fan his brow.

"We may, if we can drag him along, but he is very nearly dead beat;" and the direction in which Ned glanced showed his companion that he was speaking of a limp bundle of blue rags, which had collapsed in a heap at the first sign of a halt.

"Why not leave Phon to follow us?" asked Steve in a low tone. Low though the tone was, the bundle of blue rags moved, and a worn, shrivelled face looked piteously up into Ned's.

"No, no, Steve," replied Corbett. "All right, Phon, I'll not leave you behind, even if I have to pack you on my own shoulders."

Thus reassured, the Chinaman collapsed once more. There was not a muscle in his body which felt capable of further endurance, and yet, with the gold so near, and his mind full of superstitious horrors, he would have crawled the rest of the journey upon his hands and knees rather than have stayed behind.

"Thank goodness, there it is at last!" cried Corbett a minute later, shading his eyes with his hand. "That smoke I expect rises from somewhere near our claims;" and the speaker pointed to a faint column of blue which was just distinguishable from the surrounding atmosphere.

"I believe you are right, Ned. Come, Phon, one more effort!" and Steve helped the Chinaman on to his legs, though he himself was very nearly worn out.

Ned took up the slender pack which Phon had carried until then, and added it to the other two packs already upon his broad shoulders. After all the three packs weighed very little, for Ned's companions had thrown away everything except their blankets, and Steve would have even thrown his blanket away had not Ned taken charge of it. Ned knew from experience that so long as he sleeps fairly soft and warm at night a man's strength will endure many days, but once you rob him of his rest, the strongest man will collapse in a few hours.

As for their food, that was not hard to carry. Each man had a crust still left in his pocket, and more than enough tobacco. Along the trail there were plenty of

streams full of good water, and if bread and water
and tobacco did not satisfy them, they would have to
remain unsatisfied. It had been a hard race against
time, and the last lap still remained to be run; but
that smoke was the goal, and with the goal in sight
even Phon shuffled along a little faster, though he was
so tired that, whenever he stumbled he fell from sheer
weakness.

The bald mountains so often alluded to in Cariboo
story are ranges of high upland, rising above the forest
level, and entirely destitute of timber at the top.

Here in late summer the sunnier slopes are slippery
with a luxuriant growth of long lush grasses and
weeds, and ablaze with the vivid crimson of the Indian
pink. In early spring (and May is early spring in
Cariboo) there is still snow along the ridges, and even
down below, though the grasses are brilliantly green,
the time of flowers has hardly yet come.

Here and there as the three hurried down they
came across big boulders of quartz gleaming in the
sun. These were as welcome to Steve as the last mile-
stone on his road home to a weary pedestrian. Where
the quartz was, there would the gold be also, argued
Steve, and the thought roused him for a moment out
of the mechanical gait into which he had fallen. But
he soon dropped into it again. A hill had risen and
shut the column of smoke out of his sight, and the
trail was leading down again to the timber.

Away far to the east a huge dome of snow gleamed
whitely against the sky-line. That was the outpost
of the Rockies. But Steve had no eyes even for the
Rockies. All he saw was a sea of endless brown hills
rolling and creeping away fold upon fold in the distance, all so like one to another from their bald ridges

to the blue lakes at their feet, that his head began to spin, and he almost thought that he must be asleep, and this some nightmare country in which he wandered along a road that had no end.

Luckily Ned roused him from this dreamy fit from time to time, or it might well have happened that Steve's journey would have ended on this side of Williams Creek in a rapid slide from the narrow trail to the bottom of one of the little ravines along which it ran.

Both men were apparently thinking of the same subject. So that though their sentences were short and elliptical, they had no difficulty in understanding each other's meaning. Men don't waste words on such a march as theirs.

"Another three hours ought to do it," Ned would mutter, shifting his pack so as to give the rope a chance of galling him in a fresh place.

"If we get there by midnight, I reckon it would do."

"Yes, if we could find the claims."

"Ah, there is that about it! Have you got the map?"

"Yes. I've got that all right. Oh, we shall do it in good time;" and Ned looked up at his only clock, the great red sun, which was now nearly overhead.

The next moment Corbett's face fell. The path led round a bluff, beyond which he expected to see the trail go winding gradually down to a little group of tents and huts gathered about Williams Creek. Instead of that he found himself face to face with one of those exasperating gulches which so often bar the weary hunter's road home in the Frazer country. The swelling uplands rolled on, it was true, sinking gradually to the level of Williams Creek, and he could see the trail running from him to his goal in fairly gentle sweeps.

all except about half a mile of it, and that half-mile lay right in front of him, and was invisible.

It had sunk, so it seemed to Ned, into the very bowels of the earth, and another hundred yards brought him to the edge of the gulch and showed him that this was the simple truth. As so often happens in this country which ice has formed (smoothing it here and cutting great furrows through it elsewhere), the downs ended without warning in a precipitous cliff leading into a dark narrow ravine, along the bottom of which the gold-seekers could just hear the murmur of a mountain stream.

It was useless to look up and down the ravine. There was no way over and no way round. It was a regular trap. A threadlike trail, but well worn, showed the only way by which the gulch could be crossed, and as Ned looked at it he came to the conclusion that if there was another such gulch between him and Williams Creek it would probably cost him all he was worth, for no one in his party could hope to cross two such gulches before nightfall.

"It's no good looking at it, come along, Steve!" he cried, and grasping at any little bush within reach to steady his steps, Ned began the descent.

Who ever first made that trail was in a hurry to get to Williams Creek. The recklessness of the gold miner, determined to get to his gold, and careless of life and limb in pursuit of it, was apparent in every yard of that descent, which, despising all circuitous methods, plunged headlong into the depths below.

Twice on the way down Steve only owed his life to the stout mountain weeds to which his fingers clung when his feet forsook him, and once it was only Ned's strong hand which prevented Phon from following a great flat stone which his stumbling feet had sent tobogganing into the dark gulf below.

For two or three minutes Ned had to hold on to Phon by the scruff of the neck before he was quite certain that he was to be trusted to walk alone again. Even Steve kept staring into that "dark-profound" into which the stone had vanished in a way which Corbett did not relish. Though he had never felt it himself, he knew all about that strange fascination which seems to tempt some men, brave men too, to throw themselves out of a railway-carriage, off a pier-head, or down a precipice, and therefore Ned was not sorry to be at the bottom of that precipitous trail without the loss of either Steve or Phon.

"Say, Ned, how does that strike you? It's a 'way-up' bridge, isn't it, old man?" and the speaker pointed to a piece of civil engineering characteristic of Cariboo.

Two tall pines had grown upon opposite edges of the narrow ravine in which the gulch ended. From side to side this ravine was rather too broad for a single pine to span, and far down below, somewhere in the darkness of it, a stream roared and foamed along. The rocks were damp with mist and spray, but the steep walls of the narrow place let in no light by which the prisoned river could be seen. In order to cross this place, men had loosened the roots of the two pines with pick and shovel, until the trees sinking slowly towards each other had met over the mid-stream. Then those who had loosened the roots did their best to make them fast again, weighting them with rocks, and tethering them with ropes. When they had done this they had lashed the tops of the trees together, lopped off a few boughs, run a hand-rope over all, and called the structure a bridge.

Over this bridge Ned and his comrades had now to pass, and as he looked at the white face and quaking legs of Phon, and then up at the evening sky, Ned turned to Steve and whispered in his ear: "Pull yourself together, Steve. This is a pretty bad place, but we have got to get over at once or not at all. That fellow will faint or go off his head before long."

Luckily for Ned, Steve Chance had plenty of what the Yankees call "sand."

"I'm ready, go ahead," he muttered, keeping his eyes as much as possible averted from the abyss towards which they were clambering.

"I'll go first," said Corbett, when they had reached the roots of the nearest pine; "then Phon, and you last, Steve." Then bending over his friend he whispered, "Threaten to throw him in if he funks."

Of course the bridge in front of Corbett was not the ordinary way to Williams Creek. Pack-trains had come to Williams Creek even in those early days, and clever as pack-ponies are, they have not yet developed a talent for tree climbing. So there was undoubtedly some other way to Williams Creek. This was only a short cut, a route taken by pedestrians who were in a hurry, and surely no pedestrians were ever in a much greater hurry than Steve and Ned and Phon.

Consider! Their all was on the other side of that ravine; all their invested wealth and all their hopes as well; all the reward for weeks of weary travel, as well as rest, and shelter, and food. They had much to gain in crossing that ravine, and the slowly sinking sun warned them that they had no time to look for a better way round. They must take that short cut or none. And yet when Ned got closer to the rough bridge he liked it less than ever. Where the trees should have met and joined together a terrible thing had happened. Ned could see it now quite plainly from where he stood. A wind, he supposed, must have come howling up the gulch in one of the dark days of winter, a wind so strong that when the narrow gully had pent it in, it had gone rushing along, smashing everything that it met in its furious course, and amongst other things it had struck just the top of the arch of the bridge.

The result was that just at the highest point there was a gap, not a big gap, indeed it was so small that some of the ropes still held and stretched from tree to tree, but still a gap, six feet wide with no bridge across it, and black, unfathomable darkness down below. Ned Corbett was one of those men who only see the actual danger which has to be faced, the thing which has to be done—that which is, and not that which may be. For instance, Ned saw that he had to jump from one stout bough to another, that he would have to cling to something with his hands on the other side, and that it would not do to make a false step, or to clutch at a rotten bough.

That was all he saw. So he leapt with confidence (he had taken twenty worse leaps in an afternoon in the gymnasium at home for the fun of the thing), and of course he alighted in safety, clambered down the other pine-tree trunk, and landed safe and sound on the farther shore. He had never stayed to think of the awful things which would have happened if he had slipped; of that poor body of his which might have gone whirling round and round through the darkness, until it plunged into the waters out of sight of the sun and his fellow-men.

But all men are not made after this fashion. When

Ned turned towards the bridge he had just passed his face turned white, and his hands, which had until then been so firm trembled. What he saw was this. Phon had been driven ahead of Steve, as Corbett and Steve had arranged. As long as the big broad trunk of the pine was beneath him, with plenty of strong boughs all round him to cling to, Phon had listened to Steve and obeyed him. Now it was different. Phon had come to the end of the pine, to the place from which Corbett had leaped, and nothing which Steve could say would move him another inch. Chinamen are not trained in athletics as white men are, and to Phon that six-foot jump appeared to be a simply impossible feat. Steve might threaten what he liked, but jump Phon would not. The mere sight of the horrible darkness below made his head reel, and his fingers cling to the rough pine like the fingers of a drowning man to a plank.

And now Ned noticed a worse thing even than this Phon had been driven to the very end of the tree by Steve, and Steve himself was close behind him. The result was that the weight of two men had to be borne at once by the thin end of what, after all, was but a small pine, and one extended almost like a fishing-rod across the ravine. So the tree began to bow with the weight, and then to lift itself again until it was swinging and tossing, swaying more and more after every recoil, so that at each swing Ned expected to see one or both of his friends tossed off into the gulf below. There must come an end to such a scene as this sooner or later, and Ned could see but one chance of saving his friend.

"Chance," he shouted, "hold tight! I am going to shoot that cursed Chinaman!"

The miserable wretch heard and understood the

words, and saw the Winchester, the same which had sent the runaway cayuse spinning down the stone-slide, come slowly up to Corbett's shoulder.

"Jump or I'll shoot! It's your last chance!" and Phon heard the clank of the pump as his master forced up a cartridge into the barrel of his rifle.

It was now death anyway. Phon realized that, and even at that moment his memory showed him plainly a picture of that pinto mare, whose bruised and battered body, with a great ghastly hole between the eyes, he had seen by the edge of Seton Lake. That last thought decided him, and with a scream of fear he sprang out, and managed to cling, more by sheer luck than in any other way, to the pine on the Williams Creek side of the ravine. When Ned grounded arms and reached out to help Phon across the last few feet of the bridge he was wet through with perspiration, and yet he was as cool as a new-made grave.

"Ned," said Steve five minutes later, "I would give all the gold in Cariboo if I had it, rather than cross that place again!"—and he meant it.

For a few minutes Steve's gold fever had abated, and in the terror of death even the Chinaman had forgotten the yellow metal. And yet their journey was now over, and within half an hour's walk of them lay the claims they had bought, the wonderful spot of earth out of which they were to dig their heart's desire, the key to all pleasures and the master of nine men out of every ten—gold!

Ned laughed to himself. Was a steady head and the agility of a very second-rate gymnast worth more than all the gold in Cariboo?

"WITH A SCREAM OF FEAR THE CHINAMAN SPRANG OUT."

CHAPTER XII.

A SHEER SWINDLE.

IT is hard to sever the idea of a journey's end from ideas of rest and comfort. A is the starting-point, B the goal, and no matter how distant, no matter how wild the region in which B lies, the mind of the traveller from A to B is sure to picture B as a centre of creature comforts and a haven of luxurious rest.

Thus it was then that Steve and Corbett hurried through the lengthening shadows, eager for the city that was to come, their eyes strained to catch a glow of colour, and their ears alert for the first hum which should tell of the presence of their fellow-men.

After the gloom of the northern forests, the silence of the pack-trail, and the monotony of forced marches, they were ready to welcome any light however garish, any revelry however mad it might be. Life and light and noise were what both hankered after as a relief from the silence and solitude of the last few days, and it is this natural craving for change in the minds of men who have been too much alone, which accounts for half the wild revels of the frontier towns.

As a matter of history, the first impression made by Williams Creek upon the sensitive mind of the artist Chance was one of disappointment. Perhaps it was that the heavy shadows of the mountains drowned all colour, or that the day was nearly over and the dance-house not yet open; whatever the cause Williams Creek struck Chance with a chill. It was a miserable, mean-looking little place for so much gold to come from. In his visions of the mines Steve had dwelt too much upon the glitter of the metal, and too little on the dirt and bare rock from which the gold has to be extracted; extracted, too, by hard labour, about the hardest labour probably which the bodies of men were ever made to undergo.

As his eyes gradually took in the details of the scene, Steve Chance remembered Cruickshank's glowing word-pictures of the mines, and his own gaudy map of them, and remembering these things a great fear fell upon him. Steve had accomplished a pilgrimage over a road upon which stronger men had died, and brave men turned back, and now the shrine of his golden god lay at his feet, and this is what it looked like.

In the shadow of a spur of wooded mountains, lay a narrow strip of land which might by comparison be called flat. It was lower than the bald mountains which were at its back, so the melted snows of last winter had trickled into it, until the whole place was a damp, miserable bog, through the centre of which the waters had worn themselves a bed, and made a creek.

There were many such bogs and many such creeks about the foothills of the bald mountains, but these were for the most part hidden by an abundant growth of pine, or adorned by a wealth of long grass and the glory of yellow lily and blue larkspur. But this bog was less fortunate than its fellows. Gold had been found in the creek which ran through it, so that instead of the spring flowers and the pines, there were bare patches of yellow mud, stumps rough and untrained where trees had stood, tunnels in the hillside, great wooden gutters mounted high in the air to carry off the stream from its bed and pour it into all manner of unexpected places, piles of boulders and rubbish, so new and unadorned by weed or flower that you knew instinctively that nature had had no hand in their arrangement.

And everywhere amongst this brutal digging and hewing there were new log huts, frame shanties, wet untidy tents, and shelters made of odds and ends, shelters so mean that an African Bushman would have turned up his nose at them. Instead of the telegraph and telephone wires that run overhead in ordinary cities, there were in the mining camp innumerable flumes, long wooden boxes or gutters, to carry water from point to point. These gutters were everywhere. They ran over the tops of the houses, they came winding down for miles along precipitous side-hills, and they ran recklessly across the main street; for traffic there was none in those days, or at any rate none which could not step over, or would not pass round the miners' ditch. In 1862 rights of way were disregarded up in Cariboo, but an inch of water if it could be used for gold-washing was a matter of much moment.

"I say, Ned, this looks more like a Chinese camp than a white man's, doesn't it?" remarked Steve with a shudder.

"What did you expect, Steve,—a second San Francisco?"

"Not that; but this place looks so dead and seems so still."

"Silence, they say, is the criterion of pace," quoted Ned; "but I can hear the noise of the rockers and the rattle of the gravel in the sluices. It looks to me as if men were at work here in grim earnest.—Good-day. How goes it, sir?"

The last part of Corbett's speech was addressed to a man of whom he just caught sight at that moment, standing in a deep cutting by the side of the trail, and busily employed in shovelling gravel into a sluice-box at his side.

"Day," grunted the miner, not pausing to lift his head to look at the man who addressed him until he had finished his task.

"Are things booming here still?" asked Chance.

"Booming, you bet! Why, have you just come up from the river?" and the man straightened his back with an effort and jerked his head in the general direction of the Frazer.

"That's what," replied Steve, dropping naturally into the brief idioms of the place.

"Seen anything of the bacon train?" asked the miner after a pause, during which he had again ministered to the wants of his sluice-box.

"The bacon train! What's that?"

"Brown's bacon train from Oregon. Guess you haven't, or you'd know about it. Bacon is played out in Williams Creek, and we are all going it straight on flour."

The thought of "going it straight on flour" was evidently too much for Steve's new friend, for he actually groaned aloud, and dug his shovel into the wall of his trench with as much energy as if he had been driving it into the ribs of the truant Bacon Brown.

"That will suit us royally," ejaculated Ned. "We shall have a small train here in a day or two, and there's a good deal of bacon amongst our stores."

"You've got a train acomin'! By thunder! I thought I knowed your voices. Ain't you them two Britishers as were along of Cruickshank?"

"Strike me pink if it isn't Rampike!" cried Steve,

and the next minute the old gentleman who had helped Steve in his little game of poker climbed out of the mud-pie he was making, and shook hands, even with the Chinaman.

"But where's Roberts, and where's Cruickshank?" he asked.

Corbet told him.

"Wal, as you've left Roberts with him I suppose it's all right. Did you meet any boys going back from these parts?"

"Only two, going back for grub," replied Ned.

"I guess they told you how short we were up here, and they are worse off at Antler."

"No, they said very little to us. They had a bit of a yarn with Cruickshank though. He was leading out and met them first. He didn't say anything about the want of grub to us."

"That's a queer go. Why, it would almost have paid you to go to Antler instead of coming here. You would get two dollars a pound for bacon up there."

"Ah! but you see we were bound to be here for the 1st of June, because of those claims we bought."

"Is that so? Bob did say summat about those claims. Do you know where they are?"

"Here's our map," replied Corbett, producing the authorized map of Dewd and Cruickshank, upon which the three claims had been duly marked. "Is Dewd in the camp?" he added.

"I don't know; but come along, there goes Cameron's triangle. Let us go and get some 'hash,' and we can find out about Dewd and the claims." And so saying Rampike laid aside his shovel, put on his coat, and led the way down to a big tent in the middle of the mining camp.

Here were gathered almost half the population of Williams Creek for their evening meal, the other half having finished theirs and departed to work upon the night-shift; for most of the claims were worked night and day, their owners and the hired men dividing the twenty-four hours amongst them.

Here, as on board the steamer, Rampike was evidently a man of some account; one able to secure a place for himself and his chums in spite of the rush made upon the food by the hungry mob in its shirt sleeves.

At first all three men were too busy with their knives and forks to notice anyone or hear what men were saying about themselves, but in a little while, when the edge of appetite was dulled, Ned caught the words repeated over and over again—" Bacon Brown's men, I guess," and at last had to answer point blank to a direct question, that he had "never heard of Mr. Brown before."

"These fellows hain't seen Brown at all," added Rampike. "They're looking for Dewd. Have you seen him anywhere around?"

At the mention of Dewd's name a broad grin passed over the faces of those who heard it, and one man looked up and remarked that a good many people had been inquiring kindly after Dewd lately. The speaker was a common type amongst the miners, but in those early days his rough clothes and refined speech struck Ned as contrasting strangely.

Truth to tell, he had been educated at Eton and Oxford, had thrown up a good tutorship to come out here, and here he was happy as a king, though all his classical education was thrown away, and his blue pantaloons were patched fore and aft with bits of sacking once used to contain those favourite brands of flour known respectively as "Self-rising" and the "Golden Gate."

As he rose to his feet with the names of the brands printed in large letters on either side of him, he looked something between a navvy and a "sandwich man."

"Dewd," he went on, "has been playing poker lately a little too well to please the boys. Say, O'Halloran, do you know where Dewd is?"

"Faith and I don't. If I did, Sandy M'Donald would give me half his claim for the information. Hullo, have you got here already, sonny? I was before ye though." And Ned's red-headed friend of fighting proclivities held out his hand to him over the heads of his neighbours.

"What does Sandy want him for?" asked someone in the crowd.

"You'd betther ax Sandy. All I know is that he went gunning for him early this morning, and if he wasn't so drunk that he can't walk he'd be afther him still."

"Who's drunk, Pat,—Dewd or Sandy?"

"Oh, don't be foolish! Whoever heard of Dewd touching a drop of good liquor. That's the worst of that mane shunk; he gets you blind drunk first and robs you afther."

"What, have you been bitten too, O'Halloran?" asked the tutor; and while the laugh was still going at the wry face poor Corny O'Halloran pulled, Rampike and his three friends slipped quietly out of the room.

"I guess we may as well locate those claims of yourn right away," remarked Rampike as soon as they were clear of Cameron's tent, "so as there'll be no trouble about securing them to-morrow. Not as I think any one is likely to jump 'em. Let me see your map."

Ned handed over the map before alluded to.

"Why, look ye here, these claims are right alongside the Nugget, the richest claim on the creek!" cried their friend, after studying the map for a few minutes.

"Quite so, that is what gives them their exceptional value," remarked Chance, quoting from memory Cruickshank's very words.

"Oh, that's what gives them their 'ceptional vally, is it, young man?" sneered Rampike. "Wal, I guess they ought to have a 'ceptional vally' to make it worth while working them there;" and Rampike, who was now standing by the Nugget claim alongside the bed of the creek, pointed upwards to where the bluffs, two hundred feet high, hung precipitously over their heads.

It was no good arguing, no good swearing that the map must be wrong, that Cruickshank had marked the wrong lots, that there was a mistake somewhere.

"Just one of the colonel's mistakes, that's what it is. Come and see the gold Commissioner, he'll straighten it out for you," retorted Rampike, hurrying the three off into the presence of a big handsome man, whose genial ways and handsome face made "the judge" a great favourite with the miners.

All he could do he did, and was ready to go far beyond the obligations of his office in his desire to help Cruickshank's victims. It was a very common kind of fraud after all. The colonel had drawn a sufficiently accurate map of the Williams Creek valley; he had even given accurately every name upon that map, and moreover the claims which he had sold to Corbett & Co. adjoined the Nugget claim, and had been regularly taken up and bonded by his partner and himself. Cruickshank's story indeed was true in every particular.

Gold was being taken out of the Nugget mine at the rate of several lbs. per diem; why should it not be taken out of the claims which it adjoined?

There was only one objection to Cruickshank's map,—he had not drawn it in relief. There was only one objection to Corbett's claim—the surface of it would have adjoined the surface of the Nugget claim had they both been upon the same level, only,—only, you see, they were not. There was a trifling difference of two hundred and fifty feet in the altitude of the Nugget claim and the bluff adjoining it, and Corbett's claim was on the top of that bluff. Now a claim on the top of a bluff, where no river could ever have run to deposit gold, and whither no water could be brought to wash for gold, was not considered worth two thousand dollars even in Cariboo.

CHAPTER XIII.

THE BULLET'S MESSAGE.

"WAL, those'll maybe make vallible building lots when Williams Creek has growed as big as 'Frisco, but somehow trade in building lots ain't brisk here just now."

No one answered old Rampike. Steve and Ned felt rather hurt at the levity of his remarks. It is poor fun even for a rich man to be robbed of six thousand dollars, and neither Ned nor Steve were rich men. In fact, in losing the six thousand dollars they had lost their all except the pack-train.

"It ain't no manner of good to grizzle over it," continued this philosopher, "Cruickshank has got the cinch on you to rights this time. Six thousand dollars cash, the pleasure of your company from Victoria, and your pack-train to remember you by! Ho! ho!" and although it was very annoying to Ned, and quite contrary to Rampike's nature to do so, he laughed aloud at his own grim joke.

The laugh roused Chance. He was a Yankee to the tips of his finger-nails, one of those strange beings who "bust and boom" by turns—millionaires to-day, bankrupts to-morrow, equally sanguine, happy, and go-ahead in either extreme.

"Ned," he said, his face relaxing into a somewhat wintry smile, "I guess you were right after all. Cruickshank is no Britisher, you bet."

"Glad you think so; hang him!" growled Ned.

"No Britisher could ever have planned so neat a swindle," continued Steve meditatively. "By Jove, it is a 'way up'!" and this strange young man really seemed lost in admiration at the smartness from which he himself had suffered.

"I don't see much to admire in a thief and a liar. We prefer honesty to smartness in my country, thank God!"

There was no disguising the fact that Ned Corbett was in a very ugly temper. Not being one of those who look upon the whole struggle for wealth as a game of chance and skill, in which everything is allowable except a plain transgression of the written rules of the game, he could not even simulate any admiration for a successful swindler's smartness.

Old Rampike saw his mood, and laying his hand on his shoulder gave him a friendly shake. "Never mind, sonny," he said. "It's no good calling names; and as for being stone-broke, why there isn't a man in Cariboo to-day, I reckon, who hasn't been stone-broke, aye and most of 'em mor'n once or twice."

"Oh, yes, I suppose that is so," said Ned a little wearily, but rousing himself all the same. "What can a man earn here as a digger in another fellow's claim?"

"Anything he likes to ask almost. Men who are worth anything at all as workers are scarce around these parts."

"Then we sha'n't starve, that is some consolation By the way, I have a note here for you. This confounded business nearly made me forget it;" and so saying Corbett produced from an inner pocket the little note given him by Roberts at the Balm-of-Gilead camp.

For a few moments Rampike twisted and turned the note about, trying to decipher the faint pencil-marks in the dim light. At last he got the note right side up and began to read. Evidently he hardly understood what he read at first, for those who were watching him saw that he read the note through a second time, as if looking for some hidden meaning in every word. When he had done this a vindictive bitter oath burst from between his set teeth.

"If Cruickshank ain't dead by now, my old pal Roberts is. You may bet on that. Look ye here!" and the speaker handed Ned a flattened, blood-stained bullet which he had taken from Roberts' letter.

"Do you know what that is?" he asked.

"It looks like a revolver bullet," answered Ned.

"And so it is. That's the identical bullet as Dan Cruickshank fired at a grouse and *hit a cayuse* with. Pretty shooting, wasn't it?" and Rampike ground his teeth with anger.

"What the deuce do you mean?" cried Steve in blank astonishment.

"Mean—mean! Why, that if you warn't such a durned tenderfoot you'd have tumbled to the whole thing long ago! Men like Cruickshank don't leave horses unhobbled by mistake, don't hit and scare pack-horses on a stone-slide by mistake, don't get to Williams Creek a day late by mistake. Oh, curse his mistakes! If he makes one more there'll be the best pal and the sweetest singer in Cariboo lying dead up among them pines."

"Do you mean that Cruickshank did these things on purpose?" asked Corbett slowly, his face growing strangely hard as he spoke.

"Read Rob's letter," said Rampike, and gave Ned the scrap of paper on which Rob had found time to write a brief record of the journey from Douglas, ending his story in these words—"Cruickshank means Corbett mischief, so I am staying instead of the lad. What his game is with the pack-ponies I am blowed if I know, but if I don't come in with them inside of a week, do some of you fellows try and get even with the colonel for the sake of your old pal Roberts."

For several minutes after reading this note no one spoke; each man was thinking out the situation after his own fashion.

"Will you trust me with grub for a fortnight, Rampike?" asked Ned at last.

"Yes, lad, if you like; but you won't want to borrow. Men like you can earn all they want here;" and the miner looked appreciatively at the big-limbed man before him.

"I'll earn it by and by, Rampike. I'm going after Roberts first," replied Ned quietly.

"How's that?" demanded Rampike.

"I'm going after Roberts and Cruickshank. Can I have the grub?"

"If that's your style, you can have all the grub you want if I have to go hungry for a week. When will you start?"

"It will be dark in two hours," replied Ned, "and the moon comes up about midnight. I shall start as soon as the moon is up."

"Impossible, man!" cried Chance. "I could not drag myself to the top of that first bluff unless I had had twenty-four hours' solid sleep, if my life depended upon it."

'I know, old fellow, and I don't want you to; but you see a life may depend upon it."

"But you aren't going alone, Corbett. I'll not hear of that."

"We will talk about that by and by, Steve. Let us go and turn in for a little while now. I am dead tired myself." And so saying Corbett turned on his heel and followed Rampike to his hut, where the old man found room for all three of them upon the floor.

"If Steve and I go to look for Roberts can you find a job for our Chinaman until we come back? I should not like the poor beggar to starve," said Ned, pointing to where Phon lay already fast asleep. The moment he laid down his head Phon had gone to sleep, and since then not a muscle had twitched to show that he was alive. Whatever his master might choose to arrange for his benefit the Chinaman was not likely to overhear or object to.

"Oh yes, I can fix that easy enough. I'll set him to wash in my own claim. I can afford to pay him good wages as well as feed him. Men are scarce at Williams Creek."

Again for a time there was silence in the hut, Corbett and Rampike puffing away at their pipes, and Steve Chance trying hard to keep his eyes open as if he suspected mischief. At last nature got the better of him; the young Yankee's head dropped on his arm, and in another moment he was as sound asleep as Phon.

Then Ned stood up and went over to sit beside the old miner Rampike, remarking as he did so:

"Thank heaven Steve is off at last. I thought the fellow never meant to go to sleep."

"What! Do you mean to leave him behind?" asked Rampike.

"Does he look as if he could do another week's tramping?" retorted Ned, glancing at the limp, worn-out figure of his friend. "He has pluck enough to try, but he would only hinder me."

"If that's so, I'll chuck my claim and come along too."

'Nonsense, you can't afford to lose your claim; and, besides, you couldn't help me."

"Couldn't help you! How's that?" snorted Rampike indignantly.

"A man can always hunt better alone than with another fellow. One makes less noise than two in the woods."

"But you ain't going hunting?"

"Yes I am,—hunting big game too." And there was a light in Ned Corbett's eye, as he overhauled his Winchester, that looked bad for an enemy.

"You ain't afraid of—losing your way?" asked Rampike. He was going to say "You ain't afraid of

Cruickshank, are you?" but a look on Corbett's face stopped that question.

"No, I'm used to the woods," Ned answered shortly; and then again for a while the two men smoked on in silence.

Presently Corbett knocked the ashes out of his pipe, and put it away carefully in his pocket.

"Do you work in the night-shift on your place?" he asked Rampike.

"Either me or my partner is there all the while."

"Shall you be there to-night?"

"I'll be going on at midnight, but I'll fix up a pack with some grub in it for you before I go."

"Thank you, I'll leave that to you, if I may. Will you call me before you go? I mean to try to get all the sleep I can before the moon is up."

"Well, lie down right now. I'll call you, you bet. You're a good sort for a Britisher—give us a shake;" and Rampike held out a hand as hard and as honest as the pick-handle to which it clung day after day.

Perhaps it was the thought of his old friend's danger which made Rampike blind and careless, or perhaps it was only his natural clumsiness. In any case he steered very badly for his own door, so badly indeed that he tripped over Chance's prostrate form, dealing him a kick that might have roused a dead man. But Steve only turned over restlessly in his sleep, like one who dreams, and then lay as still again as ever.

Ned smiled. "No danger of waking him, I think, when I want to go. Poor old Steve! the loss of the money does not seem to spoil your sleep much."

Five minutes later, when Rampike had gone out to get together the provisions which his guest needed, anyone listening to that guest's regular breathing would have been of opinion that the loss of the dollars troubled Ned Corbett as little as it troubled Steve Chance.

CHAPTER XIV.

WHAT THE WOLF FOUND.

ABOUT midnight Rampike returned to his hut, and as the moonlight streamed through the doorway across the floor, Corbett rose without a word and joined the old miner outside.

"You didn't need much waking, lad."

"No; and yet I slept like a top. But I *felt* you were coming, and now every nerve in my body is wide awake."

Rampike looked at his companion curiously.

"You're a strong man, Ned Corbett, but take care. I've known stronger men than you get the 'jim-jams' from overwork."

Ned laughed. He hardly thought that a man who had not tasted liquor for a month was likely to suffer much from the "jim-jams."

"That's all right," said Rampike testily. "You may laugh, but I've seen more of this kind of life than you'll ever see, and I tell you, you'd better stay where you are."

"What! and let Cruickshank go?"

"What are you going to do with Cruickshank when you catch him?"

"Bring him back to look at the *mistake* he made about my claims," answered Corbett grimly.

"And suppose Cruickshank don't feel like coming back? It's more than likely that he won't."

"Then it will be a painful necessity for Roberts and myself to pack him back."

"If you get him back the law can't touch him, and the boys won't lynch him just for swindling a tenderfoot."

"The law can't touch him?"

"Why, certainly not. If you were such a blessed fool as to buy claims without a frontage on the crik, that's your business. He didn't say as they weren't on the top of a mountain."

"But no mountain was shown on his map," argued Corbett.

"I guess he'd say as he couldn't draw maps well and the one Steve Chance copied was the best he knew how to make. He sold you what he said he'd sell you, and if you didn't ask any questions that's your fault."

This was a new view of the case to Corbett, and for a moment he felt staggered by it, but only for a moment. After all, it was not for the sake of the claims that he had made up his mind to pursue Cruickshank.

"Thanks, Rampike, for trying to make me stay here. I know what you mean, but I am not as nearly 'beat' as you think I am, and I wouldn't leave old Roberts alone with that scoundrel even if I was. Have you got the grub there?"

"Well, if that's your reason for going I've no more to say, except as I reckon Roberts is pretty good at taking care of himself. However, a pal's a pal, and if you mean to stay by him, I'll not hinder you. Here's the grub;" and so saying he helped Ned to fix a little bundle upon his shoulders, taking care that whatever weight there was should lie easily in the small of his back. "It's only dried venison," continued Rampike, "and I didn't put any bread in. Bread weighs too much and takes up too much room. You can go it on meat straight for a week, can't you?"

"I'll try to. Give Chance a helping hand if you can. He is a regular rustler if you can get him any work to do."

"Don't worry yourself about your pals. You are going to look for Dick Rampike's old partner, and you may bet your sweet life that he won't let *your* pals starve."

The two men, who had been walking slowly through the mining camp, had now reached the foot of the trail by which Ned had arrived at Williams Creek.

"Well, good-bye, Rampike," said Ned, stopping and holding out his hand. "It's no good your coming any farther. Don't let Steve follow me."

"Good-bye, lad; I'll see that Steve Chance don't follow you. He ain't built to go your pace," he added, looking after Ned, "if he wanted to, but there'll be me and some of the boys after you afore long, if there's going to be any trouble;" and with this consoling reflection in his mind, the old hard-fist returned to his cabin, pulled off his long gum boots, and lay down on the floor beside the still sleeping Chance and Phon.

Mr. Rampike had not as yet had time to furnish his country residence, and after all, in his eyes a bed was rather a useless luxury. 'What's the matter with a good deal floor?' he often used to ask; and as he never got a satisfactory answer, he never bothered to build himself a bunk.

Meanwhile Ned Corbett was standing for a moment

on the top of a bluff above Williams Creek, whence he could still see the lights of the camp, and still hear faint strains of music from the dance-house and the monotonous "clink, clink" of the miner's pick. The next moment he turned his back upon it all; a rising bank shut out the last glimpse of the fires and the last faint hum of human life. The forest swallowed them up, and Ned was alone with the silence.

Never in all his life had he been in so strange a mood as he was that night.

It seemed to him that every nerve and muscle in his body, every faculty of his brain, had been tuned to concert pitch. All his old calmness had deserted him, and in place of it a very fire of impatience devoured him. Wherever the trail allowed of it he broke into a long swinging run, and yet, though the miles flew past him, he was not satisfied. On! on! a voice seemed to cry to him, and in spite of his speed the voice still urged him to further efforts. That was the worst of it. Instead of the silence the forest seemed full of voices, —not voices which spoke to his ear, but voices which cried to the soul that was within him. The shadows were full of these inarticulate cries, the night air throbbed with them, all nature was full of them, and of a secret which he alone seemed unable to grasp.

But it was no good standing still to listen, so he pressed on until he came to the bridge of pines where the day before Phon had clung, swinging between this world and the next. Here Corbett hesitated for the first time, standing at the top of that arch of pines, looking across the black gulf in which the unseen waters moaned horribly. If his foot slipped or his hands failed him for the tenth part of a second, he would drop from the moonlight into eternal darkness, leaving no trace behind by which men could tell that Ned Corbett had ever existed.

For a moment a cold horror seized him, he clung wildly to the boughs round him and looked backwards instead of forwards. But this fit only lasted for a moment, and then the bold English blood came back to his heart with a rush. "Good heavens!" he muttered, "am I turning Chinaman?" and as he muttered it he launched himself boldly across the gap, caught at the rope to steady himself, and having crossed the bridge set his face firmly once more for the bald mountains above him.

All through the night Corbett maintained that long swinging stride, climbing steadily up the steep hills and passing swiftly down the forest glades, tireless as a wolf and silent as a shadow.

When the dawn came he paused in his race, and sat down for a quarter of an hour to eat a frugal meal of dried meat. Had he been living the normal life of a civilized man in one of the cities of Europe, he would have needed much less food and eaten much more. All civilized human beings overeat themselves. Perhaps if the food at the Bristol or the Windsor was served as dry and as little seasoned as Rampike's venison, less would be eaten and more digested.

Breakfast over, Ned resumed his course. Even during his hurried meal he had been restless and anxious to get on. Fatigue seemed not to touch him, or a power over which mere human weariness could not prevail, possessed him.

As the air freshened and the stars paled, the tits and "whisky-jacks" began their morning complaints, their peevish voices convincing Ned that they had been up too long the night before. A little later the squirrels began to chatter and swear angrily at him as he passed, and a gray old *coyoté* slinking home to bed stood like a shadow watching him as he went, wondering, no doubt, who this early-rising hunter might be, with the swift silent feet, white set face, and stern blue eyes which looked so keen and yet saw nothing.

Then the sun rose, and at last, taking a hint from the tall red-deer, Ned threw himself down on the soft mosses, trusting in the sun to warm him in his slumbers, as it does all the rest of that great world which gets on very well without blankets.

Until the shadow had crept to the other side of the tree under which he lay, Ned Corbett slept without moving; then he rose again, ate a few mouthfuls of dried meat, took a modest draught of the white water which foamed and bubbled through the moss of the hillside, and again went on.

One day went and another came, and still Corbett held on his course, and on the third day he had his reward. At last on the trail in front of him he saw the tracks of horses, nine in number, all of them shod before and behind as his own had been, and the tracks of *one* man driving them.

That was singular. There were two men left with Ned Corbett's pack-train. Where had the other gone to? Backwards and forwards he went, bending low over the trail and scrutinizing every inch of it, but he could see no sign of that other man. Perhaps he had tired and had found room upon one of the least laden of the pack animals. It would be hard upon the beast and most uncomfortable for the rider, but it was possible.

Or perhaps the tracks of the man who "led out" had been quite obliterated by the feet of the beasts which followed him. That too was possible, and Ned remembered how he had noticed upon the trail that a horse's stride and a man's were almost exactly the same length, so that it might be that for a few hundred yards at any rate one of the animals had gone step for step over Cruikshanks or old Rob's tracks.

But this could not have lasted for long; either the man or the beast would have strayed a yard or two from the track once in the course of a mile; but Corbett had examined the tracks for more than a mile, and still the story of them was the same: "nine pack-horses driven by one man over the trail nearly a week ago;" that was the way the tracks read, and Ned could make nothing else out of them.

There was one thing, however, worth mentioning. Corbett had hit upon the tracks on the path by which he himself had come from the Balm-of-Gilead camp to Williams Creek, at a point as nearly as he could judge five miles on the Williams Creek side of that camp. So far then the pack-train had followed him, but at this point it had turned away almost at right angles to follow a well-beaten trail which Corbett and Steve had overlooked when they passed it a week earlier.

"That, I suppose, is where we went wrong, and this must be the proper pack-trail to Williams Creek," soliloquized Ned, and then for a moment he stood, doubting which way he should turn. Should he follow his pack-train, or should he go back until the tracks told him something of that other man, whose feet had left no record on the road?

The same instinct which had urged him on for the last three days, took hold upon him again and turned him almost against his will towards the old Balm-of-Gilead camp.

It was nearly dark when he reached it, and he would

perhaps have passed it by, but that he stumbled over the half-burnt log which had been used as the side log for his own fire. Since Ned had camped there a little snow had fallen, a trifling local storm such as will take place in the mountains even in May, and this had sufficed to hide almost all trace of the camp in that rapidly waning light.

As well as he could, Corbett examined the camp, going carefully over every inch of it; but the only thing he could find was a cartridge belt, hung up on the branch of a pine,—a cartridge belt half full of ammunition for a revolver. This he at once recognized as belonging to Roberts.

"By Jove, that's careless," he muttered, "and unlike the old man. I should have thought at any rate that he would have found out his loss before he got very far away, and have come back for the belt."

In another quarter of an hour it was too dark to see his hand before his face, so making the best of a bad business Ned sat down at the foot of a big pine, and leaning his back against it tried to doze away the time until the moon should rise and enable him to proceed on his way. But though Corbett's muscles throbbed and his limbs trembled from over-exertion, no sleep would come to him. In spite of himself his brain kept on working, not in its ordinary methodical fashion, but as if it were red-hot with fever. Indeed poor Ned began to think that he was going mad. If he were not, what was this new fancy which possessed him?

For some reason beyond his own comprehension his brain would now do nothing but repeat over and over again the refrain of Roberts' favourite song. The tune of "the old pack-mule" had taken possession of him and would give him no peace. Without his will his fingers moved to the time of it; if he tried to think of something else his thoughts put themselves in words, and the words fell into the metre of it, and at last he became convinced that he could actually with his own bodily ears hear the refrain of it, sad and distant as he had last heard it before leaving that camp.

There it came again, wailing up out of the darkness, the very ghost of a song, and yet as distinct as if the singer's mouth had been at his ear—

"Riding, riding, riding on my old pack-mule."

When things had gone as far as this, Ned sprang to his feet with a start. There was no doubt about *that* weird note anyway; and though it was but the howl of a wolf which roused him from his doze, Ned shuddered as the long-drawn yell died away in the darkness, which was now slowly giving way to the light of the rising moon.

Brave man though he was, Ned Corbett felt a chill perspiration break out all over him, and his heart began to beat in choking throbs. The wolf's weird music had a meaning for him which he had never noticed in it before. He knew now why it was so sad. Had it not in it all the misery of homeless wandering, all the hopelessness of the Ishmael, whose hand is against every man as every man's hand is against him, all the bitterness of cold and hunger and darkness? Was his own lot to be like the wolf's?

"Great Scott, this won't do!" cried the lad, and snatching up his pack he blundered away upon the trail, prepared to face anything rather than his own fancies.

As he moved away down the trail Corbett thought

that he caught a glimpse of the beast, whose hideous voice had dispelled his dreams and jarred so roughly upon his nerves.

Fear makes most men vicious, and Corbett was very human in all his moods, so that his first impulse on seeing the beast which had frightened him was to give it the contents of his revolver. Stooping down to see more clearly, he managed to get a faint and spectral outline of his serenader against the pale moonlight, and into the middle of this he fired. A wolf's body is not at any time too large a mark for a bullet, even if it be a rifle bullet; but a wolf's body is a very small mark indeed for a revolver bullet at night, and so Ned found it, and missed. To his intense surprise, however, the gray shadow was in no hurry to be gone. Though the report of the revolver seemed curiously loud in the absolute silence of a northern night, the wolf only cantered a few yards and then stood still again, and again sent his hideous cry wailing through the forest aisles.

"Curse you, you won't go, won't you?" hissed Ned, his nerve completely gone, and his heart full of unreasonable anger; and again he fired at the brute, and this time rushed in after his shot, determined if he could not kill him with a bullet to settle matters with the butt.

But the wolf vanished in the uncertain light as if he had really been a shadow, and his howl but the offspring of Corbett's fancy. For a few yards Ned followed in the direction in which the beast seemed to have gone, until his eyes fell upon a swelling in the snow, near to which the wolf had been when the first shot was fired.

What is that other sense which we all of us possess

and for which there is no name,—that sense which is neither sight nor hearing, nor any of the other three common to our daily lives? Before Ned Corbett's eyes there lay a low swelling mound of snow, smooth white snow, still and cold in the pale moonlight. There were ten thousand other mounds just like it in the forest round him, and yet before *this* mound Corbett stood rooted to the ground, whilst his eyes dilated and he felt his hair rising with horror, and in the utter stillness heard his own heart thundering against his side.

Until that moment Ned Corbett had never looked upon the dead. He had heard and read of death, and knew that in his turn he too must die; but as it chanced, he had never yet seen that dumb blind thing which live men bury, saying this *was* a man. And yet it needed not the disappointed yell of that foul scavenger to tell him what lay beneath the snow.

Slowly he compelled himself to draw near, and stooping he completed with reverent hands what the claws of the hungry beast had already begun, and then the moon and the man, with wan white faces, looked down together upon all that remained of cheery old Rob. Corbett knew at last why there had been no peace for him in the forests that night. There was no mystery about his old comrade's death. The whole foul story of murder was written so large that the woods knew it, and were full of it. This was the story which the shuddering pines had whispered all along the trail, and at last Corbett had grasped their secret and knew what the voices kept saying.

Just where the curly hair came down upon his friend's sturdy neck, was a small dark hole; a trifling wound it looked to have killed so strong a man, and yet when the bullet struck him there, Roberts had fallen without knowing who had struck him.

Then for one moment, perhaps, the man who did this thing had stood glaring at what he had done, more afraid of the dead man at his feet than his victim had ever been of any man. The position of the body told the rest of the story. Though he could kill him, Cruickshank dared not leave those death-sharpened features staring up to heaven appealing for vengeance against the murderer, so he had seized the corpse by its wrists and dragged it away from the campfire, away to where the dark balsams threw their heaviest shadows, and there left it, its arms stretched out stiff and rigid for the snows to cover and hide until it should melt away into the earth whence it came.

And what was Corbett to do? Men do not weep for men—their grief lies too deep for that—and, moreover, there is nothing practical in tears.

And yet what was Corbett to do? He might hide the dead again for awhile, but in the end he would be meat for the wolf and the raven.

"Oh God!" he cried in the bitterness of his spirit, "is this nothing unto Thee? Dost Thou see what man has done?"

And even then, while the infinitely small pleaded from the depth of the forest to the Infinitely Mighty, a little wind came and shook the tops of the pines, and the dawn came.

Thereafter, as far as Corbett knew, time ceased. Only the pines went by and the trail slipped past under his feet, until, in spite of all his efforts, and although the trees seemed still to go past him, he himself stood still. Then there came a humming in the air and the thunder of a great river in his ears, and the earth began to rise and fall, and suddenly it was night!

. . . .

It was on a Monday morning that Ned Corbett started from Williams Creek to search for Cruickshank, and on Saturday old Bacon Brown from Oregon brought his train into Antler, and with it a tall, fair-haired man, whom he had found upon the trail some fifteen miles back he said—a man whom he guessed had had the "jim-jams" pretty bad, "and come mighty nigh to sending in his chips, you bet."

CHAPTER XV.

IN THE DANCE-HOUSE.

"CHASSEY to the right, chassey to the left, swing your partners round, and all promenade!" sang Old Dad, fiddler and master of ceremonies at Antler, British Columbia.

It was early in June. The moon was riding high above the pine-trees, and the men of the night-shifts were dropping in one by one for a dance with Lilla and Katchen before going to supper.

Claw-hammer coats and boiled shirts were not insisted upon in the Antler dance-house, so most of the men swaggered in in their gray suits and long gum boots, all splashed with blue mud, and took their waltz just as we should take our sherry and bitters, as a pleasant interlude between business and dinner.

Some fellows found time to eat and sleep, and a few were said to wash, but no one could afford to waste time in changing his clothes at the Cariboo gold-mines in '62. When your overalls wore out you just handed your dust over the store-keeper's counter and got into a new pair right there, and some fellows took off their gum boots when they lay down for a sleep. Wasn't that change enough?

At any rate the hurdy girls were content with their partners, and their partners were all in love with the "hurdies."

Now, it may be that some unfortunate person who knows nothing of anything west of Chicago may read this book, and may want to know what a "hurdy" is or was, for, alas! the "hurdies," like the dodo, are extinct.

Be it known then to all who do not know it already, that the hurdy-gurdy girls (to give them their full title) were douce, honest lassies from Germany, who, being fond of dancing and fond of dollars, combined business with pleasure, and sold their dances to the diggers at so many pinches of dust per dance. It was an honest and innocent way of earning money, and if any sceptic wants to sneer at the gentle hurdies, there need be no difficulty in finding an "old-timer" to argue with him; only the arguments used in Cariboo are forcible certainly, and might even seem somewhat "rocky" to a mild-mannered man.

Well, now you know what a "hurdy" was, and when I tell you that a troop of hurdies had just come up from Kamloops, you will understand that Antler was very much *en fête* on this particular June night.

Indeed, the long wooden shanty known as the dance house was full to overflowing, full of miners having what they considered a good time—dancing in gum boots, drinking bad whisky, singing songs, and swearing wonderfully original "swears." But there was no popping of pistols, no flashing of bowie-knives at Antler. That might do very well in Californian mining camps, but in British Columbia, in early days, even the strong men had been taught by a stronger to respect the law.

So Old Dad took command in the noisy room, and was under no apprehension for his personal safety. He might be dead drunk before morning or "dead-broke" before the end of the season, but there was very little chance that a stray bullet would end his career before that terrible time came round when the camp would be deserted, and he would have to sneak away to the lower country to earn his living by pig-feeding and "doing chores."

But the pig-feeding days were far distant still, so that this most dissolute yet tuneful fiddler continued to incite his clients to fresh efforts in dancing.

There were those, though, even at Antler, who were too staid, or too shy, or too stolid to dance, and for the benefit of such as these small tables had been arranged, not too far from the refreshments—small tables at which they could sit and smoke in peace.

At one of these, in a pause between the dances, a tall, fair-haired girl, all smiles and ribbons, came to a halt before a solitary, dark-visaged misanthrope, who sat abstractedly chewing the end of an unlit cigar.

"What's the trouble, Colonel? Have you anyone murdered?"

The words were lightly spoken, and a laugh rippled over the speaker's pretty face, but no answering smile came into the smoker's deep-set eyes. On the contrary, he sprang to his feet with so fierce an oath that Lilla started back, and the smokers at the next table turned

LILLA ACCOSTS THE COLONEL IN THE DANCE-HOUSE.

with savage scowls to see who it was who dared to swear at their little German sweetheart.

"By mighty, I believe the girl's right!" said one of these; "the fellow looks pretty scared."

"Like enough. A fellow who cain't speak civil to a woman might do anything," growled another. This last was a Yankee, and Yankees have a great respect for the ladies, all honour to them for it.

Meanwhile the colonel and the dancing-girl stood facing each other, the smile dying out of her face as the scowl died out of his. She was half-frightened, and he had overheard his neighbours' remarks, and recognized the necessity for self-control.

"I beg your pardon, Lilla. What a brute you must think me! But don't you know better than to wake a sleeping dog suddenly?"

"But no dog is so mean as to bite a woman," protested Lilla.

"That's so, and *I* only barked. I've been so long packing all alone that I have lost my company manners. Won't you forgive me, Lilla?" and he held out his hand to her. Now it was part of Lilla's business to pour oil upon the troubled waters of society at Antler, and, besides, the colonel was an old acquaintance and excellent dancer, so Lilla took his hand.

"Well, I'll try, but you pay me a fine. See, not once have you asked me to dance this time in Antler. Now dance with me."

"Is that all, Lilla? Come then." And so saying he offered the girl his arm, and walked away with her to another part of the room out of ear-shot of the angry Yankee.

"I wanted to talk to you, Lilla," he began; but just then the music struck up, and the girl, who had quite recovered her spirits, beat the ground with a pretty impatient toe, exclaiming, "The talk will keep; come on now, we mustn't lose a bar of it." And then, as her partner steered her gracefully over the floor, she gave a little contented sigh and muttered, "So you have not forgotten. Ach, himmel! this is to dance."

And indeed the dark-faced man might have committed many crimes, but he was not one to trample upon a woman's tenderest feelings by treading on her toes, tearing her dress out at the gathers, and disregarding good music.

On the contrary, he had a perfect ear for time, steered by instinct, and held his partner like one who was proud of her and wanted to show her off to advantage.

When the music ceased, and not until then, Lilla and the colonel stopped dancing, and the girl had just enough breath left to say in a tone of absolute conviction:

"You *must* be a good man, I think, you dance so well."

"Of course I'm a good man, Lilla," laughed her partner. "Why should I not be?"

"Well, I don't know, but you frightened me pretty bad just now. What was it with you?"

"Oh, nothing—at least nothing much. I was sulky and you startled me. Are you never sulky, Lilla?"

"What is that sulky, *traurig*?" asked the girl.

"No, not quite. More like what you feel when a frock won't fit you, Lilla."

"So! I understand: well, wherefore are you sulky?"

"I can't sell my freight at my price. Just think what rough luck it was for me that Bacon Brown got in so soon after me. And after bringing the stuff so far and *at such a cost too!*" and again for a moment the colonel's face looked white and drawn in the lamp light.

The Frazer river trail was a bad one, but once its perils were passed there seemed to be no reason why an old packer should turn pale at the mere memory of them.

"Ach, sacrifice!" cried the girl. "You sell your bacon a dollar a pound, and you call that sacrifice. Have you no shame?"

"All very well for you, Lilla. You are a girl who owns a gold-mine; I'm only a poor packer. By the way, have you done anything more about Pete's Creek since last season?"

"No, but I think I'll do something soon."

"Better send me to find it for you, Lilla, before someone else gets hold of it, and give me a share in it for my work. I'll take you, and you keep the creek. How will that do?"

"And what do I become—ach, I mean what shall I get for my share?"

Her partner laid his hand upon his heart and made her his most impressive bow, but the girl only burst out laughing merrily. Perhaps the noise and bright lights of a dance-house are unfavourable to sentiment.

"Ach so, Colonel. Bacon a dollar a pound, and you will trade yourself for the richest gold-mine in Cariboo and me! *Danke schön*," and she curtsied to him laughingly.

"As you please, Lilla. But will you bet me that I don't know where your creek is?"

"I know you don't know anything about it, except what I told you last fall."

"Don't be too sure. You'd better trust me, Lilla. It isn't the other side of the Frazer in the Chilcotin country, is it?"

"I told you so much, and then—"

"It isn't up at the head of the Chilcotin?"

"On which bank?"

"The right."

"Ach so! I knew you didn't know," and then the girl stopped, and for a moment suspicion looked out from her simple blue eyes. Lilla wasn't quite sure whether her dancing partner had not been trying to pump her.

But the colonel saw the look, and knowing that he had obtained all the information which he was likely to get, he deftly turned the conversation into a fresh channel.

"Of course it's only my chaff, Lilla. I would rather have the pretty gold on your head than all the gold in Pete's Creek, even if there was such a place, which I doubt. But who is the new invalid you are nursing?"

"A Britisher as you are, Colonel; only I find him better-looking," replied Lilla mischievously.

"He might easily be that, Lilla. I'm getting old, my dear, with waiting for you. But how did you find this new treasure?"

"Bacon Brown brought him in."

'Brown brought him in! When?"

"Three days from to-day—when his train came along."

"Where did he find him? Is he one of his men?"

"Ach no. I tell you he is English not Yankee. Brown found him dying on the trail."

"On the trail! Where?"

"I don't know quite where, but somewhere between

this place and where the trail forks for Williams Creek."

Whilst the girl had been speaking her companion had shifted his position, so that he now stood with his back to the light, so that no casual observer would have noticed even if his face should turn white and his hand shake.

"What is your friend like, and what was the matter with him, Lilla?" asked the colonel after a while, with a certain show of carelessness, dropping out his words disjointedly between his efforts to light a cigar.

"Well, I can hardly tell you, he lies down all the time. He is too weak to stand up, but he looks a fine man, tall and big—oh, very big, and hair like a Deutscher's, and blue eyes, more blue, I think, than mine;" and she opened those pretty orbs very wide to let her questioner see how very blue eyes would have to be to be bluer than her own.

"Is that so, and Lilla is half in love with him already? Oh, Lilla, Lilla! And when will this beautiful person be well again?"

"Don't talk foolishness," replied the girl, blushing furiously. "How could I love a man who has the 'jim-jams?'"

"The 'jim-jams!' What! from drink?"

"I don't know. But there, there's the music, come along;" and once more Lilla bore away the best waltzer in Antler to the tune of some slow rhythmical German air.

During the dance the girl said nothing, and after it was over she left her partner for someone else (mind) you, dancing meant business for Lilla); but towards the end of the evening she sought out the colonel again, and leading him on one side, said:

"What will you do when you have sold your freight?"

"I don't know. Anything. Why?"

"I have a fancy, and you shall not laugh at me. Pete gave me the map to find his creek when he died. That is good. Now comes another Englishman, also dying. I am, what do you call it—*abergläubig?*"

"I don't know superstitious perhaps?"

"Perhaps superstitious. Suppose this man gets well, he has no money, he is dead-broke, and very young. Do you see?"

"I see. You say he is ill and a 'dead-beat.' Most of your patients are that way, Lilla."

"No, he is not a 'dead-beat.' I think he is—ach, well no matter. But see here, if you will give money for the outfit and grub, and take this man along when he is well again, I will give you the map, and you two can take half the mine between you. Is that good?"

"But why give him a quarter of your mine?"

"I give you a quarter also; and I tell you Pete was English, and you say you are English, and he is English. I think Pete would have liked it so, and this shall bring me luck."

"As you please, Lilla. I would go for you for nothing. Shall I have the map to-night?" And at that moment the light fell upon the man's face, which he had moved somewhat during the conversation, and showed that the mouth was twitching and the eyes glittering with strong excitement which would not be entirely suppressed.

"No, not to-night. When Corbett is well. I may change my mind before then, you know, and give you all the mine, and myself too—who knows!"

And with a nod and a smile, half mocking, half

friendly, Lilla the hurdy girl turned on her heel and left the dancing-room for a little poorly furnished chamber, where, behind a Hudson Bay blanket hung up as a curtain, lay Ned Corbett in the first quiet sleep he had enjoyed since Bacon Brown found him insensible upon the trail which leads to Antler

CHAPTER XVI.

THE PRICE OF BLOOD.

IT was neither day nor night in Antler, but that time between the two when the stars are fading and the moon has set and the sun has not yet risen.

The men of the night-shift had gone back to the claims; the hurdy girls had all followed Lilla's example and slipped away to their own rooms, and though the big dancing hall was still open, the only people in it were a few maudlin topers dozing over their liquor.

Out in the main street there was no light, no light either of sun or moon; no light at all except one feeble ray which flickered from Lilla's window, and fell upon the black water which hurried through the wooden boxes laid across the highway.

By and by a man came out of the gloom, blundered heavily over the boxes, and swore savagely below his breath as if the boxes had consciously conspired for his downfall.

When he had picked himself up again from the mud, this night-bird stood looking fixedly towards the light. Had he swayed unsteadily from side to side, and perhaps fallen again, there would have been nothing worth watching about him. Rye whisky, the fresh night air, and the ditches laid across the roads, used often to persuade very honest gentlemen to pass their nights beside the gutter. But this man stood firmly upon his feet, looking steadily at the light ahead of him. Presently he appeared to have made up his mind, for after looking up and down the road to see whether anyone was watching him, he stole up to the window and crouched beside it in such a position that he could peer in unseen.

Inside the room the light fell upon bare wooden walls, from which hung a little mirror, and a man's coat and broad-brimmed hat. There was a rifle in one corner, and half the room appeared to be partitioned off from the rest by a bright red Hudson Bay blanket hung up as a curtain. In spite of the rifle and the coat an expert would have decided at once that the room was a woman's room. There was a trimness about it not masculine, a cleanliness not Indian. Whatever a red lady's virtues may be, cleanliness and order are not among them. But the figures upon which the light fell explained the anomaly of a rifle and a mirror hung side by side in a miner's shack, and explained, too, why a room in which hung a miner's coat and hat was swept and garnished and in order.

In a bunk against the wall lay a fair-haired man, his eyes shut in sleep, with one powerful arm thrown limp and nerveless upon the outside of his bed. The man who watched him felt a nervous twitching at his throat as his eyes rested upon the big brown hand, contrasting so strongly with the white linen upon which it rested; for Lilla had given her patient of her best, and Ned Corbett was sleeping between the only pair of sheets in Cariboo.

The worst was evidently over for Corbett. The fever, or whatever his disease had been, had left him, worn and pulled down it is true; but the peacefulness of his sleep, the calm child-like restfulness of his face, told both his watchers that unless a relapse took place his young life would be as strong in him as ever before many days had passed.

The colonel, peering in at Lilla's face as she sat and watched her patient, saw very little chance of a relapse whilst *she* was Corbett's nurse. If tender care and ceaseless watching would save him, Corbett would be saved. The colonel fancied, indeed, that he saw even more than this. His eyes ever since very early days had peered deep into the hearts of men and women; not from sympathy with them, not even from idle curiosity, but to see what profit could be made out of them. Now he thought that he recognized in Lilla's eyes, and in the caressing touch of her hand as she brushed back Corbett's yellow hair, something which he had often seen before, something which he had generally turned to his own advantage at whatever cost to the woman.

"The little fool!" he muttered. "She has got stuck on him because he has blue eyes and yellow hair like a Deutscher. Great Scott, what simpletons these women are!

Perhaps the colonel's guess as to the state of Lilla's heart was a shrewd one, perhaps not. At any rate if the girl was in love with her handsome patient she was not herself conscious of it as yet, and as she sat crooning the tender words of a German love song, she was unconscious that they had any special meaning for her.

"*Du du liegst mir im Hertzen*," she sang; but as she sang, she believed that the only feeling which stirred her heart for the sick man at her side was one of pity for a helpless bankrupt brother.

For some time Lilla sat dreaming and crooning scraps of German songs, and then a thought seemed to strike her, and she drew from her bosom a little leather case. Opening this she drew from it what looked like an old bill, and indeed it was an old billhead, frayed and torn as if it had been carried for many, many months in some traveller's pocket. But there was no account of goods delivered and still unpaid for upon that dirty scrap of paper. As Lilla turned it to catch the light, the man at the window had a glimpse of it, and started as if someone had struck him.

"Old Pete's map, by thunder!" he exclaimed; and so loudly did he speak, or so noisy was his movement as he tried to obtain a better view of that precious document, that Lilla heard something, and replacing the paper in her pocket rose and came to the window.

There was only a thin partition of rustic boarding and the bosom of a woman's dress between the most reckless scoundrel in Cariboo and the key to Cariboo's richest gold-mine. He could hear her breathing on the other side of that thin partition, and he knew that his strong fingers could tear it down and wrench away that secret before the woman and the sick man her friend could even call assistance. But he dared not do the deed. Life was still more than gold to him, and he knew that earth would be hardly large enough to hide the man who should wrong Lilla from the vengeance of the hard-fists she had danced with and sung to in their merry moods, and nursed like a sister in their sickness.

"No." he muttered, when Lilla had resumed her

seat, "I daren't do it, and I daren't stay another hour. If that fool gets his wits back the cat will soon be out of the bag, and the only question of interest to me will be,—'Is it to be Begbie or Lynch?' If the boys knew, I believe it would be Lynch!" and muttering and grinding his teeth, a prey to rage and baffled greed, Colonel Cruickshank turned and retraced his steps to his own quarters.

Once, and only once, he stopped before he reached them, and stood with knitted brows like one who strives to master some difficult problem. At last a light came into his face, and his coarse mouth opened in an evil grin—"I will, by Jove I will! It will be as safe there as anywhere. Cruickshank, my boy, you shall double the stakes and go for the pot. If I had only seen more of that map—"

The rest of his sentence was lost as he entered the snack where his goods were stored, and half an hour later, when the sun was still only colouring the sky a faint saffron along the horizon, he strode up to the store of Ben Hirsch, general dealer, money-changer, and purchaser of gold-dust at Antler.

Old Ben was fairly early himself that morning. He had smoked so much the night before (being a German Jew) that he really needed a breath of fresh air to pull him together, before he engaged in another day of chicanery, bargaining, and theft. But the sight of the dashing colonel at such an hour in the morning considerably astonished him. There was something wrong somewhere, of that he felt quite certain, and wherever there was anything wrong there was profit for the wise old Jew. So his beady eyes twinkled beside his purple beak, and he gave the man he looked upon as his prey the heartiest greeting.

"Goot-mornin', Colonel, goot-mornin'. Ach, vot a rustler you are! No vonder zat you make much gold. Haf you zold ze pacon yet?"

"Not a cent's worth, uncle. Will you buy?"

"Ach! you laugh at me. I haf no monish, you know I haf no monish. Ze freight eats up all ze profit."

"Keep that for tenderfeet, Ben," replied Cruickshank roughly. "Freight on needles won't bring them up to fifty cents apiece, even in Cariboo. Will you buy or won't you? I've no time to talk."

"Vot is your hurry, Colonel? Ze pacon and ze peans von't shpoil."

The colonel turned to go.

"*Ach, himmel!*" cried the Jew, throwing up his hands deprecatingly. "How these English Herren are fiery. Colonel, dear Herr Colonel, pe so goot as to listen."

"Well, what is it? I'll give you five minutes in which to make a bid. After that I'm off straight to Williams Creek."

"Pacon is cheap zere, Colonel; almost cheaper zan here. Put I vill puy. Are ve not from of olt befreinded? Vot you zay, twenty-five cents ze pound?"

"Twenty-five fiddlesticks! Do you think I don't know the market prices?"

But it is not worth while to record all the haggling between Hirsch and Cruickshank. It was a match between the Jew, cool, crafty, and cringing, and the Christian (save the mark!), hurried, and full of strange oaths as become a soldier, "sudden and quick in quarrel."

From the very outset the colonel had one eye on Ben and the other on the door, and his ears seemed pricked to catch the tramp of men who might be coming in pursuit. Of course the Jew saw this, and every time the colonel started at some sudden sound, or reddened and swore at his obstinate haggling, Ben's ferret-like eyes gleamed with fresh cunning and increased intelligence.

Like an expert angler he had mastered his fish, and knew it, and meant now to kill him at his leisure, without risking another struggle. And yet (to maintain the metaphor) this fisher of men all at once lowered his point and seemed to let his captive go.

"Vell, colonel, all right. Suppose you give ze ponies in, I give you your price."

"You're a hungry thief, Ben. The ponies are worth the money; but I am not going to do any more packing, so take them and be hanged to you.'

"Goot. It is a deal zen."

"Yes, if I may keep the pinto. I want a pony to pack my tools and blankets on."

"Tools. Vot! you go prospecting, eh?"

"Yes. I think so."

"Ach so! By and by you strike it rich. Then you bring your dust to old Ben—eh, colonel?"

"Maybe. But where are those dollars?"

"How vill you have them, colonel,—in notes or dust?" asked the Jew.

"In dust, of course; those flimsy things would wear out before I could get them down the Frazer. Besides, I've heard that your notes aren't always just like other people's, Ben;" and the colonel pushed over a little pile of dirty "greenbacks."

"Ach, these are goot notes; but the gold is goot too, Colonel. Vill you veigh it?"

"You bet I will," replied the colonel, making no parade of confidence in his friend. There was good gold in old Ben's safe, but the tenderfoot who did not know good gold from bad often got "dust" of the wrong kind. This Cruickshank knew, so that he was careful to examine the quality of the dust in the two small canvas bags, and careful, too, in the weighing of them —trying the scales, and leaving no hole open for fraud to creep through.

At last even he was satisfied.

"Yes, Ben, that will do—it's good for the money."

"Goot dust, isn't it? very goot dust and full measure. See!" and the old Jew put it in the scales again. "But, *donner und blitzen*, vot vants ze sheriff so early?"

The last part of the sentence was jerked out at the top of his voice by the dealer in gold as he turned excitedly to stare out of the little window on his left.

"The sheriff! Did you say the sheriff? Give me the gold. Where is he?"

Cruickshank had turned as white as the dead, and his hand shook as if he had the palsy, but for all that he managed to snatch up the two small canvas bags from the counter and hide them away in the bosom of his flannel shirt.

"I zink I zee him go into ze dance-house. But vot is your hurry, colonel? shtay and vet ze deal. Vot, you von't! Ah vell, ze rye is not pad." And so saying Mr. Benjamin Hirsch filled a small glass for himself, and with a wink drank to his departing guest.

Ben Hirsch was certainly right in calling Colonel Cruickshank a rustler, a Yankee term for a man who does not let the grass grow under his feet. Half an hour after Ben's cry of "Sheriff" the colonel stole out of Antler, driving old Job in front of him, with blankets, gold-pan, and all the rest of a prospector's slender outfit, securely fastened upon the pony's back.

As soon as he was well out of sight of the camp, the fugitive diverged from the main trail, and took instead a little-used path, leading direct over a difficult country to Soda Creek, on the Frazer. Along this he drove his pony at a speed which made that wall-eyed, cow-hocked quadruped grunt and groan in piteous fashion. In all his days Job had never before found a master who could and would get a full day's work out of him, without giving him a single chance to wander or even knock his packs off amongst the timber. At last, when the sun had begun to go west, Cruickshank paused, sat down upon a log, and lit his pipe. As he smoked and thought, the lines went out of his face, until he almost looked once more the oily, plausible scoundrel whom we first met in Victoria.

"Yes," he muttered, "it was a bold game, but I made my bluff stick. Why, if old Ben knew that I didn't have even a pair to draw to, wouldn't he 'raise Cain?'" And so saying, he put his hand inside his shirt and drew out the two little bags of gold-dust, weighing them nicely in his hands, and regarding them as lovingly as a mother would her first-born. For a minute or two his fingers played with the strings which fastened the mouth of each sack, but finally thought better of it and put them back into his pocket without untying them. To this man life was a game of poker, and for the present he considered that he had risen a winner though the odds had been against him, and with his winnings in his pocket he smacked old Job on the quarters, held up his head, and felt ready for a fresh deal.

And old Ben—what of him? Did he hurry away to secure the pack-ponies and their loads, or to see what the sheriff wanted at the dance-house? Not a bit of it. *He* knew (none better) that the sheriff was away at Williams Creek, and he knew, too,—he knew enough of human nature to be sure that Dan Cruickshank would never return to Antler unless he was brought back against his will. He had sold his packs and his ponies for two little bags of gold ("of gold, ho, ho!" chuckled the Jew), and even if he should find anything wrong with the gold he would not dare to come back to claim his packs.

"I vonder vot Dan has peen up to," mused the son of Israel. "He play ze carts a leetle too vell for his friends, I know, put it must pe zomething worse zan zat. Ach vell, it was ver goot zat I knew a leetle how to conjure;" and still chuckling and muttering to himself, he took from a shelf just below the counter two small bags similar to those in Cruickshank's shirt front, and put them tenderly and reverently away in his safe. *They* contained good gold-dust.

Those which Cruickshank was carrying away contained a good many things, the price of innocent blood for instance, but Ben Hirsch would not have given many dollars for all that they contained. Whilst the colonel was looking for the sheriff, Ben had substituted bags of copper pyrites for bags of gold.

CHAPTER XVII.

CHANCE'S GOLD-FEVER RETURNS.

"WELL, Steve, what is the news? I can see that you are just bursting with intelligence. Out with it, little man."

"Bell has struck it rich again. It's a fortune this time, they say."

"Is that all? Poor Bell! He'll be drunk, then, at Victoria the whole of the winter. I shouldn't be surprised if this second stroke of luck killed him."

The speakers were our old friends Ned Corbett and Steve Chance, and when Steve joined him Ned was sitting with his long gum boots tucked under a table in the Antler dance-house, smoking his evening pipe.

It was nearly a month since Cruickshank had stolen away from Antler, and since then Ned had recovered all his old strength and vigour.

At first he had brooded incessantly over Cruickshank's escape, but as the days went by he realized that there was no chance for him, without knowledge of the country and without funds, against a man like the colonel, with a fortnight's start of him. Together with one or two miners to whom he had told his tale he had made an attempt to follow Cruickshank's tracks, and had succeeded in tracking him and his pony as far as the main trail to Soda Creek. Here the tracks, which were already old, became confused with others, and sorely against their will the pursuers had to give up the chase.

"Cruickshank has got clean away with you this journey, partner, and I guess you may as well own up to it," was the verdict of one of his comrades.

And Ned, recognizing the justice of it, threw up the sponge, and owned himself beaten for the time; but although he said no more about the claims or the packs or the comrade of whom he had been robbed, he consoled himself with the thought that life was long and had in it many chances, and that whenever his chance came, however late, it would find his hand as strong and as quick to take vengeance as it was to-day.

As soon as his story had become known, and men had seen what manner of man he was, Ned had found no difficulty in getting employment in the claims, and, indeed, he had done so well that he had been induced to send a message to his friends at Williams Creek, in answer to which Steve and Phon had hastened to join him at Antler. Rampike promised to come up later on in the fall, but as yet he had plenty to do in his own claim.

For a full fortnight the three comrades had worked away steadily with pick and shovel, and now, in spite of all his troubles, Ned was his own cheery self again, proud of the strength which enabled him to do almost as much as two other men, and content with the work which kept him supplied with all the necessaries of life. But if Ned Corbett was content, his comrades were not. Steve hated the daily labour for daily wage, and Phon was hardly strong enough for the work, and anxious to go off prospecting on his own account.

"What a phlegmatic old cuss you are, Ned! Don't you envy Bell a bit?"

"Not I. Why should I? I am strong and well again, thank God. I've plenty of fresh air and hard work, and I'm earning ten dollars a day—"

"And spending eight. You won't make a fortune that way."

"Who said that I should? Who said that I wanted to? Why, my dear chap, just think for a moment. If I did make a fortune I should have to stop at home and invest it and look after it. *Stop at home*, do you hear, Steve?"

"You'll die a pauper, Ned," asserted Chance solemnly.

"And you, perhaps, a millionaire. Poor old chap! I'm

sorry for you. I am indeed. Well, Lilla, what can I do for you?" and Ned, rising, took off his hat, as if he had been saluting a duchess.

"The boys want a song, Ned. Will you sing for them?" asked the girl, her pretty eyes brightening and her cheeks flushing as she took Ned's hand. Somehow, though Ned had often sought her, he had seen very little of his gentle nurse since he had become convalescent.

"Bother the boys!" quoth this young man of big muscle and limited intelligence. "I'm not going to do any work to-night. I have earned enough money for the day; but," he added quickly as he saw the girl's look of disappointment, "I'll sing for you, little sister, and you can give the money to the next dead-beat you nurse back again to life."

"I never nursed any dead-beats," began Lilla.

"Oh no, of course not. Never heard of Ned Corbett, or Pete of Lost Creek, or any of that crowd, did you, Lilla? Now I'm going to sing;" and with that he threw back his head, and sang in a full rich baritone a song of his Canadian lumbering days:—

A SONG OF THE AXE.

When winter winds storm, and the snow-flakes swarm,
    And the forest is soft to our tread;
When the women folk sit, by their fires fresh lit,
    Oh, ho, for the toque of red!
With our strong arms bare, it's little we care
    For politics, rates, or tax;
Let the good steel ring on the forest king—
    Oh, ho, for the swing of the axe!

Your diamonds may glitter, your rubies flame,
    Our gems are but frozen dew;
Yet yours grow tame, being always the same,
    Ours every night will renew.

> Let the world rip: tighten your grip,
>   Make the blades glitter and shine;
> At it you go, swing to each blow,
>   And down with the pride of the pine!
>
> For the trees, I ween, which have long grown green
>   In the light of the sun and the stars,
> Must bend their backs to the lumberer's axe,
>   Mere timber and planks and spars!
> Then oh, ho, ho! for the carpet of snow!
>   Oh, ho, for the forest of pine!
> Wealth shall be yours, with its business and bores,
>   Health and hard labour be mine!

"*Health and hard labour be mine!*" thundered a score of voices, and a score of strong labour-hardened hands came crashing down upon the rough deal tables. "Bravo, Ned!" "That's your sort for Cariboo!" "Mate, we'll wet that song if you please," and a dozen other similar expressions of approval rewarded Ned for his efforts, but Steve Chance did not go as far as the rest of the audience.

"A pretty good song, Ned," he said, "with lots of shouting in it, but no sense."

"Give us a better, little one," replied his friend good-naturedly. "Ah, Lilla, you are a brick—I beg your pardon, but I don't know the German for a fairy who brings a thirsty man just what he wants;" and Ned buried his moustache in a foaming glass of Lager.

"That beats all the champagne and such like trash into fits," he added with a sigh of satisfaction as he put down the empty glass. "Now, Steve, beat my song if you can."

"Beat it! No trouble to do that. If the boys don't shout themselves silly over my chorus I'll take a back seat."

"You wouldn't stay there if you did," laughed Ned; "but drive on, my boy."

Thus adjured, Steve got up and sang with a spirit and go of which I am unable to give any adequate idea, the song of—

THE YANKEE DOLLAR.

With sword or shovel, pick or pen,
   All strive to win the yellow ore;
And "bust or boom," our natural doom,
   Is but to love the dollar more.

Chorus.

The Yankee doodle dollar, oh!
I'm no saint or scholar, oh!
I only know, that high or low,
All love the Yankee dollar, oh!

In miner's ditch some strike it rich,
   And some die in the collar, oh!
But live or die, succeed or sigh,
   All strive to win the dollar, oh!

"Chorus, gentlemen,—'*The Yankee doodle dollar* oh!'" sang Chance, and the whole room rose to him and sang as one man—

The Yankee doodle dollar, oh!
I'm no saint or scholar, oh!
I only know, that high or low,
All love the Yankee dollar, oh!

There was no question as to Steve's victory. Ned had stirred the hearts of a few, and pleased all, but Steve had played upon the principal chord in the heart of Antler, and for weeks the men hummed the empty words and whistled the frivolous, ranting little air of "*The Yankee doodle dollar, oh!*" until even its author was sick of it.

"You see, Ned, everyone thinks the same except

you," said Chance, when the applause had somewhat moderated. "Why the deuce are you so pig-headed? Now that we have saved a few dollars why should we not go prospecting and make our pile like other people? I'm sick of all this picking and scratching in other men's claims."

"'Yo mun larn to scrat afore yo peck,'" replied Ned stolidly, quoting a good old Shropshire proverb; "and 'scratting' for ten dollars a day doesn't seem to me to be very badly-paid labour."

"You forget, Ned, that this cain't last. How do you mean to live during the winter?"

"Sufficient unto the day—" began Ned, and then suddenly altering his tone he added, "What is it that you want me to do, Steve?"

"What do I want you to do? Why, what any other man in Cariboo would do if he had half your chance. Take Lilla's offer and go and look for Pete's Creek for her."

"Pete's Creek! Why, my dear Steve, you don't seriously believe in that cock-and-bull story, do you?"

"Don't you believe Lilla?" retorted Chance.

'Of course I believe Lilla," replied Corbett hotly, "but she only tells the story as it was told to her."

"By a dying man who knew that he was dying, to a woman who had nursed him for weeks like a sister! According to you, Pete must have been a worse liar than Ananias, Ned."

"I didn't say Pete lied either, but Pete may not have been sane when he died. You know that he had been drinking like a fish before Lilla got hold of him."

"Yes, and slept out a couple of nights in the snow. I know that. But he died of pleurisy, not of the jim-jams."

"Well, have your own way, but nothing will make me believe in that creek. It had too much gold in it," replied Corbett. "And even if I did believe in it, why should I take Lilla's gold? Hasn't she done enough for me already?"

"Perhaps. But if you don't get it for her, I guess someone else will come along and find it for himself."

"Why don't you go for it, Steve, if you believe in it?"

"So I would if Lilla would trust me; but you see Lilla is not spoons on me, and she is on you."

Corbett flushed to the roots of his yellow hair.

"Don't talk rot, Chance, and leave Lilla's name alone."

"I'm not talking rot," said Chance seriously. "But say, Ned, do you mean to marry that girl?"

"Marry your grandmother! I don't mean to marry anyone, and no one is such a fool as to want to marry me."

"All right, Ned, don't lose your temper; but I know, old chap, that you would not like to get Lilla talked about, and the boys are beginning to say that Lilla got rid of her heart when you got rid of your fever."

'The boys are a parcel of chattering idiots, whose mouths will get stopped pretty roughly if they talk like that before me," growled Ned. "But really, Steve, this is too ridiculous. Fancy anyone wanting to marry me!" and the speaker looked down with a grin at his mud-spattered, much-mended pants, passed his hand meditatively over a rough young beard of three months' growth, and burst out laughing.

Ned Corbett was heart-whole, and he did not see why everyone else should not be as lucky in that respect as himself.

CHAPTER XVIII.

ON THE COLONEL'S TRAIL AGAIN.

THE day after the conversation recorded in the last chapter happened to be Sunday—a day which at Antler differed very little from any other day, except that a few tenderfeet, mostly Britishers, struck work on that day, and indulged in what some of their friends called a "good square loaf." Ned Corbett was one of these Sunday loafers. Of course there was no church at Antler, nor any parson except upon very rare occasions. But Ned had an ear for the anthems which the mountain breezes are always singing, and an eye for nature's attitude of reverence towards her Creator.

Every Sunday it was Ned's wont to go out by himself, and lie on a rock in the sun out of hearing of the noise of the great mining-camp, saying nothing at all himself, but thinking a good deal, and keeping quite quiet to hear what nature had to say to him.

As he was coming away from such a loaf as this, he met Lilla wandering up the banks of a mountain stream, gathering berries and wild flowers.

Ned thought that his little friend had never looked prettier than she did at that moment—her soft yellow hair blown out by the breeze, her little figure moving gracefully amongst the boulders, the colour of wild roses in her cheeks, and a deep strong light in her blue eyes, like the light of the stars when there is frost in the northern sky.

For a little while he watched her, as she hummed a

song amongst the flowers and added fresh treasures to the already overgrown bouquet in her hand.

'If she would take a man just as he is, she would make a sweet little wife for a Cariboo miner," thought the young man; "that is, if he meant always to remain a Cariboo miner. But, poor child! I'm afraid she'd find a Shropshire welcome rather chilly even after Cariboo. Ah! well," he added to himself as he went jumping over the boulders to meet her, " luckily I don't want a wife, and Lilla doesn't want a husband."

The next moment Lilla and he stood face to face.

"Did I frighten you, Lilla?" he asked, picking up some flowers which the girl had dropped. "Did you think I was a grizzly?"

" Not so bad as that, Ned. But what do you up here?"

" I'm taking a 'cultus coolee,'" replied he, using the Indian phrase in use among the miners for a walk which has no object. "You are doing the same, I fancy. Let us do it together."

"What! you wish to come with me? Well, come then," replied Lilla. "You can help me carry these."

Ned took the bouquet, and after a while said, "I have been wanting to have a good talk with you, Lilla, for some time."

"So, Ned! what is it about?" She tried hard to speak in an unconcerned off-hand way, but in spite of her, her colour rose and then paled, and her voice had an unnatural ring in it. Ned looked at her. Could there be anything in what Steve suggested the other night? he asked himself, and then almost in the same second he repented him of the thought. Ned Corbett was not one of those men who twist their moustaches complacently, and conclude that every woman they meet must fall in love with them.

"I want you to tell me about Pete and his creek again," he said. "Steve Chance is awfully keen to go prospecting, and to go and look for this gold-mine of yours."

"And why not, Ned? I wish you would, for my sake."

"I would do a good deal for your sake, Lilla," he answered; "but I can't believe in this creek, you know."

"Not believe in it! Why not, Ned?"

"There was too much gold in it; the whole story is too much like a fairy tale. And then, you know, when you took him in, Pete was as penniless as I was."

"Penniless! What's that?"

"Hadn't a cent to his name, I mean, and you fed him and took care of him."

"Ach, so. Well, what has that to do with the creek?"

"People who find gold-mines ought not to be dependent upon good little girls like you for their bread and cheese. It's not natural, you know."

"Ach, now you make me to understand. But you yourself, you don't know Cariboo ways. Pete had plenty of dust, oh, lots and lots of dust, when he came down; but, of course, he blew it all in before I saw him."

To anyone not conversant with mining life that "of course" of Lilla's was delicious. To the steady-going collector of hard-earned copper and silver it seems anything but a matter of course to "blow in" a fortune in a fortnight; but then things were not done in an ordinary jog-trot fashion either in California in '49 or in Cariboo in '62.

"Oh! of course, of course!" returned Ned with a smile which he could not hide. "I beg your pardon, Lilla. I had forgotten for a moment that I was in Cariboo, and thought as if I were at home again. Well, and what was the matter with your beggared Crœsus when you found him?"

"If you mean what was the matter with Pete, I have before told you. He drink too much one night, and then he fall asleep in the snow, and when he wake in the morning he have the pleurisy, I think you call him."

It was a long sentence for Lilla, who was getting a little bit roused by the young scoffer at her side; and, moreover, her English was always best when produced in small quantities.

"And why did they bring him to you?"

"Where else could they take him? The boys can't leave their claims to nurse sick men, and at night they are too tired to nurse anyone. And besides—"

'And besides," interrupted her companion, "Lilla is never tired. Oh, dear, no! Her eyes never want sleep, nor her limbs rest after dancing with all those roughs on a floor like a ploughed field."

"Don't you call the boys roughs, Ned. They are not rough to me. Of course I had to nurse old Pete. What are women meant for?"

"Something better than camp-life in Cariboo," replied Corbett warmly; "but it is just as well for me that you don't think so."

"Well, and so I nursed him," continued the girl, disregarding Ned's last speech altogether; "and sometimes he told me where he had been, and how much gold he had found, and at last one day when he knew that he must die he told me of this creek in Chilcotin with gold in the bed of it—free gold, coarse gold in nuggets and lumps, and as much as ever you want of it."

"Why did he not bring down more of it, instead of letting you keep him as you kept me?" asked the doubter.

"*Ach, himmel!* Keep you! I didn't keep you. You are too proud, and will pay for every little thing; but old Pete, he understood Cariboo ways. To-day you strike it rich and I am stone-broke. Very well. I lend you a handful of dollars and start you again. You don't need to thank me. Any gambler would do as much. By and by I strike it even rockier than you struck it. All right, then you 'ante' up for me. That's Cariboo."

"Is it?" asked Ned, looking into the eager friendly face of this exponent of a new commercial creed. "Is that Cariboo? Well, Lilla, I expect Samaria must be somewhere in Cariboo. But finish your story about Pete."

"Oh, Pete! Well, Pete just died quietly, and he knew it was coming, and before it came he pulled out this," and the girl drew from her bosom an old frayed bill-head which we have seen before, "and gave it to me, and told me that as soon as I found— Ach, what am I saying? I forget." And Lilla suddenly brought her story to an abrupt conclusion, with stumbling tongue and flaming cheeks, for as a fact the old man had told her that this map of his was the key to much gold, and that when she should have found a man worthy of her, she was to send him to bring it to her, and it should be to her for a dowry. But this was not quite what the honest little hurdy girl cared to tell Ned Corbett at present. However, Ned never noticed her embarrassment. His eyes were busy with the document in his hand.

"It seems a good clear map, and looks as if the man who made it was quite sane," he muttered.

"Sane? What is that—'sane?'" asked Lilla.

"Level-headed" answered Ned shortly.

"You bet he was level-headed, Ned. *Ach, mein freund*, how you doubt! I tell you there are not many men in Cariboo who would not go to look for that creek, if I would let them."

Again Ned remembered Steve's words, "She'll only trust you because she has lost her heart to you."

"Did you ever give anyone a hint as to where the creek was, Lilla?"

"No, never. At least no, I didn't tell him, but one man nearly guessed once."

"Nearly guessed once?"

"Yes. He said he knew more than I thought and I had better trust him, and wasn't the creek at the head of the Chilcotin? And I said, 'Well, which side of the Chilcotin?' And then he smiled, and I felt angry. And when he said on the right bank I was glad, and I cried 'No, it isn't, I knew you didn't know.' And then he smiled more, and I saw that I had told him what he wanted to know. But after all that is not much, is it?"

"Who was the man, Lilla?"

"Colonel—Colonel—ach, I forget, there are so many colonels in America."

"True, but what was he like?" Ned had a queer fancy to know who this clever cross-examiner might be.

"A thick dark man, stout and smooth."

"With a lot of rings on his fingers?"

"Yes, always lots of rings. Oh, he was a fine man, and such a dancer!"

"Cruickshank."

"That is it—Cruickshank, Colonel Cruickshank. But how did you know, Ned?"

"Oh, I have seen him before," replied Corbett quietly.

This was indeed news to him, but he felt that he

must be very careful not to frighten Lilla, to whom oddly enough the name of the man who had robbed Corbett had never yet been mentioned. That he had been robbed of course she knew, but by one of those strange accidents which often happen, she had never heard who had robbed him.

"So that is all you can tell me about the creek is it, Lilla?" said Ned after a long pause. "Well, if you still wish me to go at the end of this week, I will go for you; if I find it you shall pay me ten dollars a day for my work, and Phon and Steve the same; and if not, —well, if not, I shall have earned a right to teaze you if you believe in such cock-and-bull stories for the future." And Ned gave Lilla her bouquet and prepared to leave her, for they had by this time reached the door of her little cottage.

"Oh no, Ned, that is not so at all, at all. If you don't find it, of course I pay the cost; and if you do, we go shares in the find."

"As you please, Lilla, but we have got to find the creek first," and so saying he turned and strode off to his own hut.

There were many reasons now why he should go to look for Pete's Creek, but the belief in Pete's Creek or the hope of finding it was not amongst them.

Cruickshank knew something of the whereabouts of the creek, Cruickshank with his insatiable love of gold; and Ned himself had tracked him towards Soda Creek, where he must cross the Frazer to get to Chilcotin.

Yes, that was it. The tables were turning at last, and if there was such a place as Pete's Creek, Ned would find Cruickshank there, and shoot him like a bear over a carcase.

CHAPTER XIX.

'GOOD-BYE, LILLA.'

IT was not Ned Corbett's nature to say much about what he felt. Like most of his countrymen Ned was reserved to a fault, and prided himself upon an impassive demeanour, suffering failure or achieving success with the same quiet smile upon his face. The English adage "Don't cry until you are hurt" had been only a part of the law of his childhood; the rest of it read according to his teachers: "and then grin and bear it."

But even Steve, who knew Corbett as intimately as one man can know another, was astounded at the readiness with which, after one wild effort to grapple with the man who had killed Roberts, Corbett had been content to settle down quietly to his daily labour in the claims at Antler.

He could understand that his friend would take his own losses quietly. Steve, like all Yankees and all true gamblers, was a good loser himself, and didn't expect to hear a man make a moan over his own misfortunes, but he had not expected to see Ned abandon his vengeance so readily.

After Lilla's incidental mention of Cruickshank, Steve began to understand his friend better. His impatience to be on the war-path again was the real thing; the assumed calmness and content had after all been but the mannerism of the athlete, who smiles a sweet smile as he waits whilst the blows rain upon him, for a chance of knocking his man out of time before his own eyes close and his own strength fails him.

"So! you've only been lying low all this time, old man, and I thought you had forgotten," said Chance, when Ned told him of his conversation with Lilla. "Great Scott, I wouldn't care to be Cruickshank!"

"Forgotten!" echoed Corbett. "Do you suppose I am likely to forget that Roberts risked his life for mine, and that Cruickshank took it—took it when the old man sat with his back to him, and his six-shooter hanging in a tree?"

"No, I don't suppose you would forget, Ned. When shall we start? Phon and myself could be ready to 'pull out' to-morrow."

"That would suit me, Steve, but I am afraid that you and Phon are embarking on a wild-goose chase. I don't believe in that creek of Pete's one bit more now than I did before I saw Lilla's map."

"That's all right, Ned; but you see Cruickshank believed in it, and so do we."

"Yes, Cruickshank believed in it, and in looking for the one we shall find the other. That is why I am going."

"I know all about that; but as long as we both want to find the same place, I don't see that it matters a row of beans why we want to find it," replied Steve. "And mind you," he added, "I would be just as glad to let a little daylight into Cruickshank as you would."

"Very well, if that is your way of looking at it, we need lose no more time. You are old enough to know your own business."

"That's what. How about a cayuse?"

"I bought one yesterday for a hundred dollars."

"A hundred dollars! Great Scott, what a price!"

"Yes, it is a good deal, but old Dad wouldn't let the beast go for less. He calculated it at so much a pound, and told me that if I knew where to get fresh meat cheaper in Antler I'd better buy it."

"Fresh meat! I like that. Has old Dad taken to selling beef upon the hoof, then?"

"Seems so. Anyway I had to pay for the bobtail almost as if I were buying beefsteak by the hundredweight."

"Well, I suppose we cain't help ourselves; we shall only be stone-broke again. It appears to be a chronic condition with us. Let's go and look at the brute."

An inspection of the bobtail did not bring much consolation to either Steve or Ned, for in spite of the smart way in which he had been docked, he was as ragged and mean-looking a brute as anyone could want to see. Besides, he was what the up-country folk call "a stud," and anyone who has ever driven these beasts, knows that they add vices peculiar to their class to the ordinary vices of the cayuse nature.

"He ain't a picture, but we've got to make the best of him," remarked Steve. "So if you'll just fix things with Lilla, I'll see about getting grub and a pack-saddle. We *might* be ready to start to-night."

This was Steve's view on Tuesday at mid-day. At five o'clock on Wednesday he was a humbler man, heartily thankful that at last he really had got together most of the things necessary for one pack-horse. The last twenty-four hours had been passed, it seemed to him, in scouring the whole country for pack-saddles, sweat-clothes, cinch-hooks, and all sort of things, which hitherto (when Cruickshank and Roberts had had charge of the train) had seemed always at hand as a matter of course.

"Hang me if the cayuse doesn't want more fixing than a Brooklyn belle," muttered Steve. "But say,

Ned," he added aloud, "do you mean to start to-night?"

In another two hours it would be comparatively dark in the narrow canyons through which the trail to Soda Creek ran, and in two hours the three travellers could not hope to make much of a journey.

"Better wait till to-morrow, boys," remarked an old miner who had been lending a hand with the packing, trying in vain to show Ned how the diamond hitch ought to go. "It ain't no manner of use starting out at this time o' day."

"I would start if it were midnight, Jack," replied Corbett resolutely. "Once we get under weigh things will go better, but if we stayed over the night in camp, something would be sure to turn up to waste another day. Are you ready there, Steve?"

"All set, sonny," replied Steve, giving a final try at the cinch for form's sake.

"Then just drive on. I am going to get the map from Lilla;" and so saying he bent his steps towards the dance-house, whilst, one leading and the other driving, his companions trudged away along the trail to Soda Creek.

When he reached the dance-house Lilla was waiting for him, and together the two turned their backs upon Antler and walked slowly away under the pines.

"So then," said Lilla, "you will really go away to-night."

"Yes, we are really going, Lilla, to look for your golden creek. Don't you feel as if you were a millionaire already? Chance does, I know, and has decided to whom he will leave his estate when he dies."

Ned spoke lightly, and laughed as he spoke. He saw that the girl was depressed, and wanted to cheer her up. But Lilla only gave a little shiver, though the evening air was far from cold.

"Don't talk of dying, Ned. It is not good to talk of. Men die fast enough out here." She was thinking, poor little soul! how very near death that gallant yellow-haired friend of hers had been when she first saw him, and perhaps death might come near him again whilst she was not by to watch over him.

Ned looked surprised at her mood, but passed lightly to another subject.

"As you please, Lilla. Where am I to find you when we come back from Chilcotin?"

"*Das weiss der lieber Gott,*" she answered, speaking half to herself. And then recovering herself she added in a firmer voice, "Either here or at Kamloops: most likely at Kamloops, if you are not back soon."

"But we shall be back soon. What ails you to-night?"

"It is nothing, Ned; but it seems as if summer had gone soon this year, and these great mountains will all be white again directly. I don't think you will get back here this fall."

"Not get back this fall! Why, surely, Lilla, you don't think that we mean to jump your claims, or make off with your gold?"

"No, no! of course not. I know you don't care for the gold, Ned, like the other men. You don't care for anything like other men, I think."

"Don't I? Just wait until I come back from Chilcotin and pour buckets of dust into your lap. See if I won't want my share then?"

"I wonder how long it will be that I must wait, Ned? I think sometimes that we shall never meet again. Tell me, do you think such atoms as we are could ever find their way to one another, up *there?* It seems so hard to lose one's friends for ever."

And the girl looked despairingly up into the great blue vault above them, wherein even the greatest of the stars are but as golden motes.

"Yes, little sister," answered Ned seriously. "I don't think that such as you will have much difficulty in finding their way up there."

After this the two were silent for some time, standing on a rise above Antler, looking out upon the deepening gloom of the evening, Ned's heart very full of tenderness towards the little woman to whom he owed so much.

It would have been so easy, Ned could not help thinking, to put his arm round her and comfort her; but then, would that be a good thing for either of them? The world was all before them, and the world was not all Cariboo.

"Come, Lilla," he said at last, "this won't do. The night air is chilling you. You must run back now. What would the boys say if their little favourite came back without her smile? By George, they would give me a short shrift if they thought that it was my fault."

"The boys! Ach, what do the boys care? All women can laugh, and dance, and sing. One woman is all the same to them as another."

Well as Ned knew his little companion, he had never seen her in this mood before, and his face betrayed the wonder which her bitterness awoke in him.

A woman's eyes are quick, even in her trouble, to note the effect of her words upon anyone she cares for, so that Lilla saw the expression in Ned's face, and tried hard to rally her courage and laugh her tears away.

After her fashion the poor little hurdy girl was as proud as any titled dame on earth, and since Ned had not said that he loved her, she would try hard to keep her own pitiful little secret to herself.

"Don't look like that, Ned. Don't you know when I am acting. But, seriously, I am cross to-night. I wanted my gold, and I wanted to keep my play-fellow too. We have been such good friends—haven't we, Ned?"

It was no good. In spite of her that treacherous voice of hers would falter and break in a way quite beyond her control. Flight seemed to her the only chance.

"Ach well, this is folly," she said. "*Auf wiedersehen*, my friend," and she held out to him both her hands.

It was a dead still evening, and just at that moment the horn of the pale young moon came up over the fringe of dark pine-trees and lit up Lilla's sweet face, finding in it a grace and purity of outline which the daylight overlooked. But even the moonlight could add nothing to the tenderness of those honest blue eyes, which had grown so dim and misty in the last few minutes, or to the sweetness of that tender mouth, whose lips were so pitfully unsteady now.

"*Auf wiedersehen*" Ned repeated after her. "*Auf wiedersehen*, Lilla,—we shall meet again."

For a while he stood irresolute. What did Shropshire or all the world indeed matter to him? he asked himself, and in another moment he might have spoken words which would surely have marred his own life and not made hers one whit happier.

Luckily just then a wild laugh broke the silence and recalled Ned to himself. It was only the owl who laughed, but it sufficed. The dangerous charm of the silence was broken, and pressing the girl's hand to his lips he dashed away up the trail.

Steve Chance and Phon had made nearly four miles and begun to pitch camp whilst he was getting that map.

CHAPTER XX.

THE ACCURSED RIVER.

THIS world is a world of contrasts, in which laughter and tears, darkness and light, unite to make the varied pattern of our lives. When Ned Corbett left Lilla standing with tears which would not be denied upon her white cheeks, he felt as if he should never laugh again, and the ball in his throat rose as if it would choke him. In spite of the pace at which he strode through the moonlit forest aisles, his thoughts dwelt persistently upon the girl he had left behind him, or if they wandered at all from her, it was only to remind him of that snow-covered camp in the forest, at which he had taken his last farewell of that other true friend of his. And yet half an hour after he had wrung poor Lilla's hands in parting, Ned Corbett stood watching his comrades, his sides aching with suppressed laughter.

Phon's voice was the first sound to warn Ned that he had almost reached the camp, but Phon and Steve were both far too absorbed in the problem before them to notice his approach.

"You sure you no savey tie 'um hitch?" asked the Chinaman, who was standing with his hand upon the pack-ropes, whilst Chance held the cayuse by the head.

"No, Phon, I no savey. You savey all right, don't you?"

"I savey one side," replied the Chinaman. "S'pose the ole man throw the lopes, I catch 'um and fix 'um, but I no savey throw 'um lopes."

"What the devil are we to do then?" asked Chance, looking helplessly at the pack and its mysterious arrangement of ropes. "If the old man does not overtake us to-night we can't start before he gets here to-morrow morning. I wonder what the deuce is keeping him?"

Phon gave a grunt of contempt at his white companion's want of intelligence. He had a way of looking upon Steve as somewhat of an ignoramus.

"What keep the ole man? You halo comtax anything, Chance. Young woman keep him of course. Young woman always keep ole man long time, all same China. You bet I savey."

"You bet you are a jolly saucy heathen, who wants kicking badly," laughed Steve. "But say, if Corbett does not come along, what *are* you going to do with the packs?"

"I fix 'um, you see," replied Phon, suddenly brightening again and taking the pony by the head.

"Now then, you hold him there—hold him tight. He heap bad cayuse;" and Phon handed the lead-rope to Chance, whilst he himself swarmed nimbly up a bull-pine under which the pony now stood. A few feet from the ground (say seven or eight) a bare limb projected over the trail, from which the Chinaman could just manage to reach the top of the packs, so as to tie them firmly to the bough upon which he stood.

This done he descended again from his perch, hobbled the pack animal, and stood back to survey his work.

He had tied up the pony's legs, and tied him up by his packs to a bull-pine. Things looked fairly safe, but Phon was not content. "You hold him tight!" he sung out; "s'pose he go now he smash everything." A minute later Phon had undone the cinch and set the pack-saddle and its load free from the pony's back, and then picking up a big stake he hit the unfortunate cayuse a hearty good thump over the quarters, and bade him "Git, you siwash!"

The result was funny. A general separation ensued, in which—thanks to a pair of active heels—(horse's) a little blue bundle of Chinese manufacture went in one direction, a hobbled cayuse went jumping away like a lame kangaroo in another, while the pack swung in all the mystery of its diamond hitch intact upon the bough of the bull-pine.

It was a quaint method of off-saddling a pack-pony, but as Phon explained when he had picked himself up again, it saved the trouble of fixing the packs next day.

But such scenes as these are of more interest to those to whom packing is a part of their daily toils than to the average Englishman. The ordinary traveller puts his luggage in the van, or has it put in for him, and glides over his journey at the rate of forty miles an hour without even seeing, very often, what kind of country he is passing through.

It is quite impossible to travel quite as fast as this through Cariboo even on paper; but I will make the journey as short as I can, though for Phon and his friends it was weary work at first, with a pack-horse which would not be driven and could not be led. When the ordinary lead-rope had been tried and found useless, Phon slipped a clove-hitch round the brute's lower jaw, after which he and Corbett together led, throwing all their weight upon the rope and pulling for all they were worth. It seemed as if this must move even a mule; but its principal effect upon the "stud" was to make him sit down upon his quarters in regular tug-of-war fashion, rolling his eyes hideously, and squealing with rage. The application of motive power (by means of a thick stick) to his other end only elicited a display of heels, which whizzed and shot about Steve's ears until he determined to "quit driving."

After this the steed proceeded some distance of his own accord, and flattering terms were showered upon him.

"After all he only wanted humouring," Ned said; "horses were just alike all the world over. Kindness coupled with quiet resolution was all that was necessary for the management of the most obstinate brute on earth."

So spoke Corbett, after the manner of Englishmen, and the "stud" poked out his under lip and showed the whites of his eyes. He knew better than that, and for some time past had had his eye upon a gently sloping bank covered with young pines and some deadfall. As he reached this he tucked in his tail, bucked to see if he could get his pack off, and failing in that let go with both heels at the man behind him, and then rolled over and over down the bank until he stuck fast amongst the fallen timber, where he lay contentedly nibbling the weeds, whilst his owners took off his packs and made other arrangements for his comfort, without which he pretended that it was absolutely impossible for him to get up again.

This sort of thing soon becomes monotonous, and our amateur prospectors found that though they were doing a good deal of hard work they were not making two miles an hour. Luckily for all concerned the "stud" died young, departing from this life on the third day out from Antler, a victim to the evil effects of about a truss of poison weed which he had picked up in his frequent intervals for rest by the roadside.

It was with a sigh of sincere relief that Corbett and Steve and Phon portioned out the pack among them, and said adieu to their dead cayuse. Whilst he lived they felt that they could not leave behind them an animal for which they had paid a hundred dollars, but now that he was dead they were free from such scruples, and proceeded upon their journey at a considerably increased rate of speed.

Flower-time was past in Cariboo, and the whole forest was full of fruit. Upon every stony knoll, where the sun's rays were reflected from white boulders or charred black stumps, there grew innumerable dwarf raspberry canes, bearing more fruit than leaves. By the side of the trail the broad-leaved salmon-berry held up its fruit of crimson velvet, just high enough for a man to pluck it without stooping, and every bush which Steve and Ned passed was loaded either with the purple of the huckle-berry or the clear coral red of the bitter soap-berry. Best of all berries to Ned's mind was that of a little creeper, the fruit of which resembled a small huckle-berry, and reminded the thirsty palate of the combined flavours of a pine-apple and a Ribston pippin.

Altogether, what with the fool-hens and the grouse (which were too careful of their young to care properly for themselves) and the berries, it was evident to Ned that no man need starve in the forests of Cariboo in early autumn; but there were broad tracks through the long grass and traces amongst the ruined bushes of another danger to man's life every bit as real and as terrible as the danger of starvation. The fruit season is also the bear season, and the long sharp claw-marks in front of the track told Corbett that the bears were not all black which used the trail at night and rustled in the dense bush by day. Though they never had the luck to meet one, Ned and Steve had their eyes skinned and their rifles loaded for grizzly every day until they issued from the forest on to the bare lands above the Frazer.

As they could not get a canoe at Soda Creek they had to tramp down stream to Chimney Creek, where a few Chinamen were washing for gold. These men, in return for some trifling gift of stores, took the party across the river, and so worked upon the mind of their fellow-countryman with stories of the great "finds" up stream of which they had heard that his eyes began to glisten with the same feverish light which had filled them at Lillooet.

The Frazer had a peculiar fascination for Phon, and no wonder, for there is something about this river unlike all other rivers — something which it owes neither to its size nor its beauty. The Frazer looks like a river of hell, if hell has rivers. From where Ned Corbett stood, high up above the right bank, he could get glimpses of the river's course for some miles. Everywhere the scene was the same, a yellow turbid flood, surging savagely along through a deep gully between precipitous mud bluffs, whose sides stained here and there with metallic colours—vivid crimson and bright yellow, made them look as if they had been poured hot and hissing from nature's cauldron, and that so recently that they had not yet lost the colours of their molten state. The rolling years are kind to most things, beautifying them with the soft tints of age or veiling them with gracious foliage, but the banks of the Frazer still look raw and crude; the gentler things of earth will have nothing to do with the accursed river, in which millions of struggling salmon rot and die, while beside its waters little will grow except the bitter sage bush and the prickly pear.

When Corbett and Chance reached Chimney Creek the fall run of salmon was at its height, and added, if possible, to the weird ugliness of the river. From mid-stream to either bank every inch of its surface was broken by the dorsal fins or broad tails of the travelling fish, while in the back waters, and under shelter of projecting rocks, they lay in such thousands that you could see the black wriggling mass from a point several hundred yards away. From the shingle down below you could if you chose kill salmon with stones, or catch them with your hands, but you could not walk without stepping on their putrefying bodies, which while they still lived and swam took the vivid crimson or sickly yellow of the Frazer's banks. They looked (these lean leprous fish) as if they had swallowed the yellow poison of the river, and it was burning their bodies alive.

And yet like the men their betters they still struggled up and up, reckless of all the dangers, though out of every hundred which went up the Frazer not three would ever find their way back again to the strong wholesome silvery sea. The glutted eagles watched for them, the bears preyed upon them, Indians speared them; they were too weak almost to swim; their bodies were rotting whilst they still lived, and yet they swam on, though their strength was spent and they rolled feebly in a flood through which, only a few months earlier, they would have shot straight and strong as arrows fresh loosed from the bow. Gold and desolation and death, and a river that roared and rattled as if playing with dead men's bones; a brittle land, where the banks fell in and the ruined pines lay, still living, but with their heads down and their roots turned up to the burning sky; a land without flowers, jaundiced with gold and dry with desire for the fairer things of earth—this is what Corbett saw, and seeing, he turned away with a shudder.

"My God!" he said, "gold should grow there; nothing else will; even the fish rot in that hell broth!"

"You aren't polite to Father Frazer, Ned. So I will propitiate him;" and the Yankee turned to the yellow river, and holding high a silver dollar he cried, "See here, old river, Steve Chance of N'York is dead broke except for this, and this he gives to you. Take his all as an offering. The future he trusts to you."

And so saying Steve sent his last coin spinning out into the gully, where for a moment it glittered and then sunk and was lost, swallowed up in the waves of the great river, which holds in her bed more wealth than has ever been won from nature by the greed and energy of man.

CHAPTER XXI.

PETE'S CREEK

FOR an hour Steve and Ned toiled steadily up the yellow banks, bluff rising above bluff and bench above bench, and all steep and all crumbling to the tread. The banks of the Frazer may possess the charm of picturesqueness of a certain kind for the tourist to whom time is no object, and for whom others work and carry the packs, but they were hateful as the treadmill and a very path of thorns to the men who toiled up them carrying a month's provisions on their backs, and wearing worn-out mocassins upon their swollen, bleeding feet. It was with a sigh of heartfelt thankfulness that Corbett and Chance topped the last bench, and looked away to the west over the undulating forest plateau of Chilcotin. Men know Chilcotin now, or partly know it, as the finest ranching country west of Calgary, but in the days of which I am writing it was very little known, and Steve and his friends looked upon the long reaches and prairies of yellow sun-dried grass, dotted here and there with patches of pine forest, as sailors might look upon the coast of some untrodden island. To Steve and Phon this yellow table-land was the region of fairy gold. It was somewhere here that the yellow stuff which all men love lay waiting for man to find it. Surely it was something more than the common everyday sun which made those Chilcotin uplands so wondrously golden! So thought Steve and Phon.

To Ned all was different. As far as the eye could see a thousand trails led across the bluffs, gradually fading away in the distance. They were but cattle trails—the trails of the wild cattle of those hills—blacktail deer and bighorn sheep, but to Ned they were paths along which the feet of murder had gone, and his eye rested on the dark islands of pine, as if he suspected that the man he sought lurked in their shadow.

"Well, Ned, which is the way? Let's look at the map," said Chance.

Ned produced the map, and together the two men bent over it.

"The trail should run south-west from the top of this ridge, until we strike what old Pete calls here a 'good-sized chunk of a crik.' That is our first landmark. 'Bear south-west from the big red bluff,' he says—and there's the bluff," and Ned pointed to a big red buttress of mud upon the further bank of the Frazer.

"That's so, Ned, but I can see another big red bluff, and there are any number of trails leading more or less south-west," replied Chance.

"Well, let's take the biggest," suggested Corbett, and no one having any better plan to propose, his advice was taken.

For some time all went well. The trail was plain enough for a blind man to follow, and the walking, after that which they had experienced in the forest and along the banks of the Frazer, was almost a pleasure to them. Unfortunately there were a few drawbacks to the pleasures of travel even in Chilcotin. In Cariboo and up the Frazer the Indians had already learnt that the white man's rifle could kill nearly as far as a man could see, and they respected the white men, or feared them, which did as well. But in Chilcotin the red men were untamed (they are less tamed still, probably, than any Indians on the Pacific coast), and it was necessary for Ned and his friends to take care lest they should blunder unasked into some hunter's camp.

This upon the evening of their first day upon these table-lands they very nearly did, but as luck would have it, they saw the thin column of blue smoke winding up from a clump of pines just in time, and slunk away into the bed of Pete's "good-sized chunk of a crik," where they lay without a fire until the dawn of the next day.

Luckily for them the nights were still fairly warm as high-land nights go, but after sundown the air is always fresh upon these high tablelands, and no one was sorry when the day broke. The expedition, Steve Chance opined, had ceased to be "a picnic." Food was becoming somewhat scarce, and already Ned in his capacity of leader had put them upon rations of one tin cupful of flour per diem, two rashers of bacon, and a little tea. A cupful of flour means about four good-sized slices of bread, and although a man can live very well upon two slices of bread for breakfast and two at dinner, with a rasher of bacon and a little weak tea at each meal, and nothing between meals except twelve hours' hard work in the open air, he ought not to be sneered at if he feels a craving for some little luxury in the way of sugar or butter, or even another slice of bread.

Every now and then, it is true, something fell to one of the rifles; but they dared not shoot much for fear of attracting the attention of wandering Indians, and besides it is astonishing how little game men see upon the march. You can march or hunt, but it is difficult to both march and hunt successfully at the same time. On the third day upon the Chilcotin table-lands, the trail which the prospectors had been following "played out." For four or five miles it had grown fainter and fainter, and now the party stood out in the middle of a great sea of sunburnt grass, with no road before them and no land-marks to guide them.

"I'll tell you what it is, Steve, we have rather made a mess of this journey. It seems to me that unless there is something wrong with the sun we have been bearing too much to the west. It looks as if we were going a point to the north of west, instead of south-west, as we intended to do," said Ned after a careful survey of their position.

"Likely enough," assented his companion. "I don't see how a fellow is to keep his course amongst all these ups and downs. Besides, we followed the trail."

"Yes, and the trail has played out. I expect it was only a watering trail, though it is funny that it seems to start out of the middle of nowhere. Let's steer by the sun and go nearly due south. We must hit off the Chilcotin in that way."

"What, the Chilcotin river? Yes, that seems a good idea. Lead on, MacDuff!"

So it was that with his companion's assent Ned turned nearly south, and hour after hour strode on in silence over the yellow downs, until the sun had sank below the horizon.

"It's time to camp, Ned," cried Steve, who had fallen a good deal behind his companions; "and that is rather a snug-looking hollow on our left. We should be sheltered from that beastly cold night-wind in there. What do you say?"

"All right, if you must stop," replied Ned, looking

forward regretfully. "But ought we not to make another mile or two before we camp?"

"You can do what you please, but I cain't crawl another yard, and don't mean to try to. Bring yourself to an anchor, Ned, and let's have grub."

Of course Ned yielded. It was no good going on alone.

"Say, Ned," cried Steve a few minutes later, "we aren't the first to camp here. Look at this."

"This" was the carcase of a mule-deer, which lay in the hollow in which Steve wanted to camp.

"Well, old chap, that spoils your hollow, I'm afraid. It is too high to be pleasant as a bed-fellow. By Jove, look here!" and stooping, Ned picked up the empty shell of a Winchester cartridge.

"The fellow who killed that deer has camped right alongside his kill," remarked Steve. "See here, he has cut off a joint to carry away with him;" and Steve pointed to where a whole quarter had evidently been neatly taken off with a knife. "It's some Indian, I reckon, out hunting."

"No, that is no Indian's work, Steve. An Indian would have cleaned his beast, and even if he did not mean to come back for the meat he would have severed the joints and laid them neatly side by side. It is almost a part of his religion to treat what he kills with some show of respect. The man who slept here was a white man."

"Cruickshank?" suggested Steve.

"Yes, I think so," replied Ned quietly. "But he must have been here some weeks ago."

"Great Scott! then we'll get the brute yet."

"We may, but he has a long start of us, and the grub is getting very light to carry;" and Ned lifted his little pack and weighed it thoughtfully. And Ned was right, the man had a long start of them.

From the evening upon which they found the ungralloched stag to the end of the month Corbett and his friends wandered about day after day looking for Pete's Creek or Cruickshank, but found neither. They had reached the Chilcotin of course, and on its banks had been lucky enough to kill one of a band of sheep, upon which they lived for some days, but they could find no traces of that stream which, according to the old miner, flowed over a bed of gold into the river. They had washed pansful of dirt from a score of good-sized streams, and Phon had let no rill pass him without peering into it and examining a little of the gravel over which its waters ran, but so far the gold-seekers had not found anything which seemed likely to pay even moderate daily wages.

Neither had they found anywhere traces of Cruickshank. Between the dead stag and the Chilcotin they had come across two or three camps, probably the camps of the man who had killed that stag, but even Corbett began to doubt if the man could be a white man. Whoever he was he had worn moccasins, had had but one pack animal with him, and there were no scraps of paper, or similar trifles, ever left about the camps to show that he had carried with him any of the scanty luxuries which even miners sometimes indulge in. It was odd that he left no Indian message in his old camps—no wooden pegs driven in by the dead camp-fire, with their heads bent the way he was going.

But this proved nothing. He might be a white or he might be an Indian. In either case it looked as if, after hunting on the left bank of the Chilcotin, he had crossed to the other bank as if making for Empire Valley, and, knowing as much as he knew about the position of Pete's Creek, Cruickshank would hardly have been likely to leave the left bank. Ned began to fear that his quest was as hopeless as Steve's.

It was a chill, dark evening, with the first menace of winter in the sky, when Ned announced that the grub would not hold out more than another week.

"We have made it go as far as possible, and of course if we kill anything we can live on meat 'straight' again for a time, but I think, Steve, we have hunted this country pretty well for Pete's Creek, and we may as well give it up," said Ned.

"And how about Cruickshank? Do you think he has cleared out, or do you think he has never been here?"

"I don't know what to think, but I expect we shall come across old Rampike on the Frazer, and I shall stop and hunt with him."

That word "hunt" has an ugly sound when the thing to be hunted is a man like yourself, and Steve looked curiously into Ned's face. Would he never get tired and give up the chase, this quiet man who looked as if he had no malice in his nature, and yet stuck to his prey with the patience of a wolf?

"What do you propose, Ned? Fix things your own way. I am sick of dry bread and sugarless tea, anyway."

Corbett laughed. He thought to himself that had he been as keen after the gold as Steve had been, he would hardly have remembered that the tea had no sugar in it. Phon, to his mind, was a much better stamp of gold-seeker than his volatile Yankee friend.

"All right! If you leave it to me, I propose that we

go down to the Frazer, following the Chilcotin to its mouth, and prospecting the sources of all these little streams as we go. You see, so far we have only been low down near the bed of the Chilcotin. What I propose to do now, is to keep along the divide where the streams rise. At any rate we shall see more game up there than down here."

"*Nawitka* and *hyas sloosh*, as the siwashes say. Any blessed thing you please, Ned, only let us get out of this before we starve. What do you say, Phon?"

"Very good, not go yet," replied the Chinaman. "S'pose not find gold down low, find him high up."

"Phon sticks to his guns better than you do, Steve," remarked Corbett.

"I daresay. A herring-gutted Chinaman may be able to live on air. I cain't."

But the morrow brought Phon the reward of his faith, and twenty-four hours from the time when Steve Chance had asked only to be allowed to "get out of the confounded country by the shortest road," he would not have left it for ten thousand dollars

This was how it happened.

About mid-day, the sun being unusually hot, a halt had been called to smoke the mid-day pipe and rest legs wearied with the steep climb from the river bed to the crest of the divide.

"Don't you think, Ned, we might be allowed a square inch of damper for lunch to-day? We are going back now, and I am starving," said Steve.

"All right. Half a damper among the three if you like, but not a mouthful more."

Even this was more than he had hoped for, so Steve chewed the heavy damp morsel carefully; not that he distrusted the powers of his digestion, but because he was anxious to make the most of every crumb of his scanty repast.

Just below where the three were sitting grew a patch of orange-coloured Indian pinks. "I guess there's water not far from those flowers," remarked Steve, "and I want a drink badly before I light my pipe."

Dry bread is apt to stick in a man's gullet however hungry he may be, so that the three went down together, and found that, as Steve suspected, the pinks were growing in a damp spot, from which oozed a tiny rill, which, as they followed it, grew and grew until the rapidity of its growth roused their curiosity, and led them on long after they had found the drinking-place they sought.

All at once it seemed as if the stream had been augmented by water from some subterranean source, for its volume grew at a bound from that of a rill to that of a good-sized mountain stream, which gurgled noisily through the mosses for a few hundred yards, and then plunged through a cleft in the rocks to reappear, three or four hundred feet below, a dark rapid mountain-torrent, running between walls of wet black rock.

"It is a queer-looking place, isn't it, Steve? Any fellow might go all over this country and miss seeing that creek. I wonder if it is worth while climbing down that place to prospect it?"

But whilst the strongest stood doubting, the weakest of the party had scrambled like a cat over the rocks, and could now be seen on his knees by the brink of the dark waters, washing as he had never washed before. At last the little blue figure sprang to its feet, and waving its arms wildly, yelled:

"*Chicamon! chicamon!* Me find him. *Hyóu Chicamon!*" (*anglice* heaps of money).

Diphtheria, cholera, the black death itself, rapid though they are in their spread, and appalling though they are in their strength, are sluggish and weak compared to the gold fever. In one moment, at that cry of "chicamon! chicamon!" (money! money!), Chance had recovered from his fatigue, Corbett had awakened from his dreams of vengeance, and both together were scrambling recklessly down the rocks to the pool, beside which Phon was again kneeling, washing the golden dirt.

In spite of his native phlegm and his professed disregard for gold, Ned Corbett actually jostled his companions in his eagerness to get to the water; and though his pet pipe dropped from his mouth and broke into a hundred pieces, he never seemed to know what had happened to him.

When Phon washed his first panful of dirt in Pete's Creek it was broad noon; when Ned Corbett straightened his back with a sigh and came back for a moment almost to his senses, it was too dark to see the glittering specks in their pans any longer.

From noon to dusk they had toiled like galley slaves, without a thought of time, or fatigue, or hunger, and yet two of these were weak, tired men, and the third, under ordinary circumstances, really had quite a beautiful contempt for the sordid dollar.

When Corbett looked at the gleaming yellow stuff, and realized what power it had suddenly exerted over him, he actually felt afraid of it. There was something uncanny about it. But there was no longer any doubt about Pete's Creek. They had struck it this time, and no mistake; and if there was much "dirt" like that which they had been washing since noon, a few months of steady work would make all three rich men for life. In most places which they had seen, the gold had been found in dust: here it was in flakes and scales, as big as the scales upon the back of a chub. In most places a return of a few cents to the pan would have been considered "good enough:" here the return was not in cents but in dollars, and yet even now what was this which Phon the Chinaman was saying, his features working as if he were going into an epileptic fit?

"This nothing, nothing at all! You wait till to-mollow. Then we see gold,—heap gold not all same this, but in *lumps!*"

And he got up and walked about, nodding his head and muttering: "You bet you sweet life! Heap gold! You bet you sweet life!" whilst the red firelight flickered over his wizened features, and dwelt in the corners of his small dark eyes, until he resembled one of those quaint Chinese devils of whom he stood so much in awe.

As far as Ned and his companions could calculate, their first seven hours' work had yielded them something like a thousand dollars-worth of pure gold; and already Ned Corbett almost regretted the price he had paid for it, as he listened to the eager, crazy chatter of his companions, and tried in vain to put together the good old pipe which he had shattered in his rush for that yellow metal, which gleamed evilly, so Ned thought, from the tin pannikin upon Chance's knee.

There was another thing which Corbett could not forget. It was true that they had found Pete's Creek and the gold, but there was no trace of Cruickshank.

CHAPTER XXII.

GOLD BY THE GALLON!

AFTER the finding of Pete's Creek there was no more talk of returning to the Frazer. In Corbett's camp the reign of gold had begun, so that no man spoke of anything or thought of anything but the yellow metal. Gold was a god to all the three of them, and Phon and Chance and Corbett alike bowed their backs and worshipped, grovelling on their knees and toiling with pick and pan and rocker all the day long. Only Corbett rebelled at all against the tyranny of the strange god, and he rebelled in thought only. Each day, in his heart, he swore should be the last which he would waste down by the creek, and yet every fresh dawn found him at his place with the others. Luckily for the gold-seekers, Pete's Creek was rich in other things besides mere gold. Trout abounded in the water, and huckle-berries grew thick some little distance down stream; and in addition to these good things Corbett soon discovered that the trails which ran thread-like over the face of the cliffs above Pete's Creek owed their existence to the feet of generations upon generations of white goats—staid stolid brutes, with humps upon their backs, little black horns upon their heads, wide frills to their hairy pantaloons, and beards worn as seafaring men used to wear them, all round their chins and cheeks.

These were the aborigines of Pete's Creek, and were if anything more confiding and more easily killed than the trout. Every morning at early dawn the gold-seekers saw the goats clambering slowly back to the lairs, in which they hid during the daytime, and just after dark the rattling stones told them that their neighbours were on their way down again to the lowlands. Whenever Ned wanted one for the pot, the stalk was a very simple thing, the goat standing looking at the approaching gunner with stony indifference, until a bullet rolled him over. Food was plentiful enough about the creek, and Ned was able to lay aside what little flour remained, keeping it until the time came when winter should make a move to some lower camping ground an absolute necessity.

So then the three had nothing to do but to gather up the gold-dust, and add pile to pile and bag to bag of the precious metal.

All worked with energy, but no one with such tireless patience, such feverish vigour, as the little Chinaman. Compared to him Chance was a sluggard, and even Corbett's strength was no match for the ceaseless activity of this withered, yellow little mortal, whose bones stared through his skin, and whose eyes seemed to be burning away their sockets.

The stars as they faded in the morning sky saw Phon come down to work; the sun at mid-day beat upon his head but could not drive him away from his rocker; and night found him discontented because the hours in which man can labour are so few and so short. As long as Phon could see the "colours" in his pan he stuck to his work, and when he could see no longer he carried his treasure to camp and kept it within reach of him, and if possible under the protection of Ned and Ned's rifle.

Even in the night season this slave of gold took no rest. In Victoria in old days the devils used to come to him, and tell him all manner of things—when to gamble and when not to gamble, for instance; now they haunted him, and filled him with fears lest someone else should snatch his treasure from him.

In spite of the absolute stillness which reigned round the creek, Phon believed that he was watched day and night, nor could Corbett's rough rebukes or Chance's chaff shake him in this belief. Twice he woke up, screaming that someone was taking away the gold, and once he swore positively that he had seen a face looking at him as he washed the rich dirt—a face which peered at him from the bushes, and disappeared without a sound before he could identify it. There were no tracks, so of course Phon was dreaming; but perhaps, even if there had been anyone watching from the place at which Phon saw the face, he would not have left a very distinct track, as the rock just there was as hard and unimpressionable as adamant.

Corbett, as he watched his servant muttering to himself and glancing nervously over his shoulder at every wind which stirred in the bush, felt convinced that the gold had turned his brain. And yet in some things Phon was sane enough. It happened that there was, in a sudden bend of the stream, a great boulder, which broke the course of the water, and sent it boiling and gurgling in two small streams about the boulder's base. From the very first this boulder fascinated Phon. For centuries it had stood in the same place, until green things had grown upon it, and gray lichens had spread over it.

It was a favourite resting-place for the white-breasted dipper on his way up stream; the fish used to lie in the shelter of it, where their struggle against the water need not be so severe, or to wait for the food which was washed off its piers and buttresses: and sometimes even the deer would come and stand knee-deep in the stream, to rub the velvet off their horns against its angles.

But Phon the Chinaman had guessed a secret which the old rock had kept for centuries—a secret which neither the birds nor the fish nor the deer, nor even those wise white-bearded patriarchs, the goats, had ever heard a whisper of.

That rock was set in gold, and Phon knew it.

Year by year the pebbles and the gravel and disintegrated rock were washed lower and lower down the bed of the stream, and all the while the gold kept sinking and staying, whilst the gravel and sand went on. But even gold must move, however slowly, in the bed of a rapid stream, and at last golden sand and flakes and nuggets all came to the bend where Phon's rock stood. Here the gold stopped. Gravel might rest for a while, and then rattle on again; pebbles and boulders might be torn away from their anchorage under the lee of the rock by the eager waters, but gold never. Once there Phon knew it would stay, clinging to the bottom, and even working under the rock itself. Knowing this Phon looked at the rock, and greed and discontent tortured him beyond endurance. He had already amassed far more gold than he could possibly spend upon the paltry pleasures he cared for; but he loved the yellow metal for itself, not for the things it can purchase, and this being so, he proceeded to match his cunning against the strength of the rock.

First he gathered great piles of quick burning wood from the banks and piled them upon his victim as if he would offer a sacrifice to mammon, and this he set fire to, bringing fresh supplies of wood as his fire burnt low. After a while the rock beneath the fire grew to a white heat, and then by means of a wooden trough which he had made, Phon turned a stream of cold water from the creek upon the place where the fire had been, and these things he continued to do for many days, until at last the giant yielded to the pigmy, and the great boulder, which for centuries had withstood the force of the stream in flood-time and the grinding ice in winter, began to break up and melt away before the cunning of a wizened, yellow-skinned imp from China.

About this time, and before the rock was finally split up and removed, Phon suggested that it would be better to try to divert the stream from its bed at some point just above the rock, so that they might be able to get at the gold when the boulder had been removed. To do this flumes had to be made, and axes were in request to hew them out. At the first mention of axes Steve became uneasy. There had been two axe-heads in the outfit originally, and he had been intrusted with one of them, and had lost it.

"I know I had it in the last camp," he asserted.

"Then you had better go back for it; the last camp is only about five hours' tramp from here. Or if you think that you can't find your way to it, I will go," remarked Corbett.

"I can find my way all right," replied Chance in an injured tone, nettled at the implied slur upon his woodcraft; "but do you think it is worth while going back for it?"

"Certainly. You could no doubt make a hundred dollars here in the time it will take you to get that axe, but a hundred dollars would not buy us an axe-head at Pete's Creek."

This argument being unanswerable, Steve took the back track, and after being away from camp all day, returned about sundown with the missing axe and an old buckskin glove.

"So you found the axe, I see?" was Corbett's greeting when the two met.

"Yes, I found it; I knew to a dot where I left it. But it was deuced careless to leave it anyway, wasn't it? By the way, you did not leave anything behind you in that camp, did you?"

"No, not I. I always go round camp before leaving to look for things. I only wonder that I did not see your axe."

"Oh, you wouldn't do that, I left it sticking in a cotton-wood tree a quarter of a mile from camp. But didn't you leave your 'mitts' behind?"

"No, my dear chap. I tell you I don't leave things behind. Here are my mitts;" and the speaker drew from his pocket a pair of buckskin gloves much frayed and worn.

"Then who in thunder is the owner of this?" exclaimed Chance, holding up a single glove very similar in make to those which Corbett wore.

"Your own glove, I expect, Steve, isn't it? I haven't seen you wearing any lately, and one wants them pretty badly amongst these rocks. You thought that you had caught me tripping, did you, my boy?" and Ned laughed heartily at his companion's crest-fallen appearance.

"No, Ned, this isn't mine," replied Steve seriously. "See here, it would hold both my hands."

"That is odd. Where did you find it, Steve?" and taking the glove in his hands Ned examined it carefully.

"You can't tell how long it has been out," he muttered, "the chipamuks or some other little beasts have gnawed the fingers; but the only wonder is that they haven't destroyed it altogether. Where did you say you found it?"

"About a quarter of a mile from camp. A bear has been round the camp since we were there, and I was following his trail for a bit to see what I could make of it when I came across this."

"Was it a grizzly's or a black bear's track which you followed?"

"I couldn't make out. The ground was hard, and I'm not much good at tracking. I could hardly be sure that it was a bear's track at all."

"It wasn't a man's track by any chance?'

"Confound it, Ned, I am not such an infernal fool as you seem to think. Yesterday you suggested that I couldn't find my way to the old camp, and now you ask me whether I know a bear's track from a man's."

"Don't lose your temper about it, old fellow. A man's track is very like a bear's, especially if the man wears moccasins and the ground is at all hard. Of course if you are certain that what you saw were bears' tracks there's an end of it. After all, this glove may have been where you found it since last summer. It might have been Pete's perhaps."

And so the matter dropped and the glove was forgotten, for there were many things to occupy the attention of Ned and Steve in those days; and as for Phon, he never even heard of the glove, being busy at the time upon some engineering work in connection with that great boulder of his at the bend in the stream.

For several days the Chinaman had ceased to wash or dig, all his time being devoted to preparations for the removal of the boulder, and at last, one morning, when the gully was full of the pent smoke of his fires, he was ready for the last act in his great work, and came to Corbett and Chance for help. On the top of the rock were the ashes of Phon's fires, and at its feet, where once the waters ran, was dry ground, while from summit to base the rock itself was split into a hundred pieces, so small as to offer no serious difficulties to the united efforts of the three men who wanted to remove them. For centuries the rock had stood upon a kind of shelf, from which the three men, using a pine-pole as a lever, pitched one great fragment after another until the whole of the rock's bed lay bare.

Then for a moment they paused, while the smoke drifted about them, and the corded veins stood out strangely upon their pale faces. Surely they were dreaming, or their eyes were tricked by the smoke! Phon had guessed that the boulder had caught and held some portion of the gold which had come down the mountain stream in the course of the last few centuries, but the sight upon which he gazed now was such as even he had only dreamed of when the opium had possession of him body and soul.

The bed of the boulder was a bed of gold—gold in flakes and lumps and nuggets; gold in such quantities that as Steve and Ned looked at it a doubt stole into their minds. Surely, they thought, it cannot be for this common, ugly stuff, of which there is so much, that men toil and strive, live and die, and are damned!

The wet pebbles amongst which the gold lay were twice as beautiful, and as Ned wiped the perspiration from his brow he thought that a quart of gold would be but a small price to pay for a quart of honest Bass. But Phon had no such fancies. With a wild cry, like the cry of a famished beast, the Chinaman threw himself into the hollow he had cleared, clawing and scratch-

"GOLD—GOLD IN FLAKES, AND LUMPS, AND NUGGETS."

ing at the gold with his long, lean hands until his nails were all broken and his flesh torn and bleeding.

Nor was Chance far behind Phon in the scramble. Together the two delved and scratched and picked about the bed-rock, amassing little piles and stacks of nuggets from the size of a pea to the size of a hen's egg, and so busy were they and so intent upon their labour that neither of them noticed Corbett, who after Phon's first wild cry had turned away in disgust, and now sat solemnly smoking on a log by the camp-fire.

Taking his pipe from his mouth, he blew away a long wreath of fragrant smoke, and as he watched it dissolve in space his thoughts fashioned themselves into these strange words:

"Confound your gold anyway! I don't want any more of it in my share of life's good things."

CHAPTER XXIII.

THE HORNET'S NEST.

AFTER the removal of Phon's boulder there was no more talk of washing with pan or rocker, no more thought of digging or mining. Even Chance and Phon were content with the quantity of gold which lay ready to their hands at Pete's Creek. The only trouble was that at Pete's Creek the yellow stuff was absolutely worthless, and that between Pete's Creek, where the gold lay, and those cities of men in which gold is of more value than anything else upon earth, were several hundred miles of wild country, where a man might be lost in the forest, or drowned in the river, or starved on the mountain, just like a beggarly *coyoté*, and that although he was richer than a Rothschild.

Steve had heard of men in Cariboo who had paid others ten dollars a day to carry their gold-dust for them, and he would gladly have done as much himself; but, unluckily, the only men within reach of him were as rich as he was, and wanted help just as badly. So Steve joined Corbett and Phon, and the three men sat together looking down upon as much wealth as would buy the life-long labour, aye, the very bodies and souls, of a hundred ordinary men, and yet they were conscious that it was about even betting that they would all three die beggars—die starving for want of a loaf of bread, though each man carried round his waist the price of a score of royal banquets!

Steve was the first to break the silence. Pointing away over the rolling forest lands, towards the bed of the Frazer river, he said:

"It looks pretty simple, Ned, and I guess we could get there and back in a week."

"Do you? You would be a good woodsman if you got to the river in a week, and a better one if you ever found your way back here at all."

"How's that? You don't mean to say that you think it possible that we shall lose the creek again now that we have found it?"

"We ought not to, Steve, but that is a bad country to get through and an easy one to get lost in;" and Corbett's eyes dwelt mistrustingly upon the dark, dense woods, the deep gullies, the impervious stretches of *brûlé*, and the choking growth of young pines which lay between the knoll upon which they sat and the distant benches of the Frazer river.

"Well what had we better do, Ned? If we don't take

care we shall get caught in a cold snap before we know where we are."

"We had better leave here to-morrow morning, I think, Steve, carrying all the gold we can with us, and make straight for the Frazer. There we may meet some miners going out for the winter, and if they have not struck it rich themselves they may be willing to pack the stuff out for us. If not, we must look for old Rampike and wait for the spring."

"What! and put up with nearly another year of this dog's life with all *that* lying there?"

"I'm afraid so, Steve. You can't order a special train from here to New York though you are a millionaire."

For a little while Steve Chance sat moodily biting at the stem of his unlit pipe, and then he asked Corbett—

'Are you going to join Rampike for his fall hunt, Ned?"

"Certainly. Why not?"

"Oh, I don't know, only I thought that you might have changed your mind;" and Chance's eyes wandered round to the pile of gold nuggets over which Phon kept guard.

"That can make no difference, Steve. I don't want what Cruickshank stole from me. I want to settle with him for my countryman's life."

"Much good that will do poor old Roberts. But as you please. We are all mad upon one subject or another. Do you still think that Cruickshank is somewhere hereabouts?"

"I don't think that he is on this side of the river or we should have come across his tracks before now, but I fancy he is somewhere in this Chilcotin country."

"You don't think that that glove could have been his?"

"You said that there were no men's tracks anywhere near it, so I suppose not."

"That's so; but I've seen some of your tracks since, Ned, which looked awfully like those bear tracks. I'm hanged if I know whether they were bear tracks after all!"

"It is a pity you were so positive about them at first then. But it is too late now in any case. If the tracks were made by Cruickshank he is far enough from here by now."

Again the conversation ceased for a time, the only sound being the rattle of Pete's Creek in the dark gorge below.

"It is a pity the goats have all cleared out. Don't you think you could find one, Ned, before we start?" asked Chance at length.

"No, I'm certain that I could not. We must be content with trout (if Phon can catch any), and the flour which I saved when we struck the creek."

"Ah, I had forgotten that. Is there much of it?"

"About half a pound apiece *per diem* for a week."

"Short commons for a hungry man, especially as the berries are nearly all gone."

"It *will* be hungry work for us until we reach the Frazer, but there is a little goat's meat left and the fish."

"Say, Phon, you think you catch plenty fish by to-morrow?"

"S'pose you come 'long an' help I catch 'em," replied Phon.

"All right, I'll come. How much gold you pack along with you, Phon?" Steve added as the three went down to the creek to fish.

"Me halo pack any," was Phon's unexpected reply.

"Halo pack any! Why, don't you want any gold?"

"Yes, me want him, but me not pack any. Me not go to-mollow. Me stop here!"

"Stop here! What, alone! How about the devils?"

Poor Phon glanced nervously over his shoulder. The shadows were growing deeper and deeper amongst the pine stems, and the trees were creaking and groaning with a little wind which generally rose about sundown.

"S'pose you want find men carry gold to Victollia, one man go catch 'em. One man plenty. S'pose two man stop here, that heap good. No one steal 'um gold then," and the speaker pointed to the bags of dust.

"Nonsense, Phon. Who do you suppose would take the gold?"

"Debil take him: debil take him, sure. Debil watch him all the time. S'pose all go, debil take him quick."

"Well, I'm afraid your friend the devil will take the stuff to-morrow morning, for to-morrow morning we all leave this place. You had better pack as much dust as you can carry if you are afraid to leave it."

"No. Me halo pack any. S'pose all go, me stop 'lone."

It was a resolute reply in spite of the man's frightened face, and the tone of it arrested Ned's attention.

"Have you ever really seen anyone about the camp?" he asked.

"No, me halo see him, me halo see him. Only me know him there. All the time he go lound an' lound and look at the gold and come closer. Me halo see him, me feel him looking all the time. Stop here, Misser Ned, stop here."

"The gold has made you crazy, Phon," said Ned, somewhat contemptuously, disregarding the piteous appeal in the man's tone and gesture. "However, if you like to stay, it will do no harm. You can catch plenty of fish, and we shall be back in a fortnight or so." And then turning to Steve, Ned added, in a lower tone: "He'll change his mind when he sees us start, and if he doesn't we cannot drag him through that country against his will."

That night the three discoverers of Pete's Creek worked as hard to collect a store of little trout as they had ever worked to gather gold, and at dawn two of the three stood ready to start on their march to the Frazer. In spite of all Ned's persuasions Phon remained firm in his resolution to stay with his treasure. For him the woods were devil-haunted; articulate voices whispered in every wind; faces of fear were reflected from every starlit pool; and yet, in spite of all the terrors which walk at night, Phon refused to leave his gold. In him greed was stronger even than fear.

"He will be raving mad before we get back," muttered Ned, as he gazed at the frail blue figure crouching over the camp-fire; "but what can we do? We can't 'pack' the fellow along with us."

"No, we cain't do that," replied Steve. "Poor beggar! I wouldn't be in his shoes for all the gold in the creek."

And as he stared in a brown study at the charred stumps and rough white woodwork in that gloomy canyon, at the broken rock and the dead fires, Chance began unconsciously to hum the air of "The Old Pack-mule."

"Confound you, Steve," cried Corbett angrily, "stop that! Isn't it bad enough to hear the winds crooning that air all night, and the waters of the creek keeping time to it? Shut up, for heaven's sake, and come along!" and without waiting for an answer Ned turned his back upon the gold camp and plunged boldly into the woods between it and the Frazer.

It had been arranged that Corbett should go ahead with the rifle, and that Chance should follow him with an axe. "Any fool can blaze a tree, but it takes a quick man to roll over a buck on the jump," had been Steve's verdict, and he had alloted to himself the humbler office.

From the moment they left camp until nightfall, it seemed to Steve that he and his companion did nothing but step over or crawl under logs of various sizes and different degrees of slipperiness. To follow the sinuous course of a mountain stream through a pine-forest may look easy enough from a distance, but in reality to do so at all closely is almost impossible.

As for Pete's Creek, it ran through a deep and narrow canyon, the walls of which were precipitous rocks, along which no man could climb. The bed of the creek for the most part was choked with great boulders, amongst which the water broke and foamed, rendering wading impossible; and along the edges of the canyon up at the top the pines grew so thick, or the dead-falls were so dense, that it was all Ned could do to keep within hearing of the creek.

The constant forking of the stream made careful blazing very necessary, and this took time, and the course of the stream was so tortuous that they had frequently to walk four miles to gain one in the direction in which they wanted to go, so that when at last they reached a bare knoll, from which they could look out over the forest, it seemed to Ned and Steve that the Frazer valley was no nearer, and the crawling folds of the great Chilcotin mountains no more distant than they had been at dawn.

But the folds of the mountains were already full of inky gloom, and it was evident that a stormy night was close at hand, so that whether they had made many miles or few upon their way, it was imperatively necessary to camp at once. Almost before the fire had been lighted night fell, a night of intense darkness and severe cold, a cold which seemed to be driven into the tired travellers by a shrill little wind, which got up and grew and grew until the great pines began to topple down by the dozen. From time to time one or other of the sleepers would wake with a shiver and collect fresh fuel for the dying fire, or rearrange the log which he had laid at his back to keep the wind off; but in spite of every effort the night was a weary and a sleepless one both for Ned and Steve, and in the morning, winter, the miner's deadliest foe, had come.

For a month or more yet there might not be any serious snowfall, but the first flakes of snow were melting upon Corbett's clothes when he got up for the last time that night and found that the dawn had come. Far away upon the distant crest of the black mountains at his back, Ned saw the delicate lace-work of the first snow-storm of the year like a mantilla upon the head of some stately Spanish beauty.

"By Jove, Steve, we have no time to lose," said Ned. "Look at that!" and he pointed to the mountains. "If this is going to be an early winter, Phon is a lost man."

"Lead on, Ned," replied Steve, "I'll follow you as long as my legs will let me, but if you can find any way of avoiding those dead-falls to-day, do so. Nature never meant me for a squirrel or a Blondin."

"The only other way if you don't like balancing along these logs is down there over these boulders, and the water there is thigh-deep in places, and cold as ice;" and Corbett pointed to the bed of the creek a hundred feet below.

"Let's try it for a change, Ned, it cain't be worse than this," panted Steve, who at the moment was crawling on his hands and knees through a mesh-work of burnt roots and rampikes.

"All right, come along," said Ned, and using their hands more than their feet, the two men crept down the rock wall of the canyon until they reached the bed of the creek.

Here things went fairly well with them at first. The water was icy cold, but their limbs were so bruised and feverish that the cold water was pleasant to them; and though the boulders over which they had to climb were slippery and hard to fall against, they were not more slippery and very little harder than the logs above. After two or three miles of wading, however, Steve's limbs began to get too numbed with cold to carry him any further, and a return to dry land became necessary. Looking up for some feasible way out of the trap into which they had fallen, Ned at last caught sight of what appeared to be fairly open country along the edge of the canyon, and of a way up the rock wall which, though difficult, was not impossible.

"Here we are, Steve," he cried as soon as he saw the opening. "Here's an open place and a fairly easy way to it. Come along, let's get out of this freezing creek;" and so saying he went at the rock wall and began to scramble up like a cat.

Steve was either too tired or too deliberate to follow his friend at once, and in this instance it was well for him that he was so, for a second glance showed him a far easier way to the upper edge of the canyon than the direct route taken by Ned.

Clambering slowly up by the easier way of the two, Steve was surprised not to find Ned waiting for him when he at length gained the top of the rocks, and still more surprised when, after waiting for some minutes, he heard a faint voice below him calling him by name.

"Steve! Steve!" cried the voice.

"What is it, and where are you, Ned?" answered Chance.

"Here, underneath you. Look sharp and lend me a hand, I can't hold on much longer!"

By Ned's tones his need was urgent, and yet Chance could not get a glimpse of him anywhere. Dropping on to his knees and crawling to the edge, Steve leaned over until half his body was beyond the edge of the cliff. Then he saw his friend, but even then he did not comprehend his peril. The rock wall at the point at which Ned had tried to scale it ended in a kind of coping, which now projected over his head; but as if to make amends for this, a stout little juniper bush offered the climber a convenient hand-rail by which to swing himself up on to the top. And yet with the juniper within reach of him, there hung Ned Corbett yelling for help.

"Why don't you get hold of the bush, Ned, and haul yourself up? I cain't reach you from here," cried Steve.

"Daren't do it!" came the short answer. "There's a hornet's nest on it!" and as Ned spoke Steve caught sight of a great pear-shaped structure of dry mud which hung from the bush over the creek.

"Well, get down and come round my way."

"Can't do it. I can't get back," answered Ned, who,

like many another climber, had managed to draw himself up by his hands to a spot from which descent was impossible.

At that moment, whilst Steve was devising some kind of extempore ladder or rope, there was a rattle of falling stones, and a cry: "Look out, Steve, catch hold of me if you can!" and as the frail hold of his hands and feet gave way, Ned made a desperate spring and clutched wildly at the very bough from which that innocent-looking globe of gray mud hung. The next moment, at the very first oscillation of their home, out rushed a host of furious-winged warriors straight for Corbett's face. Luckily for him Steve had clutched him by the wrist, and though the sudden attack of the hornets upon his eyes made Ned himself let go his hold, his friend managed to maintain his until, amid a perfect storm of angry wings and yellow bodies, the two lay together upon the top of the cliff. If Steve had let go at that moment when the hornets rushed out to war, Ned Corbett must have fallen back upon the rocks at the bottom of the canyon, and there would have been an end to all his troubles. As it was he lay upon the top of the cliffs, and realized that the worst of his troubles were but beginning.

"Are you much stung, Steve?" he asked.

"You bet I am, Ned. Look! that would hardly go into an eight-and-a-half lavender kid now," and Steve held out his right hand, which was already much swollen.

But Ned did not take any notice of it. Instead he pressed his hands against his eyes and writhed with pain, and when Steve laid his hand on him he only muttered: "My God! my God! Steve, how will you and Phon ever find your way out? I am stone blind!"

CHAPTER XXIV.

DROWNING IN THE FOREST.

PERHAPS no two men were ever in more desperate plight than were Steve Chance and Ned Corbett as they lay upon the edge of Pete's Creek canyon in the Chilcotin country on that 2d of October, 1862.

For a week at least they had been living upon very meagre rations, made up principally of brook trout and berries; for a day and a half they had been stumbling hurriedly through one of the densest mountain forests in British Columbia; and now, when Chance's strength was exhausted and the grub half gone, Ned the guide and hunter was utterly bereft of sight.

For ten long minutes the two sat silent, then Ned lifted his head in a helpless dazed way, and Steve saw that both his eyes were completely closed by the hornets' stings.

"Chance, old chap, this *is* bad luck, but it will all rub off when it's dry. There are only two things now for you to choose between, either you must go on alone and bring help for Phon and myself from the Frazer, or go back and bring Phon out with you. You and he could catch a fresh supply of trout up at the pool, enough at any rate to keep body and soul together."

"And what is to become of you, Ned?"

"Oh, I shall get all right. I must get on as best I can in the dark for a day or two, and then if you can spare me the rifle, I shall be able to forage for myself. If you *can* spare the rifle I can do with half my share of the grub."

Steve Chance laughed. It was not the time which most men would have chosen for laughing, but still Steve Chance laughed a quiet dry laugh. The Yankee didn't like hard times, and didn't pretend to, but he had got into a corner, and had not the least idea of trying to back out of it.

"Say, Ned, is that what you'd expect an 'old countryman' to do? I guess not. And if it comes to that, men don't go back on a pal in the new country any more than they do in the old. If you stay here, I stay with you. If we get out of this cursed country we get out together, and if we starve we starve together. Let's quit talking nonsense;" and Chance, whose spirit was about two sizes too big for his body, got up and busied himself about making a fire and a rough bed for his sick comrade, as if he himself had just come out for a pic-nic.

Now you may rail at Fortune, and the jade will only laugh at you: you may pray to her, and she will turn a deaf ear to your prayers: you may try to bribe her, and she will swallow your bribes and give you nothing in return: but if you harden your heart and defy her, in nine cases out of ten she will turn and caress you.

Thus it was in Steve's case.

He was as it were fighting upon his knees, half dead but cheery still, and the woman-heart of Fortune turned towards him, and from the time when he set himself to help his blind comrade things began to mend. In the first place, when he tried the creek for trout, he found no difficulty in catching quite a respectable string of fish in a little over an hour, although for the last two days he and Ned had almost given up fishing as useless outside Phon's pool. Then on the way back from his fishing he met a stout old porcupine waddling off to winter quarters. Stout as he was, the porcupine managed to move along at quite a lively pace until he reached a pine, up which he went as nimbly as a monkey; but Steve was ready to do a good deal of climbing to earn a dinner, and did it (and the porcupine, too, "in the eye").

Thanks to these unhoped-for supplies of fish and flesh meat the two companions were able to camp and rest for a couple of days, during which the inflammation in Ned's eyes abated considerably, although he still remained totally blind, in spite of the rough-and-ready poultices of chewed rose-leaves constantly prepared for him by Steve.

"Do you feel strong enough to walk, Ned, if I lead you?" asked Steve after breakfast, on the third morning in the hornet's-nest camp.

"Yes, I'm strong enough, but you can't lead a blind man through this country."

"Cain't I? I've been looking round a bit, and it's pretty clear ahead of us. I've caught a good lot of trout now, and if you will carry the rifle and the axe, Ned, I'll try if I cain't find a way out for both of us."

"And how about blazing the trail?"

"Oh, I reckon we must let that slide. We can go by the creek when we want to get in again. My blazing don't amount to much so far, anyway."

"Why not?"

"Well, it's no good raising Cain now, old man, because the thing is done. I said 'any fool could blaze a trail,' and I was wrong; seems as if I'm a fool who cain't blaze one. Anyway, I blazed all those trees for the first two days as *they came to me*, not as they passed me, and I reckon my blazes won't show much from this side of the trees."

A moment's reflection will make the whole significance of Steve's admission plain even to those who have never seen a blazed tree. In making a new trail through a thickly-timbered country it is customary to blaze or chip with the axe a number of trees along the trail, so that anyone following you has only to look ahead of him and he will see a succession of chipped trees clearly defining the path.

If the trail is to be a permanent one, the man blazing it chips both sides of the marked tree, so that a man coming from either end of the trail can see the blazes. If, however, you only want to enable a friend or pack-train to follow you, you save time and blaze the trees as you come up to them, on the side facing you as you advance. This of course affords no guidance to you if you want to return along your own trail, and this was exactly what Steve had done. But bad as his mistake was, it was too late to set it right, and realizing this Ned made light of it, hoping against hope that whenever his eyes should be opened again he would be able to recognize the country through which they had passed, and so find his way back to Phon.

But in his heart Ned never expected to see Phon or the Golden Creek again. As he trudged along in the darkness, holding on to the end of Steve's stick, he could hear the refrain of that old song following him; and though his eyes were shut he could see again both those camps in the woods, the one in which he had found Roberts dead, and the one in which, as he now believed, he had left Phon his servant to die.

As a rule Ned's mind was far too busy with the things around him to indulge in dreams and forebodings, but now that his eyes were shut his head was full of gloomy fancies and prophesies of evil.

"I can't hear the creek any longer, Steve," he said at length, as he and his guide paused for breath.

"No, and I'm afraid, old fellow, that you won't hear it again. I've lost it somehow or other, trying to get round those dead-falls."

"Are you sure that you can't hit it off again?"

"Sure! You bet I'm sure. What do you suppose that we have been going round and round for the last half hour for? I've tried all I know to strike it again."

"That's bad, but it can't be helped; steer by the sun now and the wind. The Frazer is down below us, to our left front."

For an hour leader and led blundered on in silence. Following Ned's advice Steve took his bearings carefully, and then tried to steer his course by the sun and the way the wind blew upon his cheek. But in an hour he was, to use an Americanism, "hopelessly turned round." You cannot go straight if you want to in the woods unless you have a gang of men with you to cut a road through live timber and dead-fall alike; you must diverge here to escape a canyon, there to avoid a labyrinth of young pines, and even if you try to cut across a dead-fall you will be obliged to achieve your object by tacking from point to point, just as the fallen trees happen to lie. When he took his bearings, Steve was confident that nothing could make him mistake his general direction: a quarter of an hour later, when he had sunk out of sight of the sun, in a perfect ocean of young pines, he began to doubt whether his course lay to his right or to his left. The sun was hidden from him, no wind at all touched his cheek, and in that hollow amongst the pines he could not tell even which way the land sloped. He felt like a drowning man over whom the waves were closing, and in his helplessness he became more and more confused, until at last he was hardly certain whether the sun rose in the east or in the west.

To the man who sits quietly at home and reads this it may seem incredible that a level-headed man, and no mean woodsman as woodsmen go, should ever entirely lose his head and distrust his memory of the common things which he has known all his life. And yet in real life this happens. Men will get so confused as to doubt whether the needle of their compass points *to* the north or *from* the north, and so muddled as to their landmarks as to be driven to the conclusion that "something has gone wrong" with the compass, making it no longer reliable.

As for Steve he had lost confidence in everything, and was wandering at random amongst woods which seemed endless—woods which shut out all life and stifled all hope, which laid hold of him and his comrade with cruel half-human hands, stopping and tripping their tired feet and tearing flesh as well as clothes to ribands.

"Are we getting near the bench country yet, Steve?" asked Ned at length. "We don't seem to me to be going very straight."

"How can you tell, Ned? Are you beginning to see a little?"

"Devil a bit, but it feels as if we were scrambling along side-hills instead of going steadily downhill all the time, though I daresay it is only my fancy. I'm not used to going about with my eyes shut."

"And *I* am," said Steve bitterly. "That is just what I've been doing all my life, and now we shall both have to pay for it. We may as well sit down and die here, Ned. I cain't keep this farce up any longer.

I'm clean turned round and have been all day;" and with a great weary sigh Steve Chance sank down upon a log and buried his head in his hands. He was utterly broken down, physically and mentally, by the difficulties of forest travel.

Even to the hunter these British Columbian forests are full of difficulties, but to a man like Steve they are more full of dangers than the angriest ocean. For an hour or two hours, or for half a day, a patient man may creep and crawl through brush and choking dead-fall, putting every obstacle aside with gentle temperate hand, and hoping for light and an open country; but even the most patient temper yields at last to the persistent buffets of every mean little bough, and the most enduring strength breaks down when dusk comes and finds the forest tangle growing thicker at every step.

To Steve Chance every twig which lashed him across the eyes, every log against which he struck his shins, had become a sentient personal enemy, whose silence and apathy only made his attacks the harder to bear, until before the multitude of his enemies and the darkness of the trackless woods, the young Yankee's strength and courage failed him, and he sat down ready if need be to die, but too thoroughly exhausted to make another effort for life. Had there been a ray of hope to cheer him he would have kept on, but a day's wandering in the dark labyrinths of a mountain forest, where the winds have built up barriers of fallen pines, and where the young trees rise in dark green billows above the bodies of their unburied predecessors, is enough to kill hope in the most buoyant heart.

"Don't throw up the sponge, Steve," said a voice at his elbow. "We'll reach the Frazer yet."

The speaker was blind, and though he had never

opened his mouth to complain all through that weary day, be sure that the led man had borne many a shrewd buffet which his leader had escaped. If the forest was dark to Steve, it was darker to blind Ned Corbett, but he at any rate was unbeaten still.

"I think that I shall be able to see a little to-morrow, Steve," he went on; "and I believe that I can put your head straight now."

"I don't see how even you can do that, Ned," replied Chance despondently.

"Don't you? Well, let's try. Are there any deer tracks near us?"

"Yes, here's an old one leading right past the log we are sitting on."

"That's good. Now follow that downhill, and if you lose sight of it look for another and follow that downhill too. The stags may go a long way round, but it is long odds that they will go at last to water, and all water in this country leads to the Frazer."

Ned's reasoning seemed so sound to Steve that for a time it inspired him with fresh energy, and although at nightfall he had not yet reached the promised stream, he rose again next day with some faint hope to renew the search.

But the stags of Chilcotin were neither blind nor lame nor tired, so that a journey which occupied more than a day at the pace at which tired men travel, was but an afternoon's ramble for them. For the men, their followers, the end was very near. At mid-day upon the fourth day of Corbett's blindness, he and Steve were slowly picking their way through logs and over boulders which seemed to everlastingly repeat themselves, when Ned felt a jerk at the stick by which Steve led him, and the dry sal-lal bushes crushed and the stick hung limply in his hand. There was no one holding on to the other end of it!

"What, Steve, down again?" he cried. "Hold up, old man!" But there was no answer.

"Steve," he cried again, "are you hurt?" but not even a rustling bush replied. Whatever was the matter, Steve Chance lay very still.

"Great heavens, he can't be dead!" muttered the poor fellow; and the horror of the thought made the cold perspiration break out upon his brow.

"Steve! Steve!" he cried, and falling upon his knees he groped among the bushes until his hand rested upon his comrade's quiet face. There was no blood upon either brow or cheek (Ned's questioning hand could tell that much), so no stone had struck him in his fall, and as he pressed his hand against Steve's chest a faint fluttering told Ned that life was not yet extinct. But if not extinct it was at a very low ebb, and when he had raised his comrade's head and made a rough pillow for it of logs, Ned Corbett sat down in the silence and in the darkness to wait alone for death.

He could do no more for Steve. If he wanted water he could not get it, indeed if he dared to move a yard or two away it was ten to one but that he would never find his way back again. There was food enough in his pack for one more slender meal, and probably the food in poor Chance's pack would never be wanted by him, but when that was gone, unless God gave him back his sight, strong man though he was, Ned Corbett could only sit there day by day in the darkness and starve to death. He wondered whether a death by starvation was painful, whether in such straits as his it would be unmanly to kiss the cold muzzle of his good Winchester and then go straight to his Maker and ask Him what he had done amiss that all these troubles should have come upon him.

But Ned Corbett put the thoughts away from him. Suicide was after all only a way of sneaking out of danger and away from pain—it was a form of "funking;" and though ill luck might dog him, and bully him, and eventually kill him, Ned ground his teeth and swore that it should not make him "funk."

But it did seem hard to think of Steve's sanguine hopes as they sat in their tent by Victoria's summer sea, to think of the weary pack-trail to Williams Creek, the worthless claims, old Roberts' stony face gazing piteously to heaven, the gold in piles at Pete's Creek, and all the rest of it; and then to think that their share in the play must end here, drowned in a forest of pines, lost in the dark and forgotten, whilst that thief would return to the light and live out his days amongst his fellow-men in wealth and honour.

Just at this point the bushes at Ned's feet stirred, and a faint voice murmured:

"Ned—are you there, Ned?"

In a moment Cruickshank was forgotten, and the whole pageant of the unsuccessful past vanished. Steve lived, that was enough for Ned.

"Yes, old man, of course I am. What is it?"

"Where am I, Ned, and what has happened?"

"You've tumbled down and stunned yourself, I think, Steve; but lie still a little and you'll come round all right."

"I don't think that's it, old man. I'm not in any pain, but I think (don't get riled at me)—I think I am going to send in my chips!"

"Nonsense, Steve. Don't make a blessed school-girl of yourself." Corbett spoke roughly to rouse his comrade to fresh effort, but his own voice was very husky in spite of himself.

"It's no good, Ned, you cain't get another kick out of me; and it doesn't much matter, anyway. Do you remember that Indian superstition about the owls hooting when a chief is going to die?"

"One of poor Rob's yarns, wasn't it?"

"Yes, one of Rob's. There! do you hear the owls now? There must be a dozen of them at least."

"What rubbish, Steve; and anyway you aren't a chief, and the owls only hoot for a chief's death."

Chance did not answer, but instead, from somewhere high up in the mountain forest, came a deep hollow "Whōō, whōō!" answered almost immediately from the pines just below where the white men lay.

Again and again the cries reverberated through the forest, and Chance shuddered as he heard the hollow prophecy of death, whilst Corbett, who had started to his feet, stood straining every muscle and every sense to catch each note of that weird hooting.

Suddenly a smile spread over his swollen features as he said: "Do you hear that, Steve?" and at the same moment a sharp "thud, thud" seemed to come through the forest and stop suddenly at the very edge of the clearing in which Ned stood, and Steve turning feebly on his elbow saw a beautiful black and gray face, out of which stared two great eyes, and above it were ears, long twitching ears, which seemed to drink in every forest whisper. For a moment Steve saw this, and noted how the shadow of the fluttering leaves played over the deer's hide, and then there came a sudden flash of white, and in a few great bounds the apparition vanished, clearing six-foot logs as if they had been sheep hurdles.

"A mule deer, wasn't it?" asked Ned, who in spite of his blindness seemed to have understood all that was happening.

"Yes, a mule deer, and a rare big one too. Of course I was too slow and too weak to get the rifle;" and with a groan Steve sank back upon his side and shut his eyes again.

"No matter, Steve, the owls will get him, and we shall have our share. Did you hear that?"

As Ned spoke a rifle-shot woke the mountain echoes, followed by another and another, each shot lower down the mountain than the one preceding it.

"Great Scott, how infamously they shoot!" muttered Ned. "The first fellow wounded him and he isn't down yet. Ah, there—at last!" he added, as a fourth shot was followed by an owl's cry, differing somewhat from those which had preceded the advent of the deer.

"What do you mean, Ned?" asked Chance, who had been sitting up watching and listening open-mouthed to his comrade's soliloquy.

"Mean? Why, Indians, of course. 'Whōō, whōō' means 'where are you?' and 'hè, hè' means 'I've killed, come and help me pack him home;'" and Ned put his hands to his mouth, and drawing a deep breath sent the deep sepulchral call-note of the owl echoing through the forest.

"It's life or death, Steve," he remarked; "if the Indians aren't friendly it's death, but it will be a better death anyway than starving here in the dark."

CHAPTER XXV.

IN THE CAMP OF THE CHILCOTINS.

AS the echoes of Ned's hoot died away amongst the pines, both he and Steve became conscious that they were no longer alone. Someone else had entered the clearing, and a pair of human eyes were intently fixed upon them. This both the white men knew, not by sight or hearing, but by that other sense for which we have no better name than instinct. They had not heard a rustle among the leaves, nor had Steve seen so much as a shadow upon the grass, and yet both men turned simultaneously towards the same point, and Ned, in spite of his blindness, said "*Clahowyah*" as confidently as if he held his visitor by the hand.

"*Clahowyah*" (How do?), repeated a deep guttural voice from the shadow of the pines, and as he spoke a broad-shouldered wiry redskin stepped softly over the logs to meet the whites. If he always moved as silently as he moved then, it was no wonder that the listening deer so often found themselves looking down the barrel of Anahem's Hudson Bay musket before their great ears had given them any warning of their danger.

"Thank God, we are saved," whispered Ned, as the chief's words reached him. "He has traded with whites, or he wouldn't speak Chinook. Lead me up to him."

But Anahem saw the outstretched hand as soon as Chance, and stepping quickly forward took it.

"*Mika halo nanitch?*" (You don't see?), he asked.

"*Halo!*" replied Ned, and he pointed to his swollen eyelids.

CORBETT AND CHANCE ARE FOUND BY A FRIENDLY INDIAN.

"*Mika comtax*—by and by *skookum nanitch*" (I understand, by and by you'll see all right), replied the chief, and then turning he repeated the owl's call twice, and almost immediately a low answer came to him from the woods above.

Luckily for Steve and Ned, the chief of the Chilcotins had met many white men when in his early days he had hunted on the Stikeen river, and all those whom he had met had been servants of a company which has always kept good faith with its Indian neighbours and employés. The honesty and fair dealing of the Hudson Bay Company saved the two white men's lives from Anahem and his tribesmen, as it has saved many a hundred lives both of redskins and whites since the day when the two races first met. Anahem knew that a fresh class of whites had lately come into his country—whites who cared nothing for skins and trading, but who spent all their time digging and making mud-pies by the river banks. He knew it because he had heard of them, had seen their strange canoes upon the Frazer, bottom upwards sometimes; and once he had found one of their tin cups, with something scratched upon it, hanging to a pine-tree, underneath which lay a little pile of bones which the *coyotés* had cleaned.

Probably these men, he thought, were gold-diggers, and lost as that other one had been lost, whose bones he had seen; but at any rate they were both very weak, and one was blind, so for the sake of that great Company which was honest, Anahem determined to help these men, who, within half an hour of their first meeting with the chief, lay warm and at rest within the glow of his camp-fire.

Then it seemed to Steve that their troubles fell away

from them like the forest shadows before the firelight, and it seemed already years ago since he and Ned had sat down in the bushes to die. Anahem's tribe was out for its fall hunt, and Ned and Steve had luckily wandered within the arms of the great drag-net of men, which was still sweeping the hillsides for game. As they lay by the camp-fire Ned and his companion could hear the hunters calling to each other; but the net was broken now, and the cries were the cries of the owl who has killed, not of the owl who still seeks his quarry.

Here and there high up amongst the woods Steve could see a little column of smoke, marking the spot where some belated hunter had made up his mind to pass the night. The fire would serve to cook his food and keep him warm; and if any friend chose to come and help him home with his game, the smoke would guide him. But most of the hunters brought back their game to camp that night, dragging it along the trails, or packing it on their backs, so that before Steve slept he had seen fifteen carcases brought in as the result of this one hunt.

He had often wondered in old days, how men who neither ploughed nor sowed nor kept cattle could manage to live through the long winter months: now he wondered no longer. The Chilcotins had been in camp for a week, and there were only six men amongst them who had muskets, and yet there were four great stacks of raw hides in their camp already—stacks as high as a man's head, and on every bough within a hundred yards of the fires were hanging strips and chunks of deers' meat.

The camp reminded Steve of the appearance of a hawthorn bush, in which a butcher-bird has built its nest,—the whole place was red with raw meat, and there were piles of soft gray down and hair, three and four feet high. These were the scrapings of a hundred hides, roughly cleaned by the Indian women during the week.

In such a camp as Anahem's hunger is an easy thing to cure, and that and blindness were Ned's chief complaints; and even the blindness yielded in a day or two to a certain dressing prepared for Ned by the squaws. But Steve Chance did not recover as easily as Corbett did. The prostration from which he suffered was too severe to be cured by a long night's rest and a couple of square meals. At night he lay and tossed in broken slumbers, and dreams came to him which wearied him more than if he had never slept. He saw, so he said, the gold-camp every night of his life, and Phon the only human being in it; and all the while Phon stood in a flood of gold dust, which rose higher and higher, until it swelled and broke over him and ran on a yellow heavy flood like the flood of the Frazer.

Day after day Ned waited and hoped against hope, until the Chilcotins were ready to strike their camp and go home for the winter. He had already done his utmost to persuade Anahem to search for Phon, but the chief took very little notice of him. Either he thought that Ned like Steve was rambling in his mind, or he did not understand him (for Anahem spoke very little Chinook, and Ned spoke less), or, and that is probable too, he did not think it mattered much what became of a Chinaman; and as to the gold, if it really was there, it would probably wait until the white men could go and look for it themselves. If Ned would have gone with him, Anahem would have gone perhaps to look for the creek; but Ned could not leave Chance whilst he was ill, and Steve would not get well, so that ended the matter.

There seemed only one course open to Ned, and he prepared to take it. Anahem had told him as they talked one night over the camp-fire that he had seen the smoke of a white man's fire coming from a dug-out on the banks of the Frazer.

"How long ago was that?" asked Ned.

"On my way up here, about the time of the young moon," answered Anahem.

"Then that may be Rampike," muttered Ned; and the next day he got Anahem to show him the direction in which the dug-out lay.

"Could I get there in two days?" he asked.

"A *skukum* (strong) Indian could. The sick white man can be there on the third day at nightfall."

This was enough for Ned. Next morning he bought some meat and dried salmon from his Indian friends, and guided by Anahem and followed by Chance he left the camp. If Chance's strength would hold out until they could reach the dug-out, he could nurse him there at his leisure, and by and by, when Steve was stronger, Ned and Rampike could go out together to look for Phon and Cruickshank. It was not impossible after all that they should find Phon still alive, though fish and roots and the inner bark of trees would be all that he could get to live upon. But would Chance's strength hold out? That was the trouble. He was terribly worn and weak, and his eyes shone feverishly, and he neither slept well nor eat well in spite of the fresh keen air. As he followed Anahem up a steep bluff Steve panted and his knees were unsteady, and when the chief stopped at last upon a bald ridge overlooking the pine-woods, he lay back upon his light load saying, "It's as well you've stopped, chief, at last. Another hundred yards, and I should have bucked my pack off."

Anahem looked surprised that even a sick man should complain of such a trifling hill. An old squaw would have carried two sacks (a hundred pounds) of flour up it without a murmur, and Steve's pack did not weigh half that.

"Your bones," he said, smiling rather contemptuously, "white bone, our bones wild bone," and then turning to Corbett he pointed out to him where the deep-bellied Frazer roared along in the valley below the pine-woods, and to one spot upon its banks, where, so he said, was the white man's dug-out.

"You see," he said, "where the sun will set."

"*Nawitka*" (Certainly), answered Ned.

"Now, look on the Frazer's banks under there where the sun will set, and you will see one patch all the same, like blood."

"Yes, I see it."

"Now, look to that side of it," and he waved his hand to the left, "and you will see one great mud-mountain like this;" and with his stick he drew in the sandy soil at his feet a picture of a great cathedral organ, with pipes reaching from the river to the sky.

Ned was startled by the strange likeness which the chief's picture bore to a thing which the chief could never have seen, but he held his peace and looked for the mud-mountain.

"Yes, chief," he said. "I see a great mountain of mud, but I cannot see the shape of it from here."

"Not see the shape of him! Ah, my friend not see well yet," said Anahem pityingly; and though Ned knew very well that his sight was as good as it had ever been, he said nothing.

He didn't want Anahem to think that wild sight like wild bone was better than the civilized samples of the same.

"Well, you see the mountain. By and by you come closer and see his shape. Under that mountain, in the bank on this side the river, stop one white man. You keep along this trail," and Anahem pointed to the track upon which they stood, "along the ridge, and by and by it will go downhill, and on the night of the third day you will see the white man. Good-bye," and before they knew that he was going the old chief turned, and like the shifting shadow of a cloud which the winds blow across the hillside, he moved away and was gone. There was no sound as he went—no twig snapped, no overall scraped against the bushes. In silence he had come, and in silence he had gone. For a moment the two with "parted lips and straining eyes stood gazing where he sank," for indeed it seemed to them as if the sea of the woods had opened and swallowed up their friend. Then Chance spoke:

"A creepy old gentleman, Ned; rather like one of Phon's devils."

"A deuced good devil to us, anyway. If we ever find Phon and the gold we shall owe our good luck to him, as we owe him our lives."

"Yes, I wish he had stopped. I should like to have given him a 'potlatch.'"

"Just as well that you didn't offer him anything. He might have liked this rifle, but I really doubt whether he knows enough about gold-dust to make him value that."

"That's what, Ned. But come on and let us get

through this beastly forest to those open benches below;" and Chance made as if he would burst his way through the barriers of serried pines which intervened between him and the Frazer valley.

"What, again, Steve?" cried Ned. "Isn't one lesson enough for you? If you tried that you would be lost again in ten minutes. No more short cuts for me. I mean to stick to the trail, and you must follow me;" and so saying Corbett took up his bundle and went ahead at a quiet steady pace which, in five or six hours, brought Steve to the land of his desire, where what trees there were were great bull-pines standing far apart, and giving men lots of room for their feet below and wide glimpses of heaven above their heads.

As soon as they reached the open country Chance's spirits improved, and his strength came back with his spirits, but for all that he was still so weak that the progress which Ned and he made was very slow, and their provisions were again at a perilously low ebb when they came in sight of that strange freak of nature, opposite to which dwelt (so they hoped) their old friend Rampike. The bluff was exactly as Anahem had drawn it: an organ cast in some Titanic mould, the pipes of it two hundred feet from base to summit, and stained with all manner of vivid metallic colours. At its foot was the gray Frazer, and the dull sky of early winter hung low about its head; but the organ was dumb from all eternity, unless those were its voices which ignorant men attributed to the winds and the fretting foaming river.

For awhile the two wanderers stood staring in wonder at this strange landmark, and then Steve's weary face lit up with a smile and a mist came over his eyes.

"Ned, as I hope for heaven, there's smoke!" and he stretched out his arm and pointed to where a thin blue column curled up against the sky.

Ned saw the smoke as clearly as Steve, but in spite of Steve's entreaties he absolutely refused to press on towards it.

"No, old fellow, we will camp here for a couple of hours, and you must eat and sleep. That smoke is a long way from here yet, and we may miss it to-night after all when we get low down amongst those sand-hills."

From where they stood the column of smoke looked within a stone's-throw, but Corbett knew well how the clear atmosphere of British Columbia can deceive eyes unused to measure distance amongst her mountains. So in spite of Steve's protestations the two men camped, and though he did not know it, Steve eat Ned's lunch, and Ned carried Steve's away in his pocket in case they should not be able to reach the river by nightfall. That slender ration in Ned's pocket was the very last food which the two men possessed, and Ned was already reproaching himself for his rashness in starting so poorly provided.

"What if after all Rampike should not be at the dug-out, or, if there, should be himself short of grub?"

Luckily for Steve and Ned it seemed as if fortune had almost spent her malice upon them, for that evening as they reached the edge of the last bench above the Frazer, they saw that they had steered a true course. Right below them, issuing from a little black funnel in the mud-bank itself, rose the column of smoke, and in the bed of the river, upon a sand-bar, they could see a man working a cradle.

CHAPTER XXVI.

RAMPIKE'S WINTER QUARTERS.

"HALLO, there! Hallo!" cried Steve as soon as his eyes fell upon the man and his rocker; but Steve's voice was so pitiably weak and small in a country where mud-banks are built like mountains, that it did not even wake an echo.

"Come along, Steve; it's no good shouting for half an hour yet. Look out for the prickly pears!" said Ned, and so saying he plunged into a little ravine, whose beggarly barrenness cried aloud to winter to come and hide it from the face of the sun.

"It's all very well to tell a man to look out for them," answered Steve in the peevish voice of sickness, "but there is nothing else to step on. It's all thorns and sharp stones in this confounded country."

"Never mind, stick to it, old chap."

"Just what I am doing, worse luck to it," muttered Steve, trying to tear himself away from a patch of little cacti upon which he had inadvertently sat down.

Ned turned and saw Steve's plight, and the white woe-begone face of his comrade only heightened the comedy of the position. So that there, at the last gasp, sick and worn-out, these two failures, with their stomachs empty and their soles full of thorns, stood and laughed until the tears rolled down their cheeks.

From the next step in the bench which led to the river Ned joined his deep bass to Steve's, and together they shouted their loudest to attract the man's attention. In vain. Whoever he was the man worked on, bending over his rocker, with the gold fever at his heart and the boom of the great river in his ears.

"It's no good, we must go right down to him," said Ned; and five minutes later he and Steve stood together upon the bar on which the man was at work. But so intent was he upon his rocking, or so silent was the approach of his visitors' bare and bleeding feet over the great boulders, that it was not until Ned's shadow fell upon him that the gold-worker was aware of a stranger's presence.

Then quick as thought he sprang to his feet, snatching up a Winchester as he did so, and covering his men with it before he had time to look into their faces.

"Stand off!" he roared, "or by 'Mity I'll let light through you!" and for the moment it seemed a mere toss-up whether he would shoot or not. But the men he spoke to were as reckless of life as he was. Hardship had taught them that a human life is not such a wonderfully big stake as the fat townsmen seem to think.

"You're in a tearing hurry to shoot, ain't you?" asked Steve coolly. "How would it be if we were to talk first? Don't you know us, Rampike?"

At the first sound of Steve's voice the miner had dropped his rifle into the hollow of his arm, and now he came forward, and holding out a huge hairy paw, yellow with river mud, said simply, "Shake."

It was not a very effusive greeting, but men don't "gush" much in the upper country, and yet that glimpse of a friendly face, and grip of a friendly hand, acted as a wonderful restorative upon the tired natures of both Steve and Ned. The sky itself seemed to get clearer and the mountain air less chill now that they had run against a "pal" once more.

"Wal, sonny, did you strike Pete's Creek?" was old Rampike's first question after they had all three "shaken some."

"We did so," answered Steve.

"Any 'pay' up there?"

"I should smile," replied the Yankee, using the slang of his country, and throwing down the belt of dust which he had clung to through all his wanderings.

"Why, this is free gold!"

"You bet it is; and there is enough for everyone we know and to spare," added Steve, "where that came from."

For a minute or two Rampike only turned the gold over and over in his hands and said nothing. At last he asked:

"Did you git Cruickshank?"

"No, never saw him," answered Ned.

"Praise the Lord you ain't got everything. I ain't sure as I wouldn't ruther look at him through the back-sights of this here, than find a crik like yourn;" and the old man passed his hand caressingly along the barrel of his "44·70."

"But, say, you look mighty hard set. Have you any grub along with you?"

"Not an ounce of flour, and this is the last of our meat;" and so saying Ned pulled out of his pocket the ration which he had kept for Chance.

"It's pretty lucky that I'm well heeled in the way of provisions, ain't it, else we'd all starve. Wal, come along up to the 'dug-out;'" and so saying he picked up his coat and rifle and led up to the bluff, until all three stood before the door of his winter residence.

Next to the homes of the pre-historic cavemen, and a few rude stone-heaps in which the Caucasian Ossetes live, the "dug-outs" along the Frazer river are the most miserable abodes ever fashioned for themselves by men. And yet these holes in the hill, with doors and roofs aflush with the hillside, are better adapted to resist the intense cold of a British Columbian winter than either frame-shack or log-hut.

"Come right in, lads," said Rampike, putting his foot against the planks which served him for a door, and thus rudely clearing the way for his visitors into a little dark interior with walls and floor of Frazer river mud.

A rough table, a solitary chair, and a kind of bench furnished the hovel somewhat more luxuriously than might have been expected, but unless you took a deep interest in geology the walls and general surroundings in Rampike's reception-room were distinctly crude and unpleasant.

If, however, you cared for geology, you could study specimens of the Frazer river system through the wide chinks between the boards which walled the room without even leaving your chair. Indeed, there was more "bed rock," as Rampike called it, than boarding in the composition of his walls.

But neither geology nor furniture attracted any attention from Steve or Ned. When they entered the cabin their eyes lit upon two things only, and it was a good hour before they took any real interest in anything else. The two centres of attraction were a frying-pan and a billy, round which all three men knelt and served, making themselves into cooks, stokers, or bellows, until the billy sang on the hearth and the bacon hissed in the pan.

Then for a while there was silence, and this story does not begin again until someone struck a match upon the seat of his pants. I believe it was Rampike, because, having had more experience than Steve, he could bolt his food faster. I know that it was not Ned, for he could never finish his meal until about the end of Steve's first pipe. Steve said it was because the Englishman eat so much. Ned said that in England men eat their food, in America they "swallered down their grub." "Swallerin' down your grub," he said, "was a faster but less satisfactory process than eating your food." But as I wish to remain upon friendly terms with both disputants, I cannot enter into this matter.

"Do you reckon to go in again this fall?" asked Rampike, without any prelude but a puff of tobacco smoke.

"To the creek?" said Ned, reaching across his neighbour for the billy. "Yes, we must go in, and that soon."

"What's your hurry? Steve here cain't travel, and you're pretty nigh played out though you are hard; and as for the gold, that'll stay right there till spring."

"You forget that there were three of us at Antler. Phon is up at the creek now."

"Phon! What, that Chinee! Is he up at the crik?"

"If he is alive he is," answered Ned. "He may have starved for all I know."

"Starved! not he; but you'll never see *that* heathen agen. He'd live on dirt or nothin' at all, any Chinee can do that; but you bet your life he ain't up there now. He's just skipped out to Victoria by some other road with all the dust he can pack along. That's what Phon has done."

"You don't know him, Jim, and you aren't fair to

him. No westerner ever is fair to a Chinaman. Phon will stay by the creek. My only fear is that we sha'n't be able to find the creek."

"Not find the crik, you say! Why, Ned Corbett, *you* ain't no bloomin' tenderfoot in the woods, are you? You ain't likely to forgit your way to the bank when the whole business belongs to you?"

"Perhaps not, but I've been blind for a week;" and then answering the inquiry in Rampike's eyes, Ned lighted his pipe and told the whole story of his own and Steve Chance's wanderings, from the time when they struck Pete's Creek until their return to the Frazer.

Now and again Rampike broke in upon the thread of the narrative with some pertinent question, or a comment as forcible as a kick from a mule, but he managed to keep his pipe going pretty steadily until Ned came to Steve's feat in "blazing." Then the old man's wrath broke out, and his pipe even dropped from his mouth. For a moment he looked at Steve in speechless indignation, and then he expressed himself thus:

"Strike me pink," he said, "ef a real down-easter ain't a bigger born fool in the woods than any bloomin' Britisher I ever heerd tell on. That's so."

After this there was a pause, during which Steve snored peacefully, and old Rampike, having made an exhaustive examination of the bowl of his pipe, proceeded to refill it with chips from his plug of T. & B.

At length Ned began again:

"You've been looking for the creek yourself, haven't you?"

"No. I stayed right here, making wages on that bar there."

"I wonder who made those camps then which we found along the divide. I can't think that those were Indian camps;" and Ned told his companion of the camps which he and Steve had stumbled upon during their search for Pete's Creek, as well as of that glove found by the bear tracks.

"Bear tracks!" growled Rampike, "not they. A softy who would blaze the wrong side of a tree wouldn't know bear tracks from the tracks of a gal's shoe with a French heel to it. Cruickshank's tracks, that's what *they* was, and ef you don't see more of 'em before you get your gold out of Pete's Crik you may call me the biggest liar in Cariboo!"

"You don't mean to say that you think Cruickshank would dare to dog *us*?"

"Dog *you!* That man would dog the devil for gold."

This was a new idea to Ned. If there was any truth in it, then all Phon's stories of faces seen in the pool, of eyes which watched the gold, of figures which rustled ever so lightly over the dry sal-lal on the canyon's edge, when all save Phon and the night owls slept, all these stories might be something more than the imaginings of a crazed Chinaman's brain.

For a while Ned sat silently smoking and looking thoughtfully into the embers. Then he rose, and knocking the ashes out of his pipe said:

"I am going to look for Phon to-morrow if Steve seems well enough to be left here. Shall you come?"

"Yes, I reckon I may as well. You cain't hev all the sport, sonny. I'm ruther partial to gunning myself."

CHAPTER XXVII

THE SEARCH FOR PHON.

FOR ten days or a fortnight after the conversation recorded in the last chapter, Rampike and Ned Corbett wandered about the country trying to "locate" Pete's Creek.

They started, as they had arranged to, upon the very next morning, leaving Steve Chance with ample provisions, to sleep and eat and rest himself after the hard times which he had been through, or if he wanted a little exercise and amusement there was the bar down below the dug-out upon which he could earn very fair wages by using Rampike's rocker.

From the dug-out to the mouth of the Chilcotin was no great distance, and Ned felt certain that anyone who knew his way to it could reach the camp in which he had left Phon in one day from the river's mouth. Unfortunately neither he nor Rampike knew their way to it, and still more unfortunately they went the wrong way to work to find it. At the end of a fortnight they both saw their mistakes, but it was too late to remedy them. Instead of taking up his own tracks at once and trying to follow them back through the woods to the creek, Ned had taken Rampike up the course of the Chilcotin, in the hope that he would be able to identify Pete's Creek amongst the hundred and one creeks and streams which emptied themselves into the main river from its right bank.

In this he failed signally, and when the search was over it was somewhat late to take up the back tracks, which were already faint and partly obliterated. However, there was nothing else to be done, so Rampike and Corbett started again, following the tracks step by step until they came at last to the Chilcotins' camp. Here they found dead fires and dry bones, and piles upon piles of soft gray fur, and over all these signs of slaughter more than one track of the inquisitive deer whose kinsmen had been so ruthlessly butchered all round. Where the principal camp-fire had stood, was a message written to whomsoever it might concern, a message written with twelve unpeeled sticks, each about six inches long, driven into the ground one behind the other, in Indian file, their tops or heads all bent one way, towards the south.

There were two other sticks, but these were peeled and white, and their heads bowed towards the Frazer.

Old Rampike touched the sticks with the toe of his moccasin.

"Pretty good writin', I call that," said he; "beats school-teachers' English to my mind. 'Twelve Injuns gone south, two whites gone down to the Frazer,' that's what that fellow says, and the piles of fur will tell you why they were all here, and a squint at them bones will give you a pretty fair notion when they went away."

So far, no doubt, the records were plain enough. Unfortunately it had not occurred to the Indian historians to point out from which direction those two whites had come to them, and a short distance outside the limits of the Chilcotin camp all trace of them ceased, for winter had come upon the Chilcotin uplands. The higher Ned went the colder the weather grew, until at last he felt that he had fairly entered the domain of the ice king. On the bald hills the yellow grass was hidden, and on the long pastures the little clumps of pines were powdered and plumed with snow.

All colour had gone from the landscape. There were no more red flushes of Indian pinks amongst the sun-dried grass, no more gleamings of sunlight upon lakes of sapphire blue. All was white, white, dead white, or a still more lifeless gray where the wind had swept the lakelets and left the rough ice bare.

In the glare of the winter sun, ice crystals floated instead of the mites which used to dance in the summer sunshine, and on those gray blots, which had been lakes where ducks called and shook their dripping wings, stood now the mud-huts of the musk-rats, and beside them at the edge of the ice stood their owners, rigid, silent, and watchful, as everything seemed to be in this silent winter-world. As far as the eye could see, in heaven or on the earth, there was nothing which lived or moved except those musk-rats, and you could not tell that they lived until the ice crunched under your feet. Then they vanished. There was no sound. You did not see them go, only when you looked again the little rigid figures were there no longer. Even old Rampike almost shivered as the biting wind caught him when he topped the ridge, and he drew his coat together and buttoned it as he turned to Ned.

"It's real winter up here, sonny, and I reckon it will be mighty lonesome for that heathen of yours by the crik, unless he and Cruickshank hev jined and gone into partnership. I'm beginning to think as he has got starved after all."

Ned made no reply. It *was* horribly lonesome; but if Phon and Cruickshank had met, Ned didn't think that the Chinaman would care whether the sun warmed or the winter wind froze him, whether he lay alone or in the midst of his fellow-men. Ned had a hideously vivid recollection of another snow scene, and of a certain little black bullet hole in the nape of a man's neck.

Well, after all, he reflected, death by gunshot might be preferable to a slow death by starvation and cold, and day by day it became more abundantly clear that neither Rampike nor Ned would find their way to Phon that winter.

The snow had changed the whole surface of the country so thoroughly that even had Ned passed through every inch of it with his eyes open he would never have recognized it again. There were hollows where before there had been hills, hills where there had been hollows. The drifting snow had made a false surface to the land and covered every landmark; and, moreover, the two searchers began to feel that it would not do to remain in the uplands any longer, unless they too would be cut off and buried away from their fellow-men by the tons upon tons of soft feathery stuff which the skies threatened to pour down upon them every day.

"It's no good talking, Ned, we're beat and we've got to give in. If your heathen hasn't skipped out some other way he's a corpse, that's just what he is, and we've no call to risk our skins collecting corpses," said Rampike as he sat in the dug-out, to which the two had returned after nearly three weeks' search for Phon. "The Almighty seems to have a down on you, my lad, someways, and if one may say so without harm, He seems to be standin' in with Cruickshank, but you bet He'll straighten it out by and by. Up to now Cruickshank has won every trick, and you're jest about broke; but no matter, we'll stay right with him all the while, and we'll get four kings or a straight flush and bust the beggar sky-high at the finish: see if we don't. What we've got to do now is jest to hole up like the bars. Winter's coming right away."

It was a long speech for Rampike, but the occasion was a serious one, and the old man felt that it would require all the influence which he could bring to bear to make Ned Corbett accept his defeat, and take some thought for his own safety.

"What makes you think that winter is so close?" Ned asked.

"Wal, there's a many reasons. The weather has been hardenin' up slowly all the while, and yesterday I saw the tracks of a little bunch of ewes along the top of that bench above us. The big-horns are comin' down, and when they come down you may look out for real winter. You bet."

After this there was silence for a time. Steve and Ned were thinking of the long account unsettled between themselves and Cruickshank, and a little too of the weary months during which they must lie dormant, as Rampike said, "like bears in a hole."

At last there was a clatter on the floor. Jim's pipe had fallen from his mouth, and the old man was snoring peacefully in that beauty sleep with which he generally preluded his night's rest.

As he lay there with his coat under his head and his patched flannel shirt turned up to his elbows, showing a hard sinewy forearm, Jim Rampike was a type of that strong wild manhood which flooded the West from '48 to '62, spending its force in a search for gold in spite of nature and in the face of any odds, and yet utterly careless of the gold when won.

Let those who will preach upon the sordid motives

which drew all that muscle and pluck to the West; others will remember how freely the miners squandered that for which they risked so much.

There were no misers amongst the miners of the West; the fortunes they made were mere counters in a game which they played, not for the stakes but for the sake of the game itself—for its very dangers and hardships; and, thanks chiefly to one strong man, who still lives in the country which owes him so much, their game was played in British Columbia with less loss of life and less lawlessness than in any other mining centre in America.

To Jim mining or prospecting was what big game hunting is to richer men. He had prospected alone for months in the Rockies, he had won big stakes in California in the great "rushes," and he had starved and toiled, loafed and squandered in turn, until his hair was as gray as a badger's coat and his lean frame strong and wiry as a wolf's. When he made a pile he set himself diligently to "paint the nearest town red." Drinks for every man and jewellery for every woman he met as long as the dust lasted was his motto; and if the dust which he had taken months to gather would not melt quick enough by fairer means, he would smash costly mirrors, fill champagne glasses only to sweep rows of them down with his cane until the champagne or the dust was all gone, or else he would put every cent upon the turn of a card in the hands of a man whom he knew did not play fair.

In a month at most Jim's spree was over. For that month he had been the most noticeable fool in a town of noisy roisterers; at the end of it he was "dead-broke" again and happy. Then without an idea of the eccentricity either of his own or the gambler's conduct, he would betake himself to that worthy and borrow from him enough gold to begin life again; and to the gambler's credit be it said, that he never refused to grant such a loan, never looked for interest upon it, nor troubled himself much about the return of the capital. Freely if dishonestly he came by his gains, freely at any rate he gave; and many a man owes a good turn to the very men whose delicate sense of touch drew more gold into their pockets than was ever won by any single miner's pick.

They are, after all, only symbols for which we all of us spend our lives, and if the yellow dust led the old man to live the life he loved, and which suited him, what did it matter? As Ned watched the red firelight flicker about the strong square jaw, and redden like blood on the great forearm, he felt that there was at any rate one man in Cariboo in whom he could unhesitatingly trust.

Before turning over to sleep Ned softly opened the door of the hut and looked out. The night was clear and bright, so clear that the hills opposite seemed to have come closer to the hut than they had been by day. Overhead stars and moon seemed to throb with a strange vitality, and burn with a cold fire all unlike the faint and far presentment of stars in an English sky. Nor was the boom of the river, which was as the accompaniment to every song of nature's changing moods, the only sound upon the night air. There was a voice somewhere amongst the stars—a loud clear "Honk, honk!" a cry of unseen armies passing overhead, and Ned as he listened recognized in the cry of the geese another of nature's prophecies of winter.

But the cry of the geese and the boom of the river only emphasized the solitude which reigned around.

Nature was alone on the Frazer that night, except for one great shadowy figure which Ned suddenly became aware of, moving upon the sand-bar upon which he had first seen Rampike. For a while Corbett thought that the moon was playing strange freaks with him, and so thinking he covered his eyes and changed his position. But no, it was no fancy. From side to side with a slow swinging motion the great dark bulk lurched silently along. If its tread had been as heavy as that of a battalion, Ned would not have heard it at that distance through the roar of the river, but that never occurred to him. The form gave him the idea of noiseless motion, and besides, at the second glimpse, he knew the beast that he was watching. The Lord of the Frazer walked in his own domain.

A moment before the mystery of the night had Ned Corbett in its clutches, but the sight of the grizzly banished dreams at once, and the moon a minute later looked down upon another actor in the night's drama, one who hid his shining rifle barrels beneath his ragged coat, and tried hard but in vain to still the loud beatings of his heart; for the sight of so noble a foe stirred the blood of the Shropshireman as fiercely as the sight of the gold had stirred Phon's sluggish blood. But the hunter toils in vain quite as often as his brother the gold-seeker, and when Ned Corbett reached the river bed the bear had gone—gone so silently and so speedily that but for those huge tracks in one of which both Ned's feet found room, Corbett would have vowed that what he had seen was but another shadow of that haunted river bed.

CHAPTER XXVIII.

THE KING OF THE BIG-HORNS.

"THIS here's the last day's huntin' as you'll get for quite a while, and don't you forget it."

The speaker was Rampike, and he spoke with the emphasis of conviction. Ned Corbett, who stood beside him at the door of the dug-out, seemed inclined to argue with him, but Rampike did not wait to hear what he had to say.

"You think," said the old man, "as it ain't partickler cold jest because the air is dry and there's plenty of sunshine. Wait until you get out of the sunshine and you'll know more about it. Why, look there at the old river—she don't close up for nothing."

Ned looked in the direction indicated by Rampike's outstretched hand, and noticed for the first time that on the yellow flood of the Frazer a strange white scum had risen, which seemed to gather as it drifted by so as to almost impede the river's progress in places. This was the beginning of the ice.

"There'll be a bridge to-morrow, I shouldn't wonder, as you mout drive cattle over. If you want any more huntin' you'd better get it to-day. We could do with another sheep or two." And so saying the old man went back into the cabin.

The air of British Columbia is so dry and the sunlight so bright, that until the shadows begin to fall or the wind begins to blow, it never occurs to anybody that the thermometer may have fallen to "ten below." To Ned Corbett, as he shouldered his rifle and climbed the first hill, it seemed that the weather was about what you would expect in England in October, but he changed his mind after he had been for five minutes in a narrow gully with a northern aspect into which no sunlight came. There indeed he began to wonder why, in spite of his toil, he earned no healthy glow such as exercise should bring, and even when he emerged upon the top of the bench he was almost afraid to open his mouth lest the bitter cold should creep down his throat and freeze his vitals.

But there was that upon the glittering snow-covered table-land which diverted his attention from the cold. At first he thought that the herds of some distant rancher had wandered to the Frazer, and were now feeding before him in little mobs and bunches of from ten to twenty head. There were so many beasts in sight, and in the wonderfully clear atmosphere they looked so large, their dark coats contrasting with the snow upon which they stood, that it never occurred to Ned that they were sheep.

A second glance, however, revealed the truth, just as a second thought reminded him that there was no rancher then in British Columbia from whom these herds could have wandered.

Here and there Ned could see the yellowish-white sterns of a band feeding from him, or the splendid sweep of a noble pair of horns against the clear sky. These were no domestic cattle, bred to be butchered, but a great army of big-horns driven from their mountain haunts by the advance of winter. For a while Ned lay and looked at them as they scraped away the snow to get at the sweet sun-dried grasses beneath, and then he began to consider how best he might win some trophy from them with which to adorn the hall of that long, low house of his father's which looked from Shropshire across the hills to Wales.

There were giants amongst them, Ned could see that, and his fingers itched to pull the trigger at more than one great ram; but the chiefs of the herd, nine in number, lay like nine gray images of stone in the middle of a level, park-like expanse, round which the smaller beasts fed and kept guard. For a long time Corbett lay and looked at the silent nine, with their heads turned in different directions, as if each had undertaken to watch one particular quarter for a coming foe. At last one of the nine rose slowly, and stood looking intently towards Corbett. At the moment he himself had risen somewhat upon his hands and knees to get a fairer view of the coveted horns, and possibly at a thousand yards the ram had seen enough of Ned's cap above the sky-line to make him suspicious. Had a gray-faced old ewe seen as much she would have given the alarm, but the ram was bolder or more careless.

For ten minutes Corbett had to remain as he was, his head rigid, and the spines of a prickly pear running into the palms of his hands. At the end of that time the ram lowered his head, turned round, and lay down again. It was only an odd-looking boulder, he thought, after all; but had he looked ten minutes later the ram would have missed that boulder upon the sky-line, for Ned Corbett was going at his best pace downhill to a point from which he thought that he could creep to within two hundred yards of his prey.

Ned was going at his best pace, because the sun stood so high in the heavens, that under ordinary circumstances the sheep would have already been on the move for the timber.

As it was there could not be much time to spare in spite of the temptations of the new-found pasture, and as Ned's snow-clogged moccasins kept letting him down upon the hillside, he just lay where he fell, and, in his own words, "let himself rip" until he reached the bottom. There he pulled up with a jerk, a somewhat bruised and breathless person, but utterly reckless of such small matters as bruises if he could only get up to his point of vantage in time.

Alas for the hopes of mortals! When Ned Corbett had reached the top of the opposite bank his breath was coming thick and short, and great drops of perspiration were splashing on to the snow from his brow, but there was not one single sheep in sight where half an hour before he had seen five hundred. The white table-land was empty. Ned could have seen a sparrow on it if there had been one to see, but there was no living thing there, only across and across it were the tracks of many feet, and in one place where the rams had been, long plunging tracks, and then, as it were, a road along which the herd had trotted steadily away to the timbered gulches above. That stalker's curse, the wind, had brought some hint of Ned's presence to the watchful beasts, and they had not waited for anything more.

"Confound the wind!" Ned muttered, "I'll be shot if I can understand how it happened;" and plucking a few hairs from his yellow head he let them go, and watched them as they drifted straight back into his face.

"The wind is all right now," he growled. "Well, I've not done with them yet;" and having made quite sure that the nine chiefs had gone up a certain gully, he began to make another detour in order to get above them.

Up and up he went, the snow getting deeper as he climbed higher, and the trees growing wider apart. Now and again he had to force his way through a thick place of young pines, where, as his shoulders brushed against them, the boughs discharged whole avalanches of soft, heavy snow upon his head, half blinding him for the moment. Once he saw the sunlight gleam upon what looked like a spear-head low down on the other side of a pine-bole, but as he looked a big brown ear flickered forward beside the spear-head, and next moment a great stag had risen, and for half a second stood looking at the intruder. But Ned let the stag go. He did not want stags just then, and, besides, in the green timber on the ridge where he stood there were lots of them, and all large ones. The little fellows lived lower down, it seemed.

So he pushed on, until all at once the frost got hold of him. In a moment his heart seemed to stop beating, his knee remained bent in the very act of climbing over a log, his hands stuck to his sides, and his eyes stared as if he had seen a ghost. Right below him, not sixteen paces away, stood the statue of the thing he sought. It could not be a live beast; it was too still. Only for a second Ned dared to look before he sank into the snow behind a juniper bush, but in that second he saw that what he looked on was the statue of an old, old ewe, big almost as a six-year old ram, and gray with age, her villainously-inquisitive head turned (luckily for Ned) downhill. For a few seconds the ewe stood searching the depths of the gully below, and then, without so much as a glance uphill, tossed her head in the air and walked silently forward past Corbett's hiding-place. One after another, all at the same sober pace and all as silent as shadows, ten or a dozen old ewes went by in the footsteps of the first.

Then there was a little noise—you would not have heard it anywhere else, but in the silence of the snow it was quite loud—and forty or fifty ewes and lambs went by, all, even the lambs, looking inquiringly down into the gully below, but none of them wasting so much as a glance upon the ground above them. After the lambs had gone by there was a pause, a break in the stream, and Corbett's heart began to throb louder than it had any right to. So far he had not even drawn a bead upon the sheep. Sixty beasts at least had gone by him one after another within sixteen paces, and he had let them go. He knew well from experience that the last comers would be the rams, and last of all would come the master of the flock. There was a kind of knoll just below him, and the first sight he got of each new-comer was upon this. One after another the sheep appeared, like figures upon a pedestal, at this spot, stood awhile, gazed, and then passed on. At last a ram stood there, his great horns standing out very wide from his head. "Not of much account," thought the hunter. "He's a four-year old; maybe fourteen inches round the butt—not more anyway," and he let him go.

Twice after that Ned raised his rifle and refrained. The biggest had not come yet. At last he could stand it no longer. How could he tell that the beauty before him was not the master ram? and if so, in another second he would be gone. The rifle rang through the mountains, a dozen blue grouse rattled out of the pines and swung downhill on wide, motionless wings, the ram toppled right over and went bumping down the gully out of sight. There was a wild rush of hurrying feet and the thud, thud of beasts that leapt from rock to rock, and then all was still. Rushing forward in the direction taken by the herd, Corbett found himself stopped by a ravine—a deep-cut, uncompromising cleft in the rock, bare stone on either side, and a sheer fall between of some hundreds of feet, and from side to side not less than twenty-five to thirty feet across. Ned stopped dead. This was beyond any man's power, even with a fair run and a good take-off, and yet every lamb in that band had jumped it—jumped it clear!

As he stood marvelling at the great leap before him, a stone rattled down from the other side of the ravine, and raising his eyes Corbett saw what many a man has sought season after season in vain, a ram, big and square-built as a mountain pony, with great horns curling close against his head in a perfect curve, horns which measured at the very least, eighteen good inches round the butt.

Ned had only a second to look at him in, and even before he could pull the trigger the ram had turned; but for all that Ned heard the loud smack of his bullet, and he knew that it was not the rock against which it had struck.

"Got him right on the shoulder-blade," he muttered, as he started full of hope to circumnavigate the head of the ravine. It was a long way round, but Ned got over the ground quickly, and soon found his wounded beast hobbling slowly away upon three legs. For two solid hours Ned followed his ram, who, in spite of his wound, could go just fast enough to keep his pursuer out of range.

Meanwhile the sun was sinking fast, and in spite of himself Ned had to admit that he must give up the chase. Even for an eighteen-inch head he dared not risk a night out on these mountains with the thermometer at ten degrees below zero. "Just one more ridge," he muttered to himself, "and then I'll give him up;" and so muttering he climbed painfully through the deep snow to the top of yet one more of those little ridges, over so many of which he had climbed that day. As his head came over the sky-line, Ned's heart dropped into his boots, and he felt the sickness of despair. The ram had vanished. He could see for half a mile in front of him, but there was no ram. Could it be that after all that weary tramp, and in spite of all those great splashes of blood, his prey had gathered fresh strength, and making a final effort had got clean away from him? For a moment Ned thought that it must be so, but the next his eye lighted upon what looked like a great gray boulder, a boulder though which had no snow upon it, and which moved ever so little. Then as he rushed forward the gray thing staggered to its knees, lurched heavily forward, and lay still again. A few seconds later Ned Corbett's hands clutched the solid crown of one who had been a king amongst the high places of the earth.

But there was no time for rest, much less for exultation. The crimson of the setting sun was already beginning to flush along the forest floors, and Ned, as he looked over the country below him, felt his heart grow sick at the thought that if he returned as he came he could not reach the hut before dark.

Was there no other way—no short cut? Ned rather thought that there was, and determined to try it. Instead of going up and down every gully on the face of the range, he would make for the edge of the divide and follow it round until he reached a point opposite to his camp, then he would descend, taking his chance of finding an easy way down. But before starting on his homeward journey, Ned hacked off the head of his victim and bound it (a heavy load) upon his own shoulders. If he had to stop out all night and risk death by frost-bite, he might as well take with him a souvenir of his hardships should he be lucky enough to survive them. As for the meat, Rampike and Steve could help him bring that in, later on. If the *coyotés* let it alone it would keep well enough; and Ned thought that a rag, which he had drawn through his rifle barrels and fastened to the carcase, would keep off the *coyotés*.

Having made his preparations he started, and toiled steadily until he reached the ridge, where the walking became infinitely easier. Ned had not much time to look about him, but for all that his eyes were not shut, and he could not help noticing one valley some distance away in the opposite direction to his camp. It seemed to him that he had seen that valley before, but it was far off, and the light was failing.

It was night when Ned reached the dug-out; there was a harsh grinding sound down in the river bed, and his clothes, which had been wet with perspiration, were frozen stiff and cold. But as he gazed at his ram's head, Ned Corbett was content.

CHAPTER XXIX.

PHON'S RETURN.

THE day after Ned Corbett's sheep-hunt was too cold even to go and bring in the carcase. A wind had risen, not much of a wind it is true, but just enough to drive the cold right through a man like blades of sharp steel, so that Ned and Steve and Rampike remained in the dug-out, smoking and trying to keep warm, or from time to time going to the door to watch the great river gradually yielding to the power of the frost.

The white scum of the day before had grown into blocks and hummocks of ice, and these came down grinding and roaring through the mist. In one more night the great Frazer would be fettered for the winter.

In the mist which hung over the freezing waters, everything assumed unnatural proportions. Rocks loomed out like mountains, bushes like forest trees, and a sneaking fox looked larger than a grizzly bear.

It was a weird scene, and it held Corbett and his companions fascinated until the bitterness of the cold drove them back for a few moments to their fire.

In this way they spent their day until nearly three o'clock, when the light began to fail, and Corbett, who was at the door, cried to Rampike, who was inside the hut:

"Great Scott, Jim, come here! What is that?"

"That" to which Corbett's pointing finger called attention was a strange upright mass of ice, which came riding towards them upon a little floe, a floe which later on was caught and whirled round and round in a backwater of the river just below the cabin.

"A tree, ain't it, Steve?" said Jim, appealing to Chance, who had followed him out. "A tree, I reckon, Ned, as has got wedged in somehow among the drift."

"Yes, I guess it's a tree," Steve assented. "But what with the mist and the way the thing dances around, it's mighty hard to tell what it is."

"Well, I'm getting as full of fancies as a woman,"

said Ned, "but I could have sworn when I saw it first, that that thing was a man."

"A man? By heaven, it *is* a man!" yelled Jim. "Look, look!" and with white, scared face he stared at the thing as it came circling round again in the endless, meaningless dance of the drift through the mist.

"If it's a man, it is no good standing here," said Corbett quickly. "Bear a hand to drag him ashore." And snatching a rope from the inside of the hut, he sprang down the steep bank to the shore, though the faces of his followers showed plainly enough that, terrible as dead men always are to the living, there was something about this river-waif which made him a horror greater even than the dead who die on land.

By some strange chance the body (for it was a body) had got jammed between two pieces of drift in such a manner that it stood upright, waist-high above the flood, bowing and curtseying with every movement of the water, but so coated with ice that, but for its general outline and a rag of clothing which still fluttered from it, none could have guessed its nature.

For a moment Corbett feared that it would break out of the backwater, and be whirled down the stream before he could get his rope over it; but no, the stream had not done with its plaything yet. The winter would be a long one, and what matter if this wayfarer by the Frazer tarried even a day and a night in the backwater? The rocks had stayed there for hundreds of years. There was no hurry about such things. Round and round in the same order came the hummocks, a bit of a wrecked canoe on one, on the next only the wreck of a man. Round and round whirled the long loop of Corbet's lariat, until the silent rider came bowing past him within his reach. Then the

rope flew out, and the long loop poised and settled
silently about the rider's neck. Quick as thought
Ned was jerked upon his knees, and for a moment it
seemed as if the angry river would suck him in and
add him to the number of its ghastly dancers. But
Ned was young and strong and loved life, so that he
stayed himself against a great boulder and called aloud
for help.

"Hold on to the rope!" he yelled to his comrade.
"The thing fights like a salmon!"

Do you know what it is to feel the electric thrill
which travels all down your spine when you stick in a
good fish? do you know how his every struggle vibrates
along your own nerves, until your heart almost stops
with excitement? If you do, you may be able to picture
what those three men felt as the frozen corpse plunged
and struggled on the rope, now sucked down by the
under-tow, now springing beneath the buffets of the
drifting ice. Ned shuddered and felt sick as he braced
himself against its unholy strength; but the Shropshire breed is like the bull-dog's, once fast in anything
it will never let go whilst life lasts; so that in spite of
the river, and the fear which chilled his marrow, Ned
persisted until he drew his ghastly capture hand over
hand to shore.

There is something very horrible in the helpless
way in which the head of a drowned man rolls about
when you lay him down once more upon dry land, but
even that is not so ghastly as were the actions of the
warped and rigid mummy which Corbett and his
friends carried to their cabin.

From the waist up the body was stiff and straight,
but below the waist the legs had been frozen into such
strange curves and angles, that when they laid it down

upon the floor the corpse went rolling and bumping over and over, and then lay rocking to and fro as if it would never be still. Every gust of wind set it in motion again, and the horror of the thing grew to such an extent that Ned at last rose, saying:

"I can't stand this, boys; the thing seems to be laughing at us. Let's fix it in a chair so as to keep it still until morning."

"And what are you going to do with it, then?" asked Chance.

"Bury it, I suppose, Steve. Oughtn't we to?"

"Wal, I don't want to dictate to no man, but ef you're goin' to make a practice of bringing corpses to this shanty, I quit," remarked Jim, who had been strongly opposed to robbing the Frazer of its prey from the first.

"Don't cut up rough, old chap. If your body was going down in that seething hell of waters, you'd be glad if anyone would drag you ashore and give you decent burial. Let it bide until to-morrow, Jim, and I'll bury it myself."

"Very well. That's a go. Now just lend a hand to cinch him on to this chair for the night, so as he won't be crawlin' around in the dark;" and old Jim with Ned's assistance fastened the body into a chair which stood by the rough deal board which served them for a table, and there left it.

Why is it that, to even the boldest men, the dead are so very terrible? Is it their inhuman calm, their silence, or the mystery to which they alone hold the key, that awes and chills the hottest human heart? Whatever the cause of it, the nameless terror exists, and neither strong Ned Corbett, nor scoffing Chance, nor hard old Jim were proof against it. With that *thing* sitting in their one seat waiting for the morning to come that it might be buried, all three men crept away into the furthest corner of their tiny shack, and, trembling at every log which creaked and sputtered on the hearth, covered their heads with their blankets and prayed for daylight to come.

But the hours of the night are longer than those of the day. The lesson-books say that the twenty-four hours are all of the same length, just sixty minutes of sixty seconds in each, but the lesson-books lie. Who that has lain awake from midnight till dawn will believe that the six hours before sunrise are no longer than the six which succeed sunset? Of course they are longer, but the hours of that one night in the hillside above the fast-freezing Frazer were the longest since God made the world.

Down below the listeners could hear the grinding and roaring of the frozen river, and the shriek of the rising night wind as it tore through the deep canyons. Now and again a loud report echoed in the stillness as an ice-crack spread from side to side of some frozen mountain lake, and all night long there were inarticulate murmurs and groanings of water prisoned beneath ice, and the long howling of starved wolves amongst the snow.

The Indians believe that their dead hunters assume the forms of wolves, and if so, the whole of the dead Chilcotins were out hunting, adding their hideous voices to those other voices of the night, which had in them nothing that was familiar, nothing that was in sympathy with man or man's daily life. It seemed to the sleepless listeners that their own souls had lost their way and strayed into some waste place, where it was always winter and always night, and then as they strained their ears so that they could hear the beat of each others' hearts, a terrible thing happened.

It was only a chair which creaked, but the creaking of it seemed to deaden every other sound, and nature herself held her breath to listen. There it was again! Creak, creak, creak, and a scraping sound upon the mud floor. Unless the ears of three men had gone crazy with fright, that grisly visitor of theirs was pushing its chair along the floor as if it would rise up and be gone. All through the night the noises went on: the chair creaked, the feet of the dead moved upon the floor, and once in the dim light of early dawn, one who dared to look for a moment, fancied that he saw a long lean hand move slowly across the table.

Yet even fear yields at last to sleep, and before the full dawn came there were four sleepers in that hut, —three who should wake and one who should sleep on for ever, and all four comrades, who for a little while had pursued that will-o'-the-wisp, Wealth, together.

For the dead man was Phon!

The ice shroud which had hidden him before had melted in the night, and the strength of the frost had gone out of his poor dead limbs, and in the searching white light of the day he lay huddled up on the chair, his head fallen forward upon the table, and his body a limp mass of faded blue rags.

Even before Ned raised his head they all knew him, and when Ned pointed silently to a little dark spot at the nape of the dead man's neck, no one expressed any surprise.

There had been just such another mark at the nape of dead Robert Roberts' neck.

"Two!" groaned Rampike. "My God, two of 'em, and we ain't beginning to get level with him yet!"

Before they saw the corpse upon the previous evening the men had been sitting, according to their wont, round their rough table smoking and poring over Chance's old map of British Columbia.

That map was the nearest approach to a book in their possession, and they often studied it and made yarns about it; but the night of Phon's arrival all three had bent over it with more than their ordinary interest, because Ned had told them of his fancy that he had recognized a certain valley from the main ridge. It was just in front of this map that the corpse had been placed, when Rampike had cinched it into its chair for the night.

"I guess we had better clear 'em all away," said the old man after a pause, and with a comprehensive wave of his hand he indicated the corpse and the map, the cups and the half-smoked pipes which still littered the table.

Ned and Steve came to their comrade's assistance, and the three made as if they would lift Phon from his seat, but at the very first touch all shrank back, while Chance cried out:

"Look at its hand! Look, look, it is writing!"

Like men in a nightmare the three stood, unable to move or to speak, whilst that long lean hand which lay upon the map moved slowly along. Like the finger of a clock, or a shadow upon a dial, it crept along slowly, slowly, and ever as it went they heard the grating of one long untrimmed nail against the canvas.

It seemed to the onlookers that the hand took hours to travel across three inches of the map, and then the limp body gave a lurch and slid with a soft heavy thud to the ground.

The slight movement caused by Jim's first touch had disturbed the balance of the body, out of which all the rigid strength of the frost had now gone, so that the slackened muscles left to themselves shrank up and collapsed. This was what really happened, but to Rampike and the rest it seemed that the dead wrote.

"That's jest what he's come for. Thet's the way to Pete's Crik as he's bin a showin' you, and thet's where you'll find the man as shot him and old Rob. Bear a hand, we can carry him out now. I guess there ain't no call for him here any longer." And so saying Rampike took hold of the corpse, and with Ned's assistance bore it out and laid it down upon the snow.

Upon the map upon which Phon's dead hand had rested there was a fine wet line drawn by his nail—a line which led from the very spot where the dug-out stood upon the bank of the Frazer, to a point upon the right bank of the Chilcotin, a good deal to the north of the spot at which Corbett believed that the gold-camp lay.

Steve Chance took a pencil, and whilst the others bore out the body he marked the line carefully, that it might not dry up and vanish away. Even as he did so, a wild cry which he knew well came from the bench above the cabin. It began in a low key, and rose higher and higher until it was like the wail of a banshee, then it died away sullenly, and Steve heard Rampike's voice outside the cabin calling to him:

"Come along and lend a hand, Steve. If we don't bury him pretty soon those blasted wolves will get him."

Steve hurried out, and together the three tried hard to make some sort of a grave for Phon in the hillside. They might as well have tried to dig into adamant.

"It ain't no good," growled Rampike at length; "and if you jest bury him in the snow the wolves 'll get him. Not as it matters much."

"We'd better put him back in the Frazer than leave him here," said Ned.

"That's so. He cain't stay in the cabin now as he's thawed out, but I ain't sure as we can get him back agen into the river."

Jim was right.

The earth which the Chinaman had robbed of its hidden treasure refused to receive him; the friends he had lived amongst would have none of him, now that death's seal was upon him; and even the river, which had spewed him up upon its banks, had now closed its portals against him, so that it was only after half an hour's hard labour that Chance and Corbett were able to hew out a hole in the solid ice, through which to send back its dead to the Frazer.

For one moment Ned Corbett stood with his hat in his hand, looking up to the sky, wondering whither the spark of life had gone and commending it to its Creator, and then he pushed the body head first through the hole. The ice round the spot where the three men stood was clear and still fairly thin, so that they saw, or thought that they saw, a face pressed against it for a moment, staring with wild eyes towards the world of the living, and then the stream caught it and it shot down and was gone.

The man had dreamed all his life of the golden secrets which lay in the bed of the mighty Frazer. He had looked forward to the days when he should carry the golden spoils of British Columbia to his own sunny land; but fate had mastered him, and though his body might roll amongst those golden sands, and his dead hands touch the heavy nuggets, it would profit him nothing. The dead have no need of gold!

CHAPTER XXX.

CRUICKSHANK AT LAST!

AFTER the burial of Phon there was no more rest for the men in the "dug-out." The Frazer was frozen hard, and offered a firm white way by which the three outcasts might return to some place where there were warmth and light and the voices of their fellow-men. But none of the three cared to profit by this way of escape. To them a mist seemed always to hang over the river, and the voices of the dead came to them through it; and to Ned Corbett it seemed that day and night one mournful old tune rang in his ears, and day and night Rampike polished his rifle and thought of the "pal" he had lost, and the murderer who had escaped him.

"It ain't no manner of use, Ned," he said one day towards the end of winter, when the ice was already breaking up. "I know as I might jest as well stay another month, and then go with you to look for this crik. But I cain't do it. Somethin' keeps callin' to me to git, and I mean makin' a start to-morrow whether you and Steve come or stay."

They had been together all through the dreary winter, and had hoped to go out together in the spring, back to that summer land by the sea from which they had all come. They were weary for awhile of the rush and struggle for wealth, and were pining for the smell of the salt waves and the drowsy lap of the sea upon the shore. They had talked over these things together when the noonday was dark with falling snow, and now that spring was at hand they little liked the idea of being parted.

"Hold hard, old man," said Corbett. "Let us see if we can't arrange to go together. Which way do you think of going?"

"Thar's only one way, the way as *he* showed us," answered Rampike, nodding over his shoulder towards the river down which Phon had gone to his rest.

For a few minutes Corbett made no answer, but sat staring fixedly out of the little window at the Frazer.

"It's infernal foolishness," he said at last—"infernal foolishness, I know, and yet I feel as you do, Jim. I shall never rest until I have tried Phon's way. I'm getting as superstitious as a Siwash."

"Superstitious is a mighty long word, but it don't amount to much. There's a heap of things happens as you cain't account for."

"Perhaps," assented Ned, and then took up once more Steve's ragged map of British Columbia, and studied for the hundredth time the course traced upon it by the dead man's nail.

"It runs south-south-east from here," he said.

"Yes, I know, and that'll be clar up that bluff and on to the divide, and then over a lot of gulches, I reckon, until we strike the Chilcotin. It'll be a pretty rough trail, you bet."

"Well, rough or smooth, Jim, if Steve doesn't mind waiting here for us, I'll come with you and start as soon as you please. What do you say, Steve?"

Now Steve Chance, as the reader knows, was by nature a decent obliging fellow, and, moreover, Steve had had all the rough travel that he cared about for years to come, so he answered readily enough.

"If you'll pass me your word that you'll be back

inside of three weeks, I'll stay. But you don't expect to see Cruickshank, I hope?"

"I know as we shall see him," said Rampike quietly. "Summat tells me as *his* time's up."

The very next day Rampike and Corbett started up the bluffs above the dug-out. Down below them the ice in the Frazer was already beginning to "run," but the snow on the mountain-sides lay hard and unmelted still, so that travelling without snowshoes was fatiguing in the last degree. From the top of the ridge the two men got a good view of the country through which they had to travel. The mountains, as far as they could see, followed the course of the Frazer until its junction with the Chilcotin, where they bent into a kind of elbow; in fact the two rivers and their attendant mountains formed two sides of a triangle, between which lay gulches and ravines innumerable, and the base of this triangle was the course laid out for them by Phon.

"Looks as if that Chinee corpse had bin laughin' at us after all," muttered Rampike. "A man would want wings to cross that country."

"Never mind, let's try it, Jim," said Corbett; and together the two men pressed on, floundering sometimes up to their armpits in the deep snow, and sometimes finding an easy way where the country at first sight appeared impassable.

On the third day of their journey, towards evening, they entered a narrow snow-choked canyon, which seemed to lead through the second main ridge of mountains to the Chilcotin.

As they entered this canyon Ned Corbett paused and looked searchingly up and down it, as if looking for some sign to distinguish it from its fellows.

But he found none. Like a hundred others which they had seen, this gully was deep and narrow and full of snow. The pines which grew on its sides seemed only just able to keep their heads above the white flood. Somewhere far down below, no doubt, there was a creek, which sang and flashed in the summer sunlight; but it was buried now out of sight by the snow and gagged by the frost.

"Do you think you know this here place, Ned?" asked Rampike, who had been watching his comrade's face.

"I *feel* as if I did, and yet I can't see anything, Jim, that I could swear to."

"Is that so? Well, it's no matter, because we must stick to this canyon anyway. It leads out on to the Chilcotin," replied the old man, and so saying he led on.

After a while he paused.

"Say, Ned, is that a sheep-trail across there on the other side?"

Ned looked hard in the direction indicated, shading his eyes with his hand to get a better view.

"It looks more like a bear's trail," he replied, "only the bears are all holed up still."

"It's pretty well used, whatever it is, and I guess we should find it a sight better travelling there than it is here. Shall we try it?"

As it happened the snow was exceptionally deep where the two men stood, so that they sank up to their knees at every step. A beaten trail of any kind would therefore save them an infinite amount of labour.

"Yes, let's," said Ned, with the brusqueness of a man who needs all his breath for other uses.

To get to the trail Corbett and Rampike had to cross the canyon, and in places this was almost impossible, both men sinking from time to time almost out of sight in the snow.

Twice Rampike voted that they should give up the attempt, and twice Corbett persuaded him to go on.

At last, sweating and trembling with exertion, they got clear of the worst of the snow and stood upon the edge of the trail.

For a moment no one noticed anything. They were both too tired to use their eyes even. Then a sudden gleam of triumph flashed into Rampike's face, and he swore savagely between his teeth, as he was wont to do when anything moved him deeply. Bending over the trail he scrutinized it carefully, fingering the soiled snow, and making an impression with his own foot that he might compare it with the tracks before him.

When he raised his face to Corbett's he had regained all his old coolness, but there was a cold glitter in his eyes which spoke of repressed excitement.

"What is it, Jim?" asked Corbett.

"What is it? Don't you see? It's the trail of the bar we've bin' huntin' this long while, that's what it is. I suppose we'd better toss for the shot."

The trail was the trail of a man. The moment Corbett looked carefully at it he saw that; and yet, cold-blooded as it seemed to him afterwards, he never hesitated for a moment, but when Rampike produced a coin and sent it spinning into the air, cried "Heads!" with all the eagerness of a boy tossing for first innings in a cricket match.

"Tails it is! That thar is a lucky coin to me," said Rampike; "that's why I always pack it around." And so saying he replaced an old English shilling in his pocket and began examining the lock of his Winchester, whilst Ned looked anxiously up and down the valley as if he expected every moment to see their foe come into sight.

"Oh, no fear of his comin' just yet awhile," said Jim, noticing his comrade's glances. "He went up the canyon about an hour ago, and I don't reckon as he'll be along this way agen before morning. I wonder what he's up to, anyway?"

To men like Rampike and Corbett the testimony of the trail upon which they stood put some facts beyond all dispute. That some man who wore moccasins used it at least twice a day, and had so used it for a month past, they knew as certainly as they knew anything. That he had passed along the trail within the hour they also knew, and that he was Cruickshank they guessed with a confidence which left no room for doubt.

"I guess, Ned, as this here must be Pete's Crik as we've got into."

"That is what I've been thinking for some time," replied Ned.

"Then that's his trail to the diggings from the river. But what does he want at the river so often? That licks me."

As Ned had no explanation to offer, the two stood silent for a moment, until the old man's eyes fell upon the tracks which he and Ned had made across the canyon.

"If we don't hide those we shall scare our game," he muttered. "Lend a hand, Ned, to cover some of them up."

"I guess that'll do," he admitted, after half an hour's hard work. "Looks as if a bar had come across until he smelled them tracks of his and then turned back agen. Cruickshank 'll never notice, anyway, so we may as well foller this trail to the river. Step careful into his tracks, Ned. I'd like to see what he has been at on the river."

These were the last words spoken by either Corbett or Rampike for quite half an hour, during which they followed one another in Indian file, stepping carefully into the same footprints, so that to anyone but a skilled tracker, it would appear at first sight that only one man had used the trail.

At the end of half an hour they paused. The roaring of a great river was in their ears, and the grinding of a drift ice.

"That's the Chilcotin," whispered Corbett.

"The Frazer, more like," replied Rampike. "Yes, I thought as much," he added a moment later as he came round a corner of the bluff round which the trail ran. "We've struck the junction of them two rivers. This creek runs in pretty nigh the mouth of the Chilcotin."

Almost whilst he was yet speaking, Corbett caught the speaker by the belt and dragged him down in the snow at his side.

In spite of the suddenness and roughness of such treatment the old man uttered no protest. The question he wanted to ask was in his eyes as he turned his head cautiously and looked into his comrade's face, but with his lips he made no sound.

Putting his lips to Jim's ear, Ned whispered: "There's a canoe just below us on the beach, lie still whilst I take a look at it;" and then he crawled away upon his belly until he could peer from behind a boulder on the sky-line, at the valley below.

In that valley, between steep banks and piles of great ice-worn boulders, the last two hundred yards of the Chilcotin river rushed by to join the Frazer, and amongst these boulders, at the very edge of the open water, lay a rough Indian canoe.

At the side of the canoe the trail stopped.

"So that's the carcase as we have to watch," said Rampike's voice in Ned's ear. "There's no need to keep down, lad, he ain't here. Let's go along the trail and take a look." And so saying Rampike rose and walked down to the canoe.

The sight which there met his eyes and Ned's struck both men dumb for a while with wonder.

What they saw was the work of one man, in one winter, without proper tools, without sufficient food, and with the awful odds against him of place and weather.

"The devil fights hard for his own," muttered Ned; and indeed it seemed as if one man, unaided by supernatural powers, could not have accomplished what this man had done.

Corbett forgot that the greed of gold is almost a supernatural power. Out of the trunk of a tree, felled by his own hands, the man who dwelt in this snow-choked canyon had made himself a canoe, his one tool the blade of his axe. The canoe so built was neither beautiful nor strong, but it was just strong enough for a fearless man to risk his life in, and beautiful enough, when it had its cargo on board, to tempt nine men out of ten to risk their souls to obtain it.

For the cargo of that canoe was the world's desire—the omnipotent, all-purchasing gold! In a hundred small sacks this cargo was stored away, each sack made either of deer-skin or the clothes of the man who made them. He had risked his life and sacrificed the blood of others to get the yellow dust, and now he gave the very clothes from off his back, in spite of the bitter winter cold, to make sacks to save it in. As Ned looked and counted the sacks, and thought of old Roberts and Phon, of the money wasted and the toil unrewarded, he sighed. For the first time he regretted that he had lost the toss.

"Wal, come on, Ned," said Rampike, breaking in upon this train of thought suddenly, "I'm goin' to watch right here. It's mighty lucky as we came when we did. That fellow means to skip as soon as ever the river clears."

Ned said nothing, but in silence followed his companion to a lair behind a great block of gray stone, from which they could look down upon the trail opposite to them.

"I guess it's safest here, though if the ice breaks up a bit more we sha'n't be able to get back if we want to," said Rampike; for in order to reach a position which commanded Cruickshank's trail, Rampike had led the way across the river, stepping warily across the ice, which was already split up into great pieces, which ground against each other and moved slowly with the stream.

"It's not more than a hundred yards, I reckon, and I'll back her to shoot good that far, even by moonlight," were the last words which Rampike muttered as he drew a bead upon an imaginary figure on the trail across the river, and after this silence came and wrapped the two men round.

All through the gloaming and the night, even until the dawn, there was only a great gray stone which stood upon one side of the Chilcotin and looked down upon the trail on the other side.

There was no movement anywhere save the movement of the ice in the river and of the moon as she rose and sank again in the clear night sky, nor was there any sound save the grinding of the ice as it broke into smaller and yet smaller pieces, and was borne along to join the hurtling mass which was hurrying down the Frazer.

At first the shadows crept out into the valley, and one who was watching them gripped his rifle hard, and his breath came thick and fast. Again the moon rose and the shadows fled, and all was white and motionless and dumb. After this it grew darker again; the moon had gone and a chill wind made the watchers shiver, and one of them drew a white thread out of the material of his coat, and doubled it and tied it round the muzzle of his rifle, so that it made a great knot where the sight was, serviceable instead of a sight in the half darkness. The wind was cold, and the watchers' clothes were rigid with frost, but Rampike's fingers scarcely trembled as he tied that knot, and his face was firm and cold as ice.

At last there was a sound far away up the canyon. "Crunch crunch, crunch crunch," it sounded with a regularity unlike any sound in nature. It was no rolling of the rocks, no creaking of the frozen pines, not even the tread of any beast of prey. It was the step of a man, and colonel or no colonel, the man whose tread echoed in that wintry dawn, brought with him to his doom some traces of that early training which had come to him from the drill-sergeant. In the streets of a great city a hundred men may pass and no one hears their tread, or knows that he hears it, and yet in spite of the roaring of the rivers and the grinding of the ice, this one man's tread, even in the snow, seemed like the tread of an army, and the sound of it grew and grew until Corbett knew that the heavens heard it, and that its vibrations were echoed in hell.

At the last they saw him, this man richer than all other men, this man yellow with gold and crimson with other men's blood, and what they saw was a wan, ragged figure, worn to a mere skeleton, its shoulders bent, plodding heavily along with the last load of yellow dust, stolen from Pete's Creek, hanging heavily in its hands.

For a moment Corbett doubted if this could really be that same stalwart, smooth-tongued knave who had jockeyed him out of his dollars for three useless claims, but a sharp metallic "clink" upon the rock beside him called him back to himself and reminded him that Rampike had no doubts even if he had.

Inch by inch Ned saw the long barrel of the Winchester pushed out over the rock, until it rested firmly, its deadly muzzle dark in the dim light of dawn.

Slowly Rampike lowered his head until his cheek lay against the cold metal and his eye trained the weapon upon the man who for gold had not hesitated to kill two of his fellows.

One more beat of his heart and he too would feel the kiss of the cold lead and go whither those others had gone.

"My God, I can't do it!—Cruickshank!" cried Corbett, and as he cried out he sprang to his feet and threw up Rampike's rifle.

"Cruickshank!" the cry startled the silence, so that all nature seemed to shudder at the sound, and "Cruickshank!" "Cruickshank!" the rocks repeated until the sound died away amongst the snows at the head of the canyon.

At the first sound of that cry he whose name it was

stopped, and as he turned to look across the river the white light of dawn came down and struck him across the face, so that those who looked could see the lines graven on it by fear and hunger and remorse, and then his hands went wildly up towards heaven and he fell.

The path which he had trodden so often crossed at this place a sheer slope of hardened snow, in which he had cut footsteps for himself, narrow indeed, but sufficient for the safety of a careful man. Until now he had never slipped or dreamed of slipping, and yet now with that cry in his ear, with the last load of gold in his hand, with the river almost clear enough for flight, he slipped and fell. Those who looked saw only a face full of mad fear, they heard only the clang of the metal wash-pan, which he wore as miners wear it, at his belt, and then, quick as the first ray of the dawn shoots across the mountain-side, Cruickshank shot down that ice-slope, and with a dull heavy plunge, sank in the ice-choked river.

For minutes, which seemed hours, the two men who lay behind the rock neither spoke nor moved, only they stared with wide eyes at the empty trail where he had stood, and the jostling hummocks of ice in the river amongst which he sank.

"Wal," said Rampike at last, "that's all, and I guess we take the pot." And he turned to where the canoe full of gold, the price of three men's lives, lay alone in the gray light of dawn.

Even as he spoke the canoe moved. Some will say that the ice on which it rested had been sucked away by the rising river, and that so, it slid down naturally and was borne along with all the other river waifs, —dead pines and dead men's bodies.

But Rampike, who saw the thing, says that hands

like the hands of the dead laid hold upon it and drew it away.

Then they watched it drift out amongst the ice into the Frazer, and there for a while the great river played with it, and moaned and laughed over it by turns, and then it sank, and the gold that was in it, and the sin which that gold begot, are a portion of the load which the old river is so glad to lay down as she rushes into the salt sea beyond the sand-heads at New Westminster.

L'envoi.

My story is told, and the days which I wrote of have passed away, but something is still left to remind old-timers of the rush of '62. Pete's Creek is still yielding a fair return for work done upon it by a company, whose chairman is our old friend, Steve Chance, but such pockets as that found under Phon's boulder have never been found again.

As for Ned Corbett, he is a rancher now on those yellow Chilcotin uplands, and the gold which pleases him best is that left by the sun upon his miles and miles of sweet mountain grass. If others have more gold, Ned has all that gold can purchase by the Frazer or elsewhere, work which he loves, and such health, spirits, and moderate wealth as should satisfy an honest man.

www.ingramcontent.com/pod-product-compliance
Lightning Source LLC
Chambersburg PA
CBHW032052230426
43672CB00009B/1572